# FIT, UNFIT OR MISFIT?

# FIT, UNFIT OR MISFIT?

## How to Perform Fitness for Duty Evaluations in Law Enforcement Professionals

*Edited by*

### KATHLEEN P. DECKER, M.D.

**CHARLES C THOMAS • PUBLISHER, LTD.**
*Springfield • Illinois • U.S.A.*

*Published and Distributed Throughout the World by*

CHARLES C THOMAS • PUBLISHER, LTD.
2600 South First Street
Springfield, Illinois 62704

©2006 by CHARLES C THOMAS • PUBLISHER, LTD.

ISBN 0-398-07661-8 (hard)
ISBN 0-398-07662-6 (paper)

Library of Congress Catalog Card Number: 2006040474

*With* THOMAS BOOKS *careful attention is given to all details of man-
ufacturing and design. It is the Publisher's desire to present books that are sat-
isfactory as to their physical qualities and artistic possibilities and appropriate for their particular use.* THOMAS BOOKS *will be true to those laws
of quality that assure a good name and good will.*

*Printed in the United States of America*
*CR-R-3*

**Library of Congress Cataloging-in-Publication Data**

Fit, unfit or misfit? : How to perform fitness for duty evaluations in
 law enforcement professionals / edited by Kathleen P. Decker.
   p. cm.
   Includes bibliographical references and index.
   ISBN 0-398-07661-8 -- ISBN 0-398-07662-6 (pbk.)
   1. Law enforcement--United States--Psychological aspects--
Medical examinations. 2. Police psychology--United States--Medical
examinations. 3. Police--Health and hygiene--United States--Medical
examinations. 4. Police--Job stress.  I. Decker, Kathleen P.

HV7936.P75F58 2006
363.2'2--dc22
                                           2006040474

# CONTRIBUTORS

**FABIENNE BROOKS** attended Western Washington University and subsequently received an Atlantic Fellowship in Public Policy in 1996. She is a graduate of the FBI National Academy's 180th session and the Pacific Northwest Command College in 1999. Her law enforcement career included positions as a patrol officer, field training officer, and patrol operations and precinct commander. She was also involved in media relations, major crimes investigation, and supervision. She retired in August, 2004, as Chief of the Criminal Investigations Division with the King County Sheriff's Office in Seattle, Washington, after more than 26 years of service.

Chief Brooks has extensive leadership experience. She has directed a number of programs and associations and provides international training. During her 1996 Atlantic Fellowship in Public Policy, she worked with the Office of Public Management in London, England, to provide training to community members and law enforcement officials on the topics of "Policing for Safer Communities," "Policing through Partnerships," and "From Difference to Diversity." Chief Brooks is a former president of the Black Law Enforcement Association of Washington (1981), the Washington State Chapter of the FBI National Academy Associates (2003), and is the in her second term as president of the Washington State Chapter of the National Organization of Blacks in Law Enforcement (NOBLE).

Her company, Brooks S-A-C, Inc., is a consulting firm specializing in training, expert witness evaluations, community relations, and motivational speeches. She currently provides training to a local Washington fire department on the issues surrounding harassment and hostile work environment. Chief Brooks has extensive experience developing regional partnerships between law enforcement and community organizations to achieve common goals. She is on the board of directors of the King County Sexual Assault Resource Center and the Public Defender Association. She is a trustee for the First AME Church of Seattle.

**KATHLEEN P. DECKER, M.D.,** completed her Honors Undergraduate B.S. in Biochemical Genetics at the University of Michigan. She attended Stanford University School of Medicine and received an National Institute of Health Medical Scientist Training Program Award during medical school. She then completed a residency in psychiatry as well as a Postdoctoral Fellowship in Neuropscychopharmacology at Stanford. She received a Levine Grant Fellowship and a Spunk Foundation Fellowship in 1987 and a Meyer Foundation Fellowship in 1991. Other awards include mention for Clinical Teaching Award (2nd) in 1997 at the University of Washington and she was listed in Seattle's Best Doctors for Women (Seattle Magazine) in 2003.

Her academic appointments include Acting Assistant Professor, Department of Psychiatry, University of Washington from 1992 to 1995 and Clinical Assistant Professor from 1996 to the present. While she was a full-time faculty member at the University of Washington, she was appointed Acting Director of Inpatient Services at Harborview Hospital from 1992-1993 and the Director of Inpatient Dual Diagnosis Program, Harborview Hospital in Seattle from 1992-1993. She served as Medical Director of Psychopharmacology Clinic at Harborview Hospital from 1993-1996.

Dr. Decker has performed over 175 fitness for duty evaluations for more than 40 police departments and 30 other law enforcement agencies and the Washington State Department of Corrections. She was a psychological consultant to the Washington State Department of Corrections-Armed on Duty Program from 1998 to 2002. She has performed fitness for duty evaluations for civilian agencies including the Department of Health Social Services, the State of Washington, the University of Washington, and the Washington State Investment Board.

She has testified in multiple civil proceedings involving fitness for duty issues, allegations of employment discrimination, hostile work environment, sexual harassment, disability, competence, and chemical dependency. She has testified as an expert witness in criminal cases involving assault and homicide (including capital punishment) in the states of Washington and Alaska. She currently provides pre-employment psychological evaluations to several large sheriff's offices and police departments in Washington State.

Dr. Decker has lectured and conducted workshops for the Washington Association of Sheriffs and Police Chiefs on fitness for duty evaluations since 1999. She is a member of the American Academy of Psychiatry and the Law and is currently a member of the Law Enforcement Liaison Committee. She is also an affiliate member of the Washington Association for Sheriffs and Police Chiefs, and a member of the American Psychiatric Association.

She has been active in community service throughout her career. She has served as Mentor for the University of Washington's Minority Recruitment Programs since 1994. She is an adult leader with the Boy Scouts of America and was appointed Seattle Medical Officer as well as a National Medical Officer for the National Boy Scout Jamboree at Fort AP Hill, Virginia in 2005.

**ANNE E. KIRKPATRICK, J.D.,** obtained a Bachelors degree in Business Administration from King College, a Master's degree in Counseling from the University of Memphis, and pursued post-Master's education in Counseling/Psychology. She received her Doctor of Jurisprudence from Seattle University Law School and is a licensed attorney in the state of Washington. She is a graduate of the FBI National Academy (Session #203) and the FBI's Law Enforce- ment Executive Development School (LEEDS) in Quantico, Virginia (Session #48).

She was a Memphis Police Officer from 1982 through 1986. In 1987 she joined the Redmond Police Department in Redmond, Washington. She was a uniformed patrol officer and a sergeant throughout most of her career in Memphis and Redmond. She also was assigned to the Washington State Police Academy where she was the Criminal Procedure Instructor and the Academy sergeant while employed in Redmond. In 1996, she became the Chief of Police of Ellensburg, Washington. Chief Kirkpatrick served the Ellensburg Police Department for four and half years and then became the Chief of Police of Federal Way, Washington in 2001, where she currently serves. Federal Way is the third largest city in King County and seventh largest in Washington State.

Chief Kirkpatrick has held a number of leadership and teaching positions in the law enforcement community. She has been a Commissioner for Washington State Criminal Justice Commission and is the current President of Washington State Chapter of FBI Academy Graduates. She is currently Co-Chair of the Washington Association of Sheriffs and Police Chiefs and she is Chair of King County Police Chiefs Association's Auto Theft Task Force. She has taught in a number of capacities. She was Director of Criminal Justice and an Instructor at Green River Community College in Auburn, Washington, from 1995 to 1996. She is currently an instructor at the FBI National Academy in the FBI's Law Enforcement Executive Development School.

**BRIAN J. WILSON** is a 26-year veteran of municipal law enforcement. He received his B.A. from Washington State and his M. P. A. from Seattle University in 1985. He is a graduate of the FBI National Academy (Session #196). He began as a patrol officer with the Renton, Washington Police Department and over 16 years rose to the rank of Commander. In May of 1996, he joined the Federal Way, Washington Police Department as a Deputy Chief where he is still the current Deputy Chief.

He has served on a number of committees of the Washington Association of Sheriffs and Police Chiefs and is currently a board member of the South Puget Sound Regional Emergency Mobilization Board. He has served as a member of the City of Federal Way's negotiation team and been a major contributor to successful relations with the Police Guild, the Police Support Services Association, and the Lieutenant's Association since 1996.

Deputy Chief Wilson has also been an active leader in nonlaw enforcement organizations. He is currently Vice-Chair of the Board of Directors of Woodstone Credit Union and a member of the Board of Directors of Valley Cities Counseling Services, an organization that provides mental health counseling to South King County. In addition, he has served terms as President, Vice-President, Secretary, and Treasurer of the Federal Way Youth and Family Services Board.

# PREFACE

This book is the product of a decade of clinical practice, research, and collaboration with a variety of professionals. The impetus to write the book was generated partly by a number of police chiefs and sheriffs who requested I provide "written guidelines," including practical information about the conduct and expectations of Fitness for Duty (FFD) Evaluations. In the same time frame, I have been teaching psychiatrists about this area of expertise. The book combines primary research conducted on law enforcement personnel referred for Evaluations in Washington State with reviews of research from the literature. Certain sections of the book also contain data from surveys completed by Washington State police officers regarding their views on a number of issues.

Chapter 1, entitled "Introduction to the FFD Evaluations in Law Enforcement Personnel," presents an overview of the reasons for performing FFD evaluations and an understanding of the process. The chapter outlines the reasons why such evaluations are performed and reviews expectations of the professionals conducting such evaluations. A vignette is used to illustrate some of the principles and difficulties involved in maintaining neutrality in the performance of FFD evaluations. The chapter ends with a checklist of the steps of a FFD from the agency perspective.

Law enforcement is a very high-stress occupation. There are many reasons that law enforcement professionals may experience difficulty with performance. In Chapter 2, entitled "Stress in Law Enforcement Personnel," some of the many stressors and officers' response to stress are explored. For example, there are stressors related to the intrinsic risks of working in a potentially violent environment, administrative issues, and balancing career and home life. In addition, there are the negative stereotypes of law enforcement professionals and a lack of understanding of the demands of the unusual environment in which they operate. Chapter 2 presents a discussion of these stressors as well as coping mechanisms so that the reader may better understand the sources of stress and stress responses that may result in unfit officers.

Chapter 3 is entitled "Common Causes of Unfit Officers." This chapter represents a key shift in the literature in the understanding of "unfit" officers. To date, no other publication has systematically examined the psychiatric diagnoses of unfit officers, and none which refer to the major accepted classification for psychiatric disorders, the Diagnostic and Statistical Manual for Mental Disorders (DSM-IV). Previous authors have tended to focus on behavioral reasons for referral rather than the presence (or absence) of specific psychiatric diagnoses. While many FFD evaluations are undertaken because of behavioral issues, it is important to understand why individual officers exhibit these behaviors. Original research data is presented in this Chapter on FFD Evaluations performed during a five-year period by the author. The data shed light on psychiatric diagnoses found in officers referred for FFD evaluations. Although, the study has limitations as any data set may be biased in spite of the sequential nature in its collection. Therefore, generalizing all of the results to all agencies and officers is not suggested. However, the data presented detail both major psychiatric syndromes, personality disorders, and interesting findings regarding family psychiatric history in officers found fit or unfit for duty.

Chapter 4, "Psychological Tests for Fitness in Law Enforcement Personnel," discusses many of the myriad of structured psychological tests that can be used in FFD Evaluations. The use of some of these tests in pre-employment psychological evaluations is also discussed, as it is often useful to compare pre-employment psychological test data with that obtained during the course of a FFD Evaluation. Although both psychiatrists and psychologists are qualified to perform FFD evaluations, fewer psychiatrists currently perform them. Part of this is because standard psychiatric residencies teach only cursory information regarding standardized psychological tests such as the MMPI-2, MCMI-III, and others. Psychologists' training usually includes detailed instruction and supervision regarding the interpretation of such tests. If psychiatrists intend to perform FFD Evaluations, it is important that they undertake significant education regarding the performance and interpretation of these tests, or collaborate with a psychologist who performs the structured testing.

Issues involving complex interactions of underlying medical and psychiatric conditions with various medications are becoming more important than in past decades. In part, this is due to the plethora of medications available and improved public education regarding the availability of medications. In part, it is also due to the recognition that an increasing number of law enforcement personnel are taking a wide variety of medications. Just as psychologists' training usually provides them with a more detailed understanding of psychological tests, psychiatrists' education provides them with the detailed understanding of medical and psychiatric conditions. As psychiatrists are physicians first, and specialists in psychiatry second, they possess skills at diagnosing and treating a variety of disorders which may affect officers' ability to perform their duties. A detailed knowledge of medicine and psychiatry is necessary to understand the impact of these medications on performance. Chapter 5, entitled "Medication Issues in FFD Evaluations," explores some of the potential impact that medications may have on officers' fitness. Chapter 5 presents a simplified overview so that police executives can have a framework for concerns. It is also meant to educate psychiatrists on the special skills necessary in law enforcement that may render the use of certain medications inadvisable although, such use might be acceptable in other occupations. Vignettes illustrate some of the complexities associated with medication use in law enforcement personnel.

Chapter 6, entitled "Police Officers' Expectations of Mental Health Professionals," outlines stereotypes and expectations that law enforcement personnel have regarding mental health personnel. The chapter quotes established literature as well as presenting data from a survey on Washington State local law enforcement personnel's attitudes. For evaluators, an understanding of the lack of information and misconceptions that officers have may assist them with interacting and educating officers and referring departments. For police executives, the chapter may serve as a reference to address officers' concerns prior to referral and throughout the process of a FFD evaluation. For both sets of readers, the chapter outlines some possible strategies to reduce the barriers between two disparate professions that share many of the same goals, e.g., helping others and community and individual safety.

As its title suggests, Chapter 7, "Gender and Ethnic Issues in Hiring, Stess and FFD Evaluations," reviews data regarding issues which are of special importance in different subgroups of law enforcement personnel. Literature regarding differences in hiring, stress, and FFD in different ethnic subgroups is reviewed. The chapter reviews the limited data on differences between male and female officers. Original research on gender similarities and differences based on the Washington study of law enforcement personnel referred for FFD evaluations is presented. Although the issues presented in this chapter are expected to evolve substantially as society changes, it provides a window into current practices and beliefs.

One of the least common but most stressful events for law enforcement personnel is duty death—when an officer is killed in the line of duty. Chapter 8, "Duty Death: A Major Stressor," explores several aspects of duty death. Literature regarding the nature of the stress experienced by law enforcement personnel is reviewed. Next, interviews with command staff from a department that lost an officer due to duty death (by homicide) are presented. Finally, the chapter quotes a number of police officers' comments on duty death which were made in the course of the survey of attitudes of Washington police officers. It also includes primary data that indicates interesting trends in the interventions officers believe may aid them after a critical incident. Their perceptions do not prove a specific intervention is useful. Their comments provide important insight into the nature and structure of future interventions to reduce stress.

Another uncommon but important event is detailed in Chapter Nine which is entitled "Police Suicide and Fitness for Duty." The sometimes controversial data regarding police suicide is reviewed in this chapter. Certain investigators have claimed the rate of suicide is dramatically higher amongst law enforcement personnel and others that it is no different than that of the general population. A large body of literature is reviewed which summarizes the current state of knowledge in this area. A case scenario illustrates some of the concepts involved in determining whether an officer has a low or high risk of suicide. A second scenario highlights the radically different outcomes that are possible depending on how suicidal officers are approached and respond to treatment. The chapter attempts to reconcile discrepancies between different research studies in this area.

"The Management of Misfit Officers," Chapter 10, explores some of the issues encountered when an officer is not necessarily mentally ill, but has become unsuitable for his or her current position. Examples include officers who experience personality shifts due to aging, changing priorities, as well as officers who misunderstood their own psychological makeup or the demands of the profession when they were hired. The chapter highlights some creative ways that departments and/or evaluators can work with officers to either shift roles within an agency or come to terms with their own psyche. Case scenarios are presented to illustrate fictionalized accounts of real cases in which "misfit" officers have been accommodated by agencies or shifted their focus.

Chapter 11, entitled "Legal Considerations: Discipline Versus Illness," outlines a number of legal considerations and constraints involved in the conduct of FFD evaluations. It also provides an introduction to prior case law regarding FFD issues. Clearly, a single chapter cannot be viewed as an exhaustive resource as the law changes quite rapidly. There are also local and state variations in laws and interpretations which may contradict approaches in another jurisdiction. However, there are certain overarching legal principles which are addressed in this chapter. It is presented to give both police executives and evaluators a window into the legal consequences and constraints of FFD evaluations.

I have tried to incorporate a variety of objective and subjective observations on the field of FFD in law enforcement personnel. No one resource can answer all questions, but I hope this work will stimulate thought and discussion. In addition, it will hopefully assist future attempts to better understand and treat the difficulties that law enforcement professionals encounter in the performance of their hazardous and stressful public service.

KATHLEEN P. DECKER

# ACKNOWLEDGMENTS

A large number of individuals have contributed to this book. I thank my great friend Dr. Walter van Schalkwijk for his encouragement, critical reading, and kindly prompting to finish this book. He lent his considerable literary skills to detailed editing suggestions, although the subject is outside his field. He exhibited great tenacity and encouraged me to pursue my dream. Chief Anne Kirkpatrick assisted not only with facilitation of distribution of surveys to police officers but contributed her perceptions regarding various topics. She coauthored the legal chapter. I also thank for her insistence that the topic of Fitness for Duty Evaluations needs to be more widely disseminated in the law enforcement community.

Deputy Chief Brian Wilson and (Retired) Chief Fabienne Brooks contributed both comments and constructive criticism of specific chapters. Mr. Leo Poort, Esquire (Chief Legal Counsel, City of Seattle) was kind enough to read and comment upon the legal chapter. Dr. Lawrence G. Wilson contributed valuable comments on certain chapters.

The unnamed officers who were kind enough to fill out survey forms regarding a variety of opinions are once again thanked for their participation. The author wishes the officers whose data were presented in FFD results in this book an easier, healthy future regardless of the outcome of their evaluation. Finally, I also wish to thank Dr. David Smith, Ph.D., for his influence on my career and this book. Our early collaborations on FFD evaluations fostered my career development in this area. His desire to improve and maintain the highest standards of mental health in law enforcement professionals sparked a fire in me to continue that tradition and to contribute to the literature in this area. Finally, I am deeply grateful to Mr. Michael Thomas, my editor, for his patience in the preparation of the manuscript. He and his editorial staff worked tirelessly to produce the book.

I hold myself entirely accountable for any inaccuracies in the material presented in this book and apologize for any omissions. I have tried to thoroughly research topics and quote established, controlled studies wherever possible so that the book is not based on the opinions of a single investigator. Because data is often boring to everyone except for scientists, I have tried to enliven the chapters by adding fictional scenarios wherever possible to illustrate points. The scenarios are all based on real incidents, but all of the scenarios have been altered to obscure identifiers and are usually composites of several situations.

K.P.D.

# CONTENTS

# FIT, UNFIT OR MISFIT?

# Chapter 1

# INTRODUCTION TO FITNESS-FOR-DUTY EVALUATIONS IN LAW ENFORCEMENT PERSONNEL

KATHLEEN P. DECKER

## I. THE PURPOSE

### 1.1 Why?

There are several reasons to perform FFD evaluations. First, law enforcement personnel are the guardians of public safety. It is important that guardians of public safety are themselves healthy and trustworthy (Wu, 1984). This has been stated in legal language as guaranteeing "stable, reliable and productive workforce" (*Yin v. State of California*, 95 F.3d 864).

Second, law enforcement personnel undergo extensive mental and physical testing and a training process which is highly selective. The department or agency has thus invested time, money, and education to train the officer. If officers contract a temporary or treatable mental illness which affects their ability to perform their job, they should be offered an opportunity to undergo such treatment and resume productive employment. This is codified in the Americans with Disabilities Act (ADA, 1984). Specifically, Title II of the Americans with Disabilities Act of 1990 and Section 504 of the Rehabilitation Act of 1973 seek to prohibit discrimination against individuals with disabilities on the basis of disability (42 U.S.C. § 12131, et seq., 29 U.S.C. § 794). If a psychiatrist or psychologist determines that a law enforcement professional is suffering from a disability, the employer must make reasonable accommodations to the employee rather than summarily terminating him or her on the basis of poor performance (Wu, 1984).

3

A third function of a FFD evaluation is to assist agencies in ascertaining whether a law enforcement personnel's behavior is misconduct or the result of a treatable mental illness. If the set of circumstances or the officer's behavior precipitating the FFD evaluation is found to be the result of misconduct, then disciplinary action is the appropriate course. Both referring agencies and evaluators are unanimous that recommendations regarding law enforcement disciplinary process are *not* the province of a FFD evaluator, but rather must be dealt with according to policies and procedures of the agency in accordance with local, state, and federal employment laws. Thus, determining whether an individual should receive progressive discipline is not an issue for the evaluator to determine. However, if the officer is found to be suffering from a mental health condition, the chief or sheriff may elect to defer or delay certain disciplinary steps due to mitigating circumstances until the officer returns to duty. The author encourages heads of agencies to view the disciplinary process as separate and as a parallel track to the FFD evaluation. It is important for the disciplinary process to proceed whether or not the officer is determined to have a mental illness, but the delivery of such disciplinary action may be changed on the basis of the FFD evaluation.

The conduct of these examinations is important. FFD evaluation is used as a means of evaluating the psychiatric status of an officer. Evaluators need to remember that evaluees view themselves at risk of job loss from the moment they are informed they have been required to submit to a FFD evaluation. Therefore, it is incumbent upon evaluators to maintain compassion as well as neutrality in the performance of these evaluations. Agencies must be prepared to defend the need for a FFD evaluation and not to seek these evaluations as an alternative to the disciplinary process, or as a solution for personnel issues. It is counterproductive for an agency to order the evaluation and face a lawsuit for invasion of privacy or wrongful termination (*Pettus v. Cole*, 49 Cal. App. 4th 402).

## II. THE PROCESS

### *1.2 Content of the Evaluation*

The content of the FFD Evaluation and evaluation materials is similar to that of a general mental health evaluation but has important differences. A fitness-for-duty evaluation comprises much of the same material as a general psychiatric evaluation, with some important additional information. The usual categories in an evaluation should be addressed. These include: the referral source, chief complaint, the history of present illness, past psychiatric and medical history, educational history, social history, family history, profile of substance use, allergies, mental status exam, differential diagnosis, and DSM-IV diagnoses (see Appendix I for a sample evaluation).

Several additional kinds of supplemental information are important in fitness-for-duty evaluation which distinguishes it from civilian evaluations. This information includes military history and type of discharge, careful chronology of law enforcement or corrections positions, previous complaints or commendations by supervisors, presence or absence of civilian or inmate complaints against the officer, and past or present involvement by the evaluee in legal action against the agency or institution (Varela. 1999). It is important to establish personal weapons possessed by the officer as well in light of the potential for suicide or homicide in dysfunctional officers. Finally, as most law enforcement personnel utilize physical training heavily as an outlet for stress, it is also useful to quantitate the evaluee's exercise regimen and whether there have been any recent changes in the frequency of his/her routine. Collateral information that is necessary for most evaluations includes evaluations by direct supervisor and contacts with Human Resources. Careful consideration of complaints by family members, for example, domestic violence or other pending legal complaints, may also be important. It is advisable that documents pertaining to work performance, attendance and discipline be forwarded to the evaluating professional subsequent to or along with the initial evaluation visit (Johnson, 1995, Perry, 2002, Reynolds, 2002).

## 1.3 Collateral Interviews

Specific inquiries should be made to discern the origin of problems precipitating a fitness-for-duty evaluation. The evaluator must at times differentiate individual pathology vs. workplace conflicts. Emphasis should be placed on methods to maintain neutrality and provide an impartial evaluation. In certain cases where the evaluee is resistant to the evaluation process, it may be preferable to provide the work performance and/or complaint documentation *after* the initial evaluation is performed, to allow the evaluee to present her/his side of the story first and allow the evaluator to form an unbiased first impression of the officer. The evaluator should discuss the situation with several people on the staff of the institution, not just one supervisor, to ascertain if there is specific interpersonal conflict with a supervisor or chief as opposed to problems within the officer.

It is also important for the institution to document consistent patterns of interpersonal pathology. Separate input from multiple individuals in the institution provides different perspectives on the impaired officer's problems and increases the chances that a clear pattern of psychopathology will be detected. Psychometric data (psychological testing) can provide an objective measure of cognitive impairment and/or personality disorders. These tests will be discussed in Chapter Four in more detail. Typical psychological testing to assist with diagnosis of personality disorder includes: Millon Multi-Axial Personality Inventory III, Structured Clinical Interview for DSM-IV diagnosis (SCID), and Minnesota Multiphasic Inventory (MMPI-II). These instruments should not be used alone to make such a diagnosis but can support or eliminate major personality disorder in the evaluee.

### 1.4 Confidentiality Issues

Certain confidentiality issues should be discussed early in the FFD interview with evaluees. These include (1) role of the evaluator, (2) storage of report data and (3) custody of evaluation information. The evaluator should introduce herself as an *evaluator*, not a *treating* professional to the officer, and explain the role carefully. Recommendations to the actual treating professional can be made, but the evaluator must then also be clear with the officer/treating professional whether the recommendations are suggestions or firm recommendations which should be implemented within a specific timeframe in order to return to duty. This is important because some officers or their treating professionals implement some, none, or delay implementing recommendations for weeks. It is also important to separate noncompliance in an officer from suboptimal treatment due to various medical or financial issues.

Results, which include written notes, primary data such as test results, and all memos or letters regarding a FFD evaluation are the property of the referring agency. The evaluator must avoid the pitfall of releasing such information to the evaluee, union representatives and lawyers for the evaluee, or even the officer's primary treating professional. These are all documents which can be used in adversarial proceedings against the referring agency in grievance hearings, litigation, etc. It is quite possible to convey recommendations, findings, or communicate the essence of the evaluation without sharing detailed observations which might allow opposing counsel to rebut or discredit the evaluation process or the institution. Clearly, if the officer hires an independent evaluator at her own expense, those records belong to the individual.

An increasingly important trend in FFD evaluations is the necessity of the evaluator to transmit *only* the information necessary to convey the officer's problems and the department's possible approaches to resolving the case. In other words, the evaluator need not and should not send detailed information regarding the past social history unless it is specifically germane to the officer's impairment (e.g., the officer's first wife was unfaithful or his daughter is pregnant out of wedlock). The author currently follows a policy of releasing *only* the answers to a predetermined set of questions. They are:

1. **Is the officer fit for duty in his/her current position?**
2. **If the officer is unfit for duty, what is the nature of his/her psychological impairment?**
3. **Is the impairment temporary or permanent?**
4. **Are there any treatment recommendations to restore this officer to fitness?**
5. **What reasonable accommodations are suggested to allow this officer to return to duty?**

It should be noted that in certain jurisdictions (e.g., City of Renton, Washington, see Appendix) the Police Guild has reached a formal agreement with the City to limit the feedback of evaluators to a similar short series of questions. However, agencies and evaluators should remember that detailed information may be required by the department at a later date. The above limited question format is designed to protect the evaluee's confidentiality. The evaluator, as a trained psychiatrist or psychologist, needs to ask quite detailed, personal questions to establish the psychosocial stresses and capabilities of the evaluee in order to make a judgment on risk and return to work. However, only the chief or sheriff need know details of the officer's specific diagnoses and recommendations. The evaluee's direct supervisors may need to know a much smaller body of information in order to work with the case, such as how long the employee will be off work and whether he/she will return to light duty or full duty. In the case of officers returning to work with restrictions, such as random drug/alcohol testing, a plan for the officer's confidentiality may be challenging for the agency to structure but is necessary.

## III. ISSUES REGARDING RECORDS

### *1.5 Acquiring Medical Records*

Sometimes, acquiring medical or psychiatric records may be difficult in the course of FFD evaluations. Analyzing the wealth of data accumulated during a FFD evaluation typically requires a minimum of several days. If the treating physicians for the officer do not provide health care information relevant to the evaluation immediately, the evaluator is obliged to either wait for such information (often a matter of weeks) or proceed in the absence of such information. Some officers are resistant to providing medical or psychiatric records because of they fear that "the entire department will know my business." It is important to discuss the responsibility that the evaluee has to provide *adequate* information to allow a thorough evaluation of his/her condition. Most employment contracts include such a paragraph stating that it is the responsibility of the employee to provide such information as to allow the employer to make reasonable accommodations or to assess impairment.

The evaluator should clarify that the original medical records will not be forwarded to the police department, but the CONCLUSIONS of the evaluator based on review of such material will be shared with the department. In some cases, excess confidentiality concerns or a desire to limit information because of pending litigation leads to a situation in which no records are received by the evaluator. In such cases, it should be clearly noted in the report that the conclusions were limited by the lack of proper information. In most cases, a comprehensive evaluation process should ensure that the evaluator can at least determine whether or not the individual is fit for duty even in the absence of treatment records. Some techniques to enhance transmission of such records include: paired requests by telephone, fax and return receipt requested letter, notification of a specific deadline by which information is needed due to the need to finalize the report for the department, and a reminder that that it is the responsibility of the employee to provide such information to facilitate the evaluation.

### *1.6 Storing Records*

Access to and maintenance of FFD evaluation records should be carefully controlled. The evaluator should remember that although many officers are ready and willing to address the problems raised in a FFD evaluation, some may be litigious or in search of secondary gain through the FFD evaluation. If an evaluee applies for state disability, the evaluator is *not* to disclose the FFD report. The state assumes that any named physician is a *treating* physician, and will usually request records from the evaluator, often stating that the evaluator "knows the evaluee and made a diagnosis." Such requests should be referred to the referring agency's human relations department, which can choose to release any portion of the report at their discretion to address such issues. It is common for evaluees to demand that the evaluator fill out disability paperwork, but careful explanation that the evaluator is not a treating physician and a standardized release (see attached below) help set proper expectations.

The department requesting the FFD evaluation should have a separate confidential file where the evaluation report is stored, separate from the usual personnel data. In most cases, there is no need to convey details of the findings to an officer's immediate supervisor. The chief and relevant human relations personnel should be informed of the findings and can best judge how much information needs to be shared with the immediate supervisor. In general, the minimum amount of information is desirable, but in certain cases such as substance abuse or erratic behavior, the supervisor must be cautioned to maintain vigilance for continuation of such behaviors.

Extensive discussion of the effect of the new HIPAA laws (Health Information Protection Access Act (HIPAA, 2003)) is beyond the scope of this chapter. In brief, it specifies that any covered entity must possess special software to ensure confidentiality in electronic billing. It also allows the treated individual full access to *all* his/her medical records upon demand. It is unlikely that evaluees would be deemed to be subject to the access provision as they are not patients, but evaluees. It is clear that all documents pertaining to a FFD evaluation would be included in the compliance aspects regarding electronic billing and/or data transmission to third parties. However, this is clearly an area that deserves further legal study and may eventually be challenged by individuals and/or unions (see Chapter 11).

## IV. AGENCY LIABILITY ISSUES

### 1.7 Forensic Liability Concerns

A number of forensic liability concerns should be addressed by the FFD evaluation. There are significant differences between the standards of "fitness" or disability in law enforcement personnel and civilians. The Americans with Disabilities Act provides protection for the employee and attempts to set standards for employers regarding appropriate treatment of employees with physical or mental illnesses. The Equal Employment Opportunity Commission (EEOC) regulations implementing the ADA define "mental impairment" to include any "mental or psychological disorder, such as mental retardation, organic brain syndrome, emotional or mental illness, and specific learning disabilities" (29 C.F.R. § 1630.2 (h)(2)). A more thorough review of ADA considerations is presented in Chapter 11.

However, standards of FFD in law enforcement personnel are *higher* than the minimum level of functioning for nonlaw enforcement individuals. Thus individuals may not be impaired by ADA standards but may not be fit for duty as a police officer. Specifically, they must be fit to carry firearms, make instant life and death decisions, and stand up to public and court scrutiny regarding being either "trigger-happy" or "scared" to carry out their duty. Officers must be courageous but not aggressive.

It is not possible to delineate specific psychiatric diagnoses which are categorically unacceptable in law enforcement personnel with the exception of psychosis (loss of touch with reality). It is patently obvious that the forensic risk of a psychotic officer is completely unacceptable. However, depression, attention deficit disorder, anxiety, and mood swing disorders such as bipolar disorder can vary widely in terms of both severity and treatment response. Therefore, the FFD evaluation should strive to educate the referring department about both general expectations. The evaluator may also explain why specific factors that may improve an officer's ability to return to work or make it unlikely. Discussions of specific job tasks that may be impaired and clear guidelines about how to return the officer to work gradually to maximize chances of success are important points to include in the FFD report.

Resolution can include transfer to a less critical position and/or counseling for the individual regarding appropriate nonlaw enforcement positions. In some cases, it may involve education of the institution or agency regarding the risks of low-level or treated psychiatric symptoms. At times, primary care providers certify individuals as "fit for duty" when the institution finds them unfit for return to duty. Then the psychiatrist can assist both the individual and the institution to resolve the problem.

### 1.8 Who Evaluates?

Diverse evaluating professionals can be utilized to perform a FFD evaluation. Psychiatrists and psychologists may have different expertise and limitations, which are often complementary (Coojhuize, 1992). Specifically, (testing) psychologists are very helpful with pre-employment phases (structured testing plus long clinical interviews designed to weed out antisocial or other personality disorders and ascertain minimal cognitive abilities to do the job). They can be of great value in FFD evaluations by performing detailed neuropsychological testing if dementia, post-MVA, or other cognitive decline is suspected.

Psychiatrists are essential to a FFD evaluation if there are medical *and/or* psychiatric conditions. They are the most qualified professionals to ascertain interactions between medical conditions and medications that have psychoactive effects. Some forensic psychologists who do *testing* are skilled at detecting (and weeding out) psychological disturbances but not treating them. The experience psychiatrists bring to the forensic setting of treating serious mental illness allows them to analyze and troubleshoot complex cases. Therefore, a psychiatrist is better able to deal clinically with the implications of a seriously impaired officer and to comment on the prognosis. They may also be better able to differentiate between "a little abnormal" and severe pathology. Finally, they can order MRIs, CTs, and other lab tests to rule out specific medical conditions.

Both psychologists and psychiatrists can perform FFD evaluations. Psychiatrists have an advantage of evaluating medication effects on officers and understanding the interplay of general medical and mental health issues. Psychologists often have more experience with psychometric testing. Combination of the sophisticated psychological screening as performed by (testing) psychologists with the specialized psychopharmacological and medical expertise of a psychiatrist is ideal but not required in all situations. Conclusions drawn by the combined team can lead to thorough resolution of the situation and pre-empt certain legal challenges to their conclusions. Therefore, the team approach may be preferred in complex cases although either professional can address simple cases (Oosthuizen, 1992).

### 1.9 Logistic Issues

There may be treatment obstacles which the evaluator must address. Many cities or agencies have limited mental health or chemical dependence coverage, and yet the evaluator may decide the current treatment plan is insufficient. Examples include complicated cases being treated by physician assistants or nurse practitioners, primary care doctors, or even community psychiatrists who are totally unfamiliar with the special considerations involved in law enforcement personnel. These are challenges, but the evaluator must be prepared to communicate with the existing network, demand that the HMO authorize special test procedures, give specific treatment recommendations to primary care physicians, etc. In the final analysis, if the treatment team is inadequate, it is the responsibility (in most jurisdictions) of the officer (evaluee) to obtain adequate treatment. If he/she refuses, it is grounds for termination. Other options should be exhausted first, but intervention by the evaluator can sometimes facilitate improved treatment and resolution of the case.

## V. THE EVALUATOR'S ROLE

### *1.10 Relationship to the Evaluee*

When may an evaluee become a patient of the evaluator? Adherence to the highest practice of psychiatric ethics obliges the evaluator to maintain her/his role as an impartial evaluator. This policy is frequently frustrating to law enforcement personnel for a number of reasons but is based on the ethics of clinical practice, forensic practice, and the important issue of neutrality of a FFD evaluator. The American Academy of Psychiatry and the Law (APPL) has specifically addressed the issue of the ethics of changing roles from evaluation to treatment in its most recent guidelines (AAPL, 2005):

> ". . . before beginning a forensic evaluation, psychiatrists should inform the evaluee that although they are psychiatrists, they are not the evaluee's "doctor." Psychiatrists should indicate for whom they are conducting the examination and what they will do with the information obtained as a result of the examination. There is a continuing obligation to be sensitive to the fact that although a warning has been given, there may be slippage and a treatment relationship may develop in the mind of the examinee

The American Psychological Association has a similar statement in its ethical guidelines regarding the performance of forensic evaluations (APA, 2002):

> Regardless of whether the scoring and interpretation are done by psychologists, by employees or assistants, or by automated or other outside services, psychologists take reasonable steps to ensure that explanations of results are given to the individual or designated representative unless the nature of the relationship precludes provision of an explanation of results (such as in some organizational consulting, pre-employment or security screenings, and forensic evaluations), and this fact has been clearly explained to the person being assessed in advance.

If a change in roles occurs from evaluation to treatment, it is unethical for the psychiatrist to attempt to resume an evaluation role. By definition, the treating psychiatrist or psychologist is an advocate for her/his patient. Once the line has been crossed, an evaluator can no longer be effective as an evaluator and the department must find another evaluator when a subsequent FFD evaluation is performed on the officer. If the officer undergoes further decompensation and/or the institution requests a future evaluation, the psychiatrist must decline the evaluation role. If his/her services were originally paid by an agency or an institution, the original evaluation might be independent, but the duty is *not* specifically to the evaluee. This neutrality is lost when treatment begins.

A second set of concerns regarding the assumption of a treatment role is that the testimony of the psychiatrist in court is colored by the shift to a treatment relationship. In this case, the psychiatrist may no longer be an unbiased evaluator of the employee. This may result in inability to clarify the original FFD evaluation report, and/or reduced ability to testify as a current treating professional without harming the patient. These concerns are similar to those encountered in disability determinations by psychiatrists in which similar conflicts of interest between the role of evaluator and treating psychiatrist occur.

The following example illustrates several of the pitfalls associated with changing roles. A psychologist evaluated an officer in a FFD evaluation, performing detailed neuropsychological evaluation because of a motor vehicle accident. He was retained and his services were paid for by the police department. He documented some impairment but reported that the officer was fit for duty as he had minimal impairment. The officer returned to full duty and seemed to perform reasonably well for a year. The officer sought treatment from the psychologist two years after the evaluation "because we had a good rapport" and because he was having problems at work with respect to anger management, low-grade insubordination, and had shown poor judgment. He had received two warnings under a progressive discipline process. The psychologist agreed to see him for several therapy sessions "to assist with his readjustment to work." These sessions were clearly identified as treatment and paid for by the officer directly.

A year later, the officer exhibited increasing difficulty with erratic job performance, judgment impairment and emotional volatility. Rather than terminate the officer, the Chief sought a second FFD evaluation because of her suspicions that the behavior might have something to do with damage from the previous motor vehicle accident. The psychologist offered to return to an evaluation role, but the psychologist had lost his neutrality. The department thus had to proceed to retain a second FFD evaluator, a psychiatrist familiar with neurologic damage. The officer did not understand why the psychologist couldn't do a new FFD evaluation "because I trust him." The officer was found unfit for duty by the new evaluator because of increasing neurologic deficits associated with the accident and separated from his job.

The officer sued the police department and the city for wrongful termination. The psychologist's court testimony was weakened with respect to his *initial* evaluation because he had now created a duty not to harm his client, the officer. This duty clearly conflicted with testifying that the officer had had some neurological impairment throughout his attempt to return to work. In addition, the jury did not believe the psychologist was impartial with respect to his testimony as he had been first an agent of the department and was subsequently employed by the officer. The department was unhappy with the evaluator because his testimony regarding impairment was weaker than his initial report indicated. Finally, the officer was angry with the evaluator because he "couldn't stand up for him" in court and deny any impairment in the interests of his lawsuit.

Thus, assuming multiple roles in the same case poses clear ethical and legal issues for psychiatrist and psychologist evaluators. There are many real-life pressures which tend to undermine neutrality. It is not uncommon for departments or agencies to request that the evaluating clinician "stabilize" an evaluee once he/she has delivered his/her findings. In rural areas, the officer may not have access to a psychiatrist, and even in urban areas, most psychiatrists are not aware of, nor comfortable with the special issues that arise in law enforcement personnel. Therefore, there is sometimes pressure for the evaluating clinician to assume a treatment role. Referral to another clinician is crucial to minimize any potential conflict of interest. The best way to approach these difficult cases is to offer to make specific recommendations to the most qualified treating professional in the area and maintain an exclusively evaluation role. Clearly, limitations of access to care are a major problem in clinical work but even more so in forensic cases. One strategy the author has used in such cases is to have an evaluee driven by a chaperone (another officer) to the evaluation site and/or to meet the evaluee geographically half-way to reduce the access difficulty.

Frequently the concept of completely separate treatment roles and evaluation roles is frustrating to law enforcement agencies and personnel. There is a bias to "use psychiatrists" who are familiar with the special constraints of law enforcement professionals and who may be trusted by officers because of other contacts such as critical incident debriefings or educational programs. Expectations by law enforcement professionals of mental health professionals are treated in greater detail in Chapter 6. There is often also a cost factor as the agency may attempt to cut costs by having a professional "already familiar with the case" assume both roles. Law enforcement personnel, many of whom are unfamiliar with or are threatened by mental health inquiries, may also push for treatment by the evaluating psychiatrist if they perceive a rapport with her/him. They may not want to reveal vulnerability to a new clinician, and have the same concern that the institution does of not trusting "outsiders" who know nothing of law enforcement's special demands and stresses.

In spite of all these pressures, evaluators have a duty to their client, the agency, as well as to their profession, to resist the temptation to slip into grey zones or assume several roles in the same case. Educating law enforcement personnel regarding the dangers of assuming multiple roles is important to improving and maintaining the highest standard of practice in this area.

### 1.11 Relationship to the Agency

Evaluators perform FFD evaluations as consultants. There are several important consequences of the fact that evaluators are consultants to the referring agency. First, the evaluator is to remain impartial. The highest adherence to ethics of evaluation practice dictates that the evaluator is neither an agent of the evaluating agency, nor the evaluee. This concept was explored above with reference to assuming multiple roles during the course of FFD evaluations. This issue is addressed by the American Academy of Psychiatry and the Law (AAPL) guidelines as follows:

> Forensic psychiatrists function as experts within the legal process. Although he may be retained by one party to a dispute in a civil matter or the prosecution or defense in a criminal matter, they adhere to the principle of honesty and they strive for objectivity. Their clinical evaluation and the application of the data obtained to the legal criteria are performed in the spirit of such honesty and efforts to obtain objectivity. Their opinion reflects this honesty and efforts to attain objectivity.

The pressure of being retained (and thus paid) by an agency may be significant. At times, attorneys or agency personnel may express disapproval or voice specific agendas regarding the outcome of an evaluation. It is part of the role of an evaluator in FFD evaluations to resist such pressure. He/she should perform, report, and testify as a neutral party.

Another consequence of this consultative role is that psychiatrists or psychologists performing such work must maintain malpractice liability. FFD evaluations are performed as consultants so the forensic risk to the evaluator is born solely by them. Thus, professionals seeking to perform such evaluations need to verify the limits of their malpractice coverage and proceed accordingly. This is another reason why assuming a treatment role is detrimental in the course of a FFD evaluation. If an evaluating psychiatrist assumes a treatment role, he/she becomes subject to doctor-patient issues of malpractice, as well as the original forensic evaluation malpractice issues. Clearly, having switched from the role of an evaluator whose client is the referring agency to a doctor treating an individual can create a conflict of interest which may lead to claims of malpractice.

## VI. RESULTS OF THE EVALUATION

### *1.12 Treatment Recommendations*

What is the role of treatment recommendations in a FFD evaluation? Fundamentally, the agency requesting a FFD evaluation employs the evaluator to provide recommendations to it. Therefore, it should heed the recommendations of its consultant. However, the evaluator is only a consultant and as such, the agency may choose to follow some, all, or none of her/his recommendations. The agency risks future forensic problems if it ignores key recommendations such as mandating psychiatric or substance use treatment of the officer referred for the FFD evaluation. Similarly, if an agency decides to pursue a strict disciplinary course, ignoring remediable psychiatric problems, it may have difficulty as well. However, some evaluators may make recommendations that are impossible for the agency to carry out. An example of this is the recommendation for extended psychiatric treatment *prior* to consideration of return to duty. The fact is that most agencies do not have adequate funding to maintain an officer on leave for months. Particularly in the case of small police forces, where the entire agency consists of five members, losing one indefinitely without replacing him/her can be an unacceptable practice.

Another difficulty that sometimes arises in FFD evaluations is that the officer may require complex treatment and further diagnostic testing which may limit his/her compliance with recommendations. However, it is in the best interest of both the officer and the agency to comply with such recommendations. For example, the author has had experience diagnosing a brain tumor during the course of a FFD Evaluation. In that case, psychological testing and interview disclosed cognitive problems which needed further nonpsychiatric evaluation including a brain scan (MRI) and metabolic work-up for cancer. The officer would have been terminated had the agency not pursued a FFD evaluation and he would have died of a brain tumor had he not followed FFD evaluation recommendations for further medical tests. In that particular case, he was separated on a well-deserved medical leave and pursued medical treatment for the tumor.

As will be discussed in subsequent chapters, some agencies may be located in rural or under-served areas and mandating psychiatric or substance use treatment may not be feasible. For example, in many rural communities, the nearest psychiatrist is over 100 miles away, so that an officer may not be able to see one weekly. Physician extenders such as physician assistants, nurse practitioners, and primary care physicians who attempt to provide psychiatric treatment may not have adequate expertise to manage these complex cases. As will be discussed in Chapter 5, treatment by lesser-qualified professionals or psychiatrists unfamiliar with the special constraints of law enforcement may even have contributed to the development of the FFD crisis.

It is beyond the scope of this book to resolve such real-world problems, but it is clear that the following areas need to be addressed by future mental health professionals in conjunction with law enforcement agencies. First, the problem of access to qualified mental health professionals by law enforcement personnel needs to be addressed. Second, nonpsychiatric physicians need to be educated regarding the special needs and constraints of the law enforcement community. A system of referral to qualified mental health professionals with special expertise in law enforcement issues needs to be established. Third,

HMO or other third-party insurers who want to obtain contracts with law enforcement agencies should be *required* to provide adequate mental health coverage when so mandated by the employer. Otherwise, the insurer should be informed that it is an unacceptable contract. In these days of consolidation of health care providers and insurers, if multiple law enforcement agencies pressured large HMOs or insurers to comply with such standards, it would happen.

### 1.13 Reporting Techniques

Prompt reporting of the results of a FFD evaluation is necessary to allow police departments to calculate staffing and to begin the process of reasonable accommodation or long-term planning. In addition, in the rare instances in which a FFD evaluation was unwarranted or inappropriate, the employee deserves to be returned to work as quickly as possible. Therefore, a preliminary finding may be communicated verbally within a few days (or even the next day) to the department. Any missing information should be cited to explain whether the evaluation's findings are preliminary or likely to be substantially altered in light of new information. An example of such issues occurred when an evaluee stated he had never had any episodes of domestic violence. A week after the evaluation report was submitted to the police department, evidence was discovered that the employee had been lying and had had previous episodes of domestic violence in another state. This information changed the entire course of the evaluation as it changed the potential of recurrent violence and also demonstrated duplicitous behavior on the part of the evaluee, which are grounds for dismissal.

A written report should follow addressing the components described above in 1.3. Only that information necessary to explain the nature of the officer's condition and the effects of that condition on FFD status should be shared with the department. Much of the information collected during the interview such as social history, family history of psychiatric disorders, and psychosocial factors such as marital dysfunction need not be communicated. Instead, the evaluator should address the conclusions reached by reviewing such information. In the past, FFD evaluation reports might have been released which were "comprehensive" and provided a wealth of the above information to the department. Current procedures designed to minimize the release of unnecessary personal information dictate a more conservative approach. Hence, typical reports may be much shorter, limited to answering the specific questions.

## 1.14 Conclusions

FFD evaluations may be necessary to ensure safety of an officer; protect the police department from liability; and protect the community from officers who are potentially unsafe because of depression, anxiety, PTSD, or are dangerous because of psychosis, alcohol, or drug abuse problems. It is important that the evaluator remain unbiased, impartial, and collect collateral information carefully to ensure that FFD evaluations are used appropriately and not abuse for political or administrative purposes.

The FFD evaluation requires specialized expertise on the part of the evaluator because although they are similar to general psychiatric or psychological evaluations, there are many specific considerations in the field of law enforcement. Specifically, the psychological makeup of law enforcement personnel differs in some respects from that of the general community. Exposure to levels of violence, trauma, and hostility may lead to a variety of conditions which must be evaluated in the context of their employment. Standards of mental health are in some respects higher than for civilians due to the constant high stress level of the job. The requirement that law enforcement personnel be armed, and exercise force, including lethal force, judiciously necessitates that law enforcement personnel be calm, level-headed, and relatively anxiety-free so that they may make these decisions.

There are often temptations to cross boundaries and function in both an evaluation and treatment role, especially in remote or underserved areas. However, the evaluator should remain in an evaluation role and refer the evaluee to an appropriate clinician. Once the boundary has been violated by assuming a treatment role, a conflict of interest may occur. The evaluator cannot properly advise the department in its best interest at same time as advising the officer in her/his best interest if the interest of the officer and agency conflict.

It is critical to protect officers' confidentiality while communicating effectively the information necessary to police departments and agencies so they can make the appropriate decisions regarding light duty, return to duty, or separation. Finally, disability with respect to law enforcement personnel is a different concept than in civilian or general mental health evaluations. Reporting the results of a FFD evaluation is different from reporting involved in community mental health or insurance disability reports. Evaluators should restrict their comments on disability to the specific question of the officer's job performance and avoid comments regarding disability in other spheres.

## SAMPLE FITNESS FOR DUTY EVALUATION PROCESS:

1. The agency identifies an officer whose work performance or behavior is impaired.
2. The case and process of FFD should be discussed with a team including the chief or sheriff, legal counsel, and human relations, with input from the officer's direct supervisor.
3. The agency consults an evaluator to perform the FFD evaluation. The evaluator is chosen by the agency, not the officer.
4. The agency requests a FFD evaluation be performed by the evaluator in writing. The results should be sent to the department in care of the chief or designated police executive.
5. The agency specifies questions to be answered by the evaluator. (A detailed description of typical questions is presented in the Appendices.)
6. The agency prepares a "performance data package." This includes items such as past disciplinary actions/commendations, excess sick leave charts, citizen and/or inmate complaints, police reports (esp. in DV cases). This data is sent to the evaluator *after* initial interview with officer.
7. The evaluator requests a written statement from the officer's treating professional regarding diagnosis, prognosis, and treatment plan.
8. If the pre-employment psychological evaluation report is available, the agency sends a copy to the evaluator.
9. The agency reviews evaluator's report. The chief and team request clarification of the report until the issues and recommendations are thoroughly understood.
10. The chief or sheriff discusses evaluator's recommendations with legal counsel and decides on a course of action.

11. The agency should discuss (police) disciplinary action with team described in #2. It is *not* the purview of the evaluator to comment on disciplinary issues, so disciplinary action is not discussed by the agency with the evaluator.

12. The chief or sheriff discusses the results of the FFD evaluation process with the officer as it relates to resuming work and/or disciplinary action. It is important that this information be communicated by police executive personnel who have a thorough knowledge of the situation, not by the officer's direct supervisor.

In rare cases, a second opinion may be sought at the *agency* discretion. Agencies are not required to perform a number of different evaluations, even if an officer protests the results; nor is the agency bound to accept a FFD evaluation paid for by the employee. It is prudent to have an evaluator review the results of a report paid for by the employee if he/she pursues this. It is the agency which determines fitness of its employees, not outside parties, based on the recommendations of outside evaluators.

13. If officer is off duty due to recommendations of the FFD evaluation for a substantial period of time, then he/she should be reevaluated prior to return to duty. (This is not a new evaluation-it is a FOLLOW-UP to the FFD evaluation.)

## REFERENCES

Americans with Disabilities Act of 1990, 42 U.S.C. §§ 12101 *et seq.* (West, 1993).

American Psychological Association. (2002). *Ethical Principles of Psychologists and Code of Conduct.*

American Academy of Psychiatry & the Law. (2004). *Ethical Guidelines for the Practice of Forensic Psychiatry.*

Allen, M. G., & Presant, N. L. (2000). Psychiatric evaluations by the federal occupational health procedures. *The Forensic Examiner*, Nov./Dec.:13-18.

Brodsky, C. M. (1996). Psychiatric aspects of fitness for duty. *Occup Med, 11*(4):719-727, 1996.

Callery, Y. C., & Schepis-Mallon N. (1995). Fitness for duty policy: Implementation in the workplace. *AAOHN J*, Oct;43(10):522-6.

Colledge, A. L., & Johns, R. E. (2000). Unified fitness report for the workplace. *Occup Med, 15*(4):723-736.

Johnson, E. E. (1995). Improving mental fitness reports of candidates for police officer and fire fighter. *Psychol Rep*, Feb;76(1):193-4.

Oosthuizen, H., & Verschoor, T. (1992). Cooperation between experts in fitness proceedings. *Med Law, 11*(7-8):611-22.

Perry, R. G. (1998). Fitness-for-duty testing. *Occup. Health and Safety*, April: 41-43.

Pettus v. Cole, 49 Cal. App. 4th 402.

Reynolds, N. T. (2002). A model comprehensive psychiatric fitness-for-duty evaluation. *Occup Med*, Jan-Mar;17(1):105-18, v. Review.

Varela, J. G., Scogin, F. R., & Vipperman, R. K. (1999). Development and preliminary validation of a semi-structured interview for the screening of law enforcement candidates. *Behav Sci Law*, *17*(4):467-81.

Wu, A. F., Martens, L. C., & Deger, P. (1984). The merits of a fitness-for-duty policy. *Hospitals Sep, 1*;58(17):78-82.

Yin v State of California, 95 F.3d 864.

42 U.S.C. § 12131 *et seq.*

29 U.S.C. § 794.

# Chapter 2

# STRESS IN LAW ENFORCEMENT PERSONNEL: SOURCES AND MANIFESTATIONS

KATHLEEN P. DECKER, ANNE E. KIRKPATRICK, & BRIAN J. WILSON

## I. SOURCES OF STRESS

### 2.1 Stressor Ranking

Police work is a high-stress occupation. Periodically, investigators have examined the factors which create and contribute to stress in law enforcement personnel. It was found quite early on that violence, pain, and suffering, although stressful, were not the only or, even in many cases, the primary causes of stress for police officers (Speilberger, 1981). They developed a comprehensive instrument for ranking stress called the Police Stress Scale (PSS). The most stressful components of police work were found to be a mixture of intrinsic and organizational stressors.

A classic study by Violanti examined stress in police officers in a metropolitan police department (Violanti, 1995). As shown in Table 2.1, 60 possible sources of stress were ranked using the scale developed by Spielberger (1981). Intrinsic stressors, as defined by those which relate to specific risks of police work, such as killing someone, duty death, or physical assault, were ranked as the most stressful events. However, certain organizational stressors, such as shift work and inadequate departmental support, were ranked almost as highly and were ranked as much more stressful than exposure to death or pain and suffering.

Table 2.1
RANKING OF POLICE STRESSORS: VIOLANTI, 1992

| *Stressors* | *Mean* | *Standard Deviation* |
|---|---|---|
| *Highest Ranked Stressors* | | |
| Killing someone | 79.38 | 27.88 |
| Duty death | 76.67 | 23.18 |
| Physical attack | 70.97 | 27.61 |
| Battered children | 69.24 | 30.95 |
| High-speed chase | 63.73 | 28.37 |
| Shift work | 61.21 | 29.15 |
| Use of force | 60.96 | 29.01 |
| Inadequate departmental support | 60.93 | 29.24 |
| Incompatible partner | 60.36 | 28.11 |
| Accident in patrol car | 59.89 | 28.21 |
| *Lowest Ranked Stressors* | | |
| Promotion competition | 29.46 | 26.56 |
| Promotion or commendation | 28.79 | 27.72 |
| Non-police tasks | 27.94 | 25.30 |
| Demands for high morality | 26.14 | 24.85 |
| Politics outside department | 25.48 | 26.72 |
| Strained non-police relations | 23.60 | 24.00 |
| Boredom | 23.25 | 22.43 |
| Minor physical injuries | 23.23 | 21.42 |
| Racial conflicts | 22.53 | 22.22 |

## 2.2 Have Stressors Changed?

Many stressors are ranked similarly by current officers to past studies. In spite of significant changes to the structure of police work and the demographics of the police force, many of the perceived stressors remain strikingly similar between 1992 and 2003. The survey used in the Washington study does not list all of the stressors listed in Violanti's early work, and addresses a number of new items. In Table 2.3 the stressors which are listed in both studies are ranked in order of highest value to lowest. It shows that duty death is still one of the most stressful events in police work. However, the most significant difference is that "activities related to seeking promotion" is ranked as much more stressful than in previous years. However, it should be noted that

Violanti's study did not address organizational change per se, although it had items related to organizational structure. Thus, it appears from this study that organizational change is a very important stressor for current police officers.

Exposure to death in Violanti's study did not differentiate between types of death, but in the current study, a distinction was made between different types of death that showed that exposure to accidental death victims was more stressful than civilian complaints and was significantly more stressful than exposure to victims of suicide or homicide. The following comments by Deputy Chief Wilson and Chief Kirkpatrick may yield some insight into the mind-set of current police officers on this issue.

   **D. Chief Brian Wilson:** *Viewing remains is stressful because accidental death is not expected and suicide is difficult to understand because they did it to themselves. The locus of control of death is on the dead person vs. the police officer—in other words, the officer can't do anything to help or change the outcome. That in itself is stressful.*

   **Chief Kirkpatrick:** *In some respects, vehicular death is stressful, because the bodies are often gruesome. In other respects, suicide is more stressful because the individual hurt himself. Suicide violates the sanctity of life and has a profound effect on ruining the surviving family.*

### 2.3 Primary Data on Current Stressors

The most stressful events for current police officers include a mixture of intrinsic and organizational stressors. Police work has changed significantly since 1992 in terms of increased emphasis on community policing, which in part involves increased use of communication skills and decreased emphasis on use of force. One might therefore expect some differences in the sources of stress in law enforcement personnel. An examination of stressors was undertaken for the purpose of comparing current views of police stressors in a sample population of Washington police officers in 2003. A total of 250 questionnaires were distributed to 12 police departments with 75 responses. Of the 75 responses, 18 were from urban police departments (Seattle and Tacoma), 28 were from suburbs of those cities, and the 19 were from rural areas of central Washington and northern Oregon within a 250-

mile radius of those cities. An abbreviated survey was constructed to look at major intrinsic and organizational stressors. The results are shown in Table 2.2. The event ranked as most stressful in police work was duty death, with a mixture of intrinsic and organizational stressors following. The survey was designed to highlight differences between organizational stressors and intrinsic stressors. It sought to generate an understanding of police officers' stress related to death or suffering compared to various current organizational stressors. Interestingly, the item "activities related to seeking promotion" was rated more stressful than suicide by cop.

Table 2.2
RANKING OF STRESSFUL EVENTS
BY WASHINGTON STATE POLICE: DECKER, 2006

| Stressor | Mean | Standard Deviation |
|---|---|---|
| **Highest Ranked Stressors** | | |
| Duty death | 3.48 | 2.06 |
| Activities related to seeking promotion | 3.29 | 1.23 |
| Death notification of civilian families | 2.90 | 1.56 |
| Organizational change | 2.75 | 1.20 |
| Viewing remains of victims of accidental death | 2.71 | 1.37 |
| Civilian complaints about officers | 2.70 | 1.33 |
| Viewing remains of victims of homicide | 2.59 | 1.46 |
| **Intermediately Ranked Stressors** | | |
| Suicide by cop | 2.44 | 2.12 |
| Off-duty death of partner | 2.42 | 2.24 |
| Viewing remains of victims of suicide | 2.41 | 1.15 |
| Rotating shift work | 2.33 | 1.40 |
| Lack of promotion | 2.29 | 1.42 |
| Lack of continuing training classes | 2.18 | 1.23 |
| Death notification of police officers' families | 2.16 | 2.29 |
| **Lowest Ranked Stressors** | | |
| Paperwork related to violent police calls | 2.04 | 1.10 |
| Liaison duties with police survivor families | 1.97 | 1.85 |
| Maintaining physical fitness for job | 1.89 | 0.94 |
| Continuing training classes | 1.77 | 1.01 |
| Paperwork related to peaceful police calls | 1.23 | 0.80 |

Table 2.3
COMPARISON OF STRESSFUL EVENT RANKING: 2005 VS. 1992

| Stressor from Decker, 2006 | Stressor from Violanti, 1992 |
|---|---|
| Duty death | Duty Death |
| **Activities related to seeking promotion*** | |
| Death notification of civilian families | Death Notification |
| Organizational change* | |
| **Viewing remains of victims of accidental death** | |
| Civilian complaints about officers | Public criticism |
| Viewing remains of victims of homicide | **Exposure to death** |
| Viewing remains of victims of suicide | **Promotion competition** |
| **Lack of promotion*** | Promotion or commendation |
| Lack of continuing training classes* | |
| Paperwork related to violent police calls | Non-police tasks |
| Paperwork related to peaceful police calls | |

*\* Item not listed in Violanti's study.*

## 2.4 Organizational Stressors Are Paramount

Organizational stressors are more stressful than inherent stressors for various subgroups of law enforcement professionals. In previous studies, organizational stressors were ranked six-fold greater than inherent stressors (Violanti, 1993). They found that increased job satisfaction reduced stress. It was also found that conflicting, ambiguous roles or orders caused more stress (Aron, 1992). As above, one of the major stressors for current law enforcement personnel appears to be organizational change. In the current study on Washington police officers, the item listed as "Activities related to seeking promotion" was also ranked more highly by law enforcement personnel in this study than many intrinsic stressors such as viewing victims of trauma.

The profound importance that organizational stressors have on law enforcement personnel is highlighted by another recent study conducted on U.S. Marshals (Newman, 2004) to determine stress levels and stressors. It echoed findings from a similar, earlier study on police officers (Storch, 1996) as well as the data presented above on Washington law enforcement personnel. One hundred U.S. Deputy Marshals from offices across the country were interviewed as well as surveyed anonymously. Generally, deputies scored low on the State-Trait Anxiety Inventory (Spielberger, 1983).

The main stressors identified by the respondents were related to organizational variables as did police officers above. The organizational stressors cited most often included problems with management, "bad bosses," and the work environment. Marshals who were facing retirement were more stressed. Those marshals who disliked their current assignments and those who were inclined to think about job-related illnesses or being injured while on duty were more stressed.

## II. STRESS IN SUBGROUPS

### 2.5 Gender Differences

Female officers in Washington State perceive activities related to promotion as more stressful than their male counterparts. In the current study on Washington officers, the only gender difference between male and female officers in the ranking of these items was of "activities related to seeking promotion." Female officers ranked this item more stressful than did their male counterparts ($p<0.05$). This is consistent with the literature reviewed in Chapter 7 regarding gender differences. It suggests that in this geographical region at the current time, female officers continue to be more concerned about promotion issues than their colleagues and more stressed by events related to promotion. It is interesting to note that there was no gender difference in the ranking of "lack of promotion" which may indicate that the female officers in this sample believed that promotion is possible, but found preparing for it more stressful than their colleagues.

The foregoing is not to suggest that there are no gender differences between stress and stress reduction in female and male police officers. Indeed, many studies have found significant differences (Oliver, 2004; Tougas, 2005; Thompson, 2005). It should be noted that the Washington study did not include nonwork-related stressors such as family difficulties, which have been rated significantly differently by male and female officers in other studies. In a study on "compassion fatigue" (Violanti, 2004), *both* female and male officers experienced psychological risk of trauma symptoms including compassion fatigue as they experienced more incidents of trauma during their careers. However, the male officers had a higher risk of compassion fatigue associated with shootings, and female officers with trauma involving children.

In a recent study of urban police officers (Toch, 2002), the investigators found that male law enforcement professionals endorsed more family-related stress and reported a greater impact of these problems than their female counterparts. The authors were puzzled by the findings and did not find a specific explanation. One hypothesis that was not tested was that perhaps men feel more secure about their work achievements than women or that women have more outlets for dealing with family stress. They also postulated that the apparent gender difference was actually due to differences in seniority. In their sample, 78 percent of the female officers were junior, with <10 years experience versus only 29 percent of the male officers. A further discussion of gender differences between coping mechanisms occurs in Chapter 7.

## 2.6 Aging and Stress

The effects of age and experience on perceived stress are complex. In an older study (Violanti, 1995), it was found that the highest level of stress was experienced by officers with an intermediate level of experience (6-10 years on the job). The lowest level of stress was reported by officers with 20-25 years of experience. Officers with 11-20 years of experience rated greater stress associated with organizational stresses than with inherent stressors. Another study examined the effect of family problems on perceived stress in police officers (Toch, 2002). Over 58 percent of senior officers stated that they experience family problems that affected their work, compared to only 35 percent of junior officers. Most senior officers (78%) also reported that occupational problems affected family life versus only 54 percent of the junior officers. In a recent study on 105 police officers aged 50 years and older (Gershon, 2002), the most important risk factors associated with officers' perceived work stress were maladaptive coping behaviors such excessive drinking or problem gambling and exposure to critical incidents (e.g., shootings). They found that perceived work stress was significantly associated with several psychiatric symptoms. The rate of anxiety depression somatization, posttraumatic stress symptoms, and "burnout" was higher in older officers. Alcohol abuse and inappropriately aggressive behavior were also associated with higher levels of perceived work stress. Physical symptoms of chronic back pain were also associated with higher work stress.

The current Washington study did not obtain information on the number of years on the job worked by the officers who responded to the survey. However, rank was obtained in the Washington study, which is somewhat similar to age in that higher ranked officers (level of commander and above) tend to be more experienced and therefore older. The results show that there was no statistically significant difference between the ranking of stressors between those of lower rank (less than commander) and those in command staff with the exception of one item. ***Higher-ranking officers were more stressed by organizational change.*** Organizational change was defined as a change in police chief or reorganization of the department. It was listed as separate from either promotion-seeking activities or lack of promotion. The Washington study did not address the issue of family stress compared to occupational stress.

### 2.7 Changing Ethnic Differences

The perceived stressors in certain ethnic groups are changing. In previous studies, Caucasians reported slightly higher stress than did African-Americans (Violanti, 1995). However, at that time, the representation of African-Americans in command positions was relatively low. Additionally, African-American officers rated lack of support from the department as more stressful than did Caucasian officers. The number of police officers in that particular study was very small (93 Caucasian, 5 African-Americans, and 5 Hispanic officers). As discussed in Chapter 7, although many social factors have improved, there are still some significant differences between African-American and Caucasian officers' view of stress and stress management.

In another recent study of an urban police department African-American and Caucasian police officers were asked to rate sources of perceived stress, including stressors related to race relations (Toch, 2002). Discrimination was no longer ranked as the major perceived cause of stress, but racial relations was still a significant stressor for both African-American and Caucasian officers. The majority of African-American officers (69%) and almost half (48%) of Caucasian officers felt that racial tension in the department resulted in significant stress.

The data presented in the Washington study above was not analyzed by ethnicity of the officers. The vast majority of officers in this particular study declined to identify their ethnicity in the study, citing that confidentiality of survey results would be impaired if they did so. Participants represented in the study did include African-American officers and Hispanic officers, but there was no means to verify the extent of participation of these officers in the survey results.

## 2.8 Geographic Differences

Stressors and mechanisms for stress reduction are different in different geographic regions. In a study on rural police officers from West Virginia, significant differences were noted in stress patterns compared to their urban counterparts (Oliver, 2004). Specifically, they rated higher stress associated with longer times to receive backup and reported more isolation. Female officers from this sample were more likely to be divorced. Finally, they found that higher levels of educational opportunities targeted at stress reduction reduced stress.

In the current study on Washington state police officers, Table 2.4 shows that lack of continuing education classes was rated as more stressful to rural police officers than to their urban counterparts. However, the trend did not achieve statistical significance. This trend is not surprising, as access to continuing education is restricted in two ways. First, rural officers are farther from training centers (such as Regional Training Centers). Second, the small department size and large catchment area often mean it is harder to take time off to participate or travel to educational opportunities for rural officers. This is consistent with urban police officers reporting that educational classes were more stressful than their rural counterpart. The hypothesis would be that if education is more difficult to obtain, it is valued more highly. In contrast, there was a trend for urban officers to report more stress associated with continuing education classes. This is logical, as officers who find education difficult to obtain may value it more highly, and officers compelled to undergo education may devalue it.

Other differences between stressor rankings by rural officers included higher stress related to activities related to seeking promotion, shift work, and lack of promotion. These results are consistent with the study on West Virginia officers (Oliver, 2004).

Organizational change was defined in this survey as having "a new chief or reorganization of jobs in the department." There was no statistically significant difference in the ranking of stressors between metropolitan (pooled urban and suburban) and rural officers. However, there were statistically significant differences in the ranking of stressors when divided by specific sub-region: rural officers were statistically significantly more stressed by organizational change than suburban officers ($p<0.002$). Interestingly, urban officers were less stressed by organizational change than rural officers and more than the suburban officer, although this finding did *not* achieve statistical significance. In other words, organizational change seemed to be less stressful to suburban officers than to either rural or urban officers.

The other item which was rated as statistically significantly more stressful by urban police officers than suburban police officers was viewing remains of accidental death ($p<0.04$). The most obvious explanation for this is that there may be more serious accidents resulting in fatalities in urban areas than in suburban areas. Rural police officers commented that they are more used to seeing death as farm life is still comprised of both frequent natural disasters and livestock fatalities and injuries to farmers.

Table 2.4
RANKINGS OF ORGANIZATIONAL STRESSOR BY REGION

| *Stressor* | *Mean Urban (Std. Dev.)* | *Mean Suburban (Std. Dev.)* | *Mean Rural (Std. Dev.)* |
|---|---|---|---|
| **Activities related to seeking promotion** | 3.3 (1.1) | 3.0 (1.2) | **3.7** (1.3) |
| **Rotating shift work** | 2.0 (1.1) | 2.3 (1.4) | **2.8** (1.5) |
| **Lack of promotion** | 2.2 (1.3) | 2.1 (1.3) | **2.7** (1.7) |
| **Continuing education classes** | **1.9** (0.9) | **1.9** (1.1) | 1.4 (0.8) |
| **Lack of continuing education classes** | 1.9 (1.2) | 2.0 (1.2) | **2.7** (1.2) |

Other studies on police officers from different geographical regions demonstrate regional differences in stress as well. In a recent study on the Norwegian police force (Berg, 2005), a variant of the original Speilberger PSS rating scale (NPSS) was developed and utilized to compare stressors. The Norwegian police force differs from U.S. forces in that officers do not carry guns, and the rate of civilian homicide by firearms is much lower. Therefore, the investigators adapted the PSS by changing certain critical items to reflect the lower level of violence seen in their society compared to the U.S. Thus, they converted duty death to "serious injury of a fellow officer." Thus, their results must be interpreted with some caution as stressors intrinsic to police work are different in Norwegian society. However, most of the items were retained. Their results indicate that "injuries on the job" (the analog of duty death) was still the most stressful item. They also found that organizational stressor were important stressors. One finding which was somewhat different than in U.S. samples was that urban police officers were more stressed than were rural officers by intrinsic stressors, citing a lack of support by the department. However, rural Norwegian officers experienced more job pressure stress, which may be analogous to the study on West Virginia officers (Oliver, 2004) and the study presented above on Washington officers. They also found that older officers were more stressed by job pressure and younger officers by potential injury.

Peer support was found to alleviate stress in police officers in the Norwegian study. They also looked at certain personality defense mechanisms and found that extraversion was associated with lower stress and that an external locus of control increased stress.

At the other end of the spectrum of violence, South African police officers reported a high degree of posttraumatic stress disorder (Emsley, 2003). In a sample of 117 male and seven female officers, they found that 18 percent of the officers met criteria for delayed posttraumatic stress disorder. The majority (80%) of the officers cited multiple incidents contributing to posttraumatic stress disorder, and only 13 percent to a single incident. This provides a compelling argument for the cumulative nature of violence contributing to posttraumatic stress disorder and has implications for officers who have experienced multiple critical incidents in any geographical location. They found that 67 percent of the officers suffered from major depression, 14 percent from panic disorder, and a relatively low 11 percent had comorbid alcohol dependence. It also highlights that stress in police officers depends to a great degree on the amount of violence to which they are exposed, especially in case of repeated exposure. Their findings suggest that in circumstances such as an inner-city or a war-torn area where violence is a frequent and unpredictable part of the workday, a shift from organizational stressors to intrinsic police stressors is likely to be seen.

## III. STRESS RESPONSES

### 2.9 Poor Coping Skills

Maladaptive coping mechanisms in response to stress in police remains a critical area for intervention. High levels of stress have long been linked to higher morbidity and mortality in the general population. A survey of mortality of municipal workers over a 40-year period in Buffalo, New York found that there was a higher mortality rate for police officers (Violanti, 1998). The accident rate was lower than for corresponding municipal workers, but natural, suicide, and homicide deaths were higher. A more thorough discussion of suicide in police officers is treated in Chapters 9 and 10. The early studies on police showed that officers resorted to alcohol use to reduce stress (Violanti, 1983). The strongest factor relating to alcohol use was distress. Violanti found that certain psychological coping mechanisms of cynicism, secrecy, and deviance were associated with increased stress.

A study examined causes of disability in Washington State Public Safety employees (Blum, 1998). The study was composed of a retrospective review of 3,686 police officers and firefighters retired in Washington State through examination of Pension Board statistics. They found that over 57 percent of public safety officers retired because of disability of which 90 percent was considered to be due to line-of-duty conditions. The most frequent cause of disability was back injury (48%). All in all, orthopedic injuries accounted for 72 percent of disability retirements. The most common orthopedic injuries included joint conditions including knee, neck, and shoulder injuries. Heart condition accounted for 13 percent of disability retirement. ***Only 4 percent of disability retirements were related to psychological conditions so diagnosed psychiatric disorders are a less common cause of disability retirement than physical causes.*** However, psychological stress is well-known to cause or exacerbate physical problems such ulcers and heart conditions so "burnout" may take its toll upon officers' physical health indirectly.

In a recent review, a variety of dysfunctional behaviors were associated with stress in police officers (Violanti, 1998). They found a number of health consequences such as cardiovascular problems, ulcers, and alcohol and substance abuse problems. They also found a number of psychiatric problems, including detachment, cynicism, posttraumatic stress disorder, marital problems, and aggressiveness. Finally, performance issues including early retirement and absenteeism were noted.

Another study found that cardiovascular disease prevalence did not differ significantly between the law enforcement officer and the general population (Franke, 2002). However, between age-matched, income-matched males from the same geographical region, the officers reported higher prevalence of hypertension, hypercholesterolemia, tobacco use, and elevated body mass index. Within the law enforcement officers, the best predictors of cardiovascular disease were time in the profession, perceived stress, and hypertension. Additionally, perceived stress was associated with cardiovascular disease and three CVD risk factors were significantly affected by perceived stress: cholesterol, hypertension, and physical activity. Perceived stress was affected by duration of time in the profession independent of the officers' age. Thus, this study is consistent with the other results in that perceived stress may contribute to cardiovascular disease both directly and indirectly by potentiating cardiovascular risk factors.

A sample of police officers aged 50 years and older was undertaken (Gershon, 2002). The most important risk factors associated with officers' higher perceived work stress were maladaptive coping behaviors such as alcohol abuse or gambling. Individuals with higher perceived work stress had a higher risk of various psychiatric complaints, including anxiety, depression, somatization, post-traumatic stress symptoms, other "burnout" symptoms, alcohol abuse, and inappropriately aggressive behavior. These data suggest that older workers in high-stress jobs may be at increased risk for work stress-related health problems, especially if they rely on risky health behaviors to cope with stress.

Another recent survey study of Norwegian police examined correlations between attitudes in police officers with their choice of police procedures (Burke, 2005). The officers who reported higher levels of cynicism were more inclined towards the use of force. The converse was also true in that police officers who reported higher levels of professional efficacy were more inclined to favor the use of social skills to solve problems.

## 2.10 Interventions to Decrease Stress

Treating stress requires a variety of approaches tailored to the needs of specific officers as well as departments. Table 2.5 shows the results of the Washington State study. Police officers were askd to rank interventions that they perceived as most helpful following a critical incident. Interventions were ranked from most useful (1) to least useful (11). The interventions that were ranked as the most useful were immediate debriefing by supervisor and peer discussions without supervisors present. These were followed by discussion with spouse next, then immediate debriefing by psychiatrist. The remaining interventions were ranked significantly lower. Essentially officers completely discounted the strategy of ignoring critical incident stress which was framed as "No discussion: just get back to work."

Table 2.5
RANKING POSTCRITICAL INCIDENT INTERVENTIONS

| INTERVENTION | Mean Rank | Standard Deviation |
|---|---|---|
| Immediate debriefing by supervisor | 2.8 | 3.1 |
| Delayed debriefing by mental health professional | 3.8 | 2.0 |
| Discussion with other family members (than spouse) | 4.1 | 2.6 |
| Peer discussion without supervisor present | 4.2 | 3.1 |
| Discussion with spouse | 4.7 | 2.8 |
| Immediate debriefing by mental health professional | 4.8 | 2.8 |
| Informal discussions over coffee, drinks, etc. | 6.2 | 2.6 |
| Individual discussion with religious figures | 6.4 | 3.0 |
| Discussions with best friend or other nonlaw enforcement contacts | 6.9 | 2.5 |
| Delayed debriefing by supervisor | 6.9 | 3.1 |
| No discussion, just get back to work | 10.6 | 1.1 |

Additionally, no statistically significant differences were found between the rankings of possible interventions to decrease stress after critical incidents by command staff versus lower-level officers. In other words, both command staff and line staff endorsed similar interventions to reduce stress after critical incidents. Immediate debriefing by supervisors, although not designed as a therapeutic intervention but as an organizational necessity and a legal necessity, appears to function as a stress-reducing mechanism for police officers. This issue was discussed with both command staff and line staff representing several different police departments. They explained that the reason this intervention is helpful is that it helps them reorganize their thinking, return to work with a clear idea of the sequence of events, and to move through the incident. A detailed analysis of these interventions is discussed in Chapter 8.

One limitation of this study is that it did not document *actual* improved functioning, only police officers' perceptions of stress reduction. A recent study (Carlier, 2000) on British police officers examined improvement in 243 officers who had experienced trauma due to critical incidents. The debriefed officers reported a high degree of satisfaction with debriefing. However, the investigators found no difference between psychological morbidity between the groups at 24 hours posttrauma or at 6 months posttrauma. Surprisingly, one week posttrauma, the debriefed officers actually exhibited significantly *more* posttraumatic stress disorder symptoms than those who did not undergo nondebriefing. Thus, the high levels of satisfaction with debriefing reported by the debriefed officers were *not* reflected in positive outcomes. It may also indicate that individual psychological makeup is a more important determinant than short-term interventions to reduce the incidence of PTSD. Of course, debriefing strategies may vary, as well as a number of other factors. The British study highlights the need for more outcome studies and for prospective analysis of the outcome of various stress reduction techniques.

A number of approaches have been utilized by different departments to assist with police stress. These include institutionalized programs such as Employee Assistance Programs, as discussed in Chapter 9. A great deal of recent literature has been written in recent years about the role of peer counseling (Madonna, 2002). Chaplains have had a historic role in reducing officer stress and some agencies still utilize them as primary providers for counseling of officers.

The COPS (Concerns of Police Survivors) organization has a variety of practical and emotional networking tools to assist with the grief and adjustment process. This organization serves both surviving family members of police officers killed in the line of duty as well as their surviving fellow officers.

Individual counseling can be an effective method for reducing stress in certain individuals. However, some investigators found that "planful problem-solving" and distancing mechanisms were the most effective at reducing stress after traumatic incidents (Violanti, 1993). Accepting responsibility and escape/avoidance behaviors actually increased perceived stress. In general, police officers are chosen to be well-grounded and matter-of-fact rather than abstract or introverted, so counseling may not work for all. It is theoretically possible that female officers may benefit more from verbal methods of stress reduction than male officers based on traditional female stress-reduction techniques of verbal release. However, it may also be that female police officers are less verbal than females in the general population and more similar to their male counterparts in this regard.

Many studies have documented the important role that exercise plays in stress reduction and in the treatment of depression. Law enforcement professionals are typically chosen to be physically healthy at hiring. It is a logical conclusion that increased exercise might assist law enforcement personnel in managing stress. One study evaluated changes in the physical activity, fitness, and body composition of 103 Finnish police officers during a 15-year period (Sorensen, 2000). No significant correlations were found between physical activity and work ability or perceived physical or mental job stress. However, this may reflect the higher baseline level of physical fitness seen in police versus many civilians—in other words, they are held to a higher standard of fitness and are more interested in maintaining fitness than civilian counterparts.

### 2.11 Conclusions

The first striking observation made in this chapter by comparing stressors that police commonly experience is that a number of the essential characteristics of police work result in similar stress compared to prior decades. Although society has undergone many changes, law enforcement personnel still experience organizational stressors as more severely than intrinsic job stressors such as violence. In part, this is likely because they are *chosen* to handle violence better than most civilians. Between an enhanced ability to tolerate action and stress and a decreased ability to pursue paperwork and remain behind a desk, law enforcement personnel continue to experience activities related to seeking promotion, organizational change, and civilian complaints as more stressful than a variety of violent incidents.

An examination of gender differences between male and female police officers reveals many similarities but a few differences. Differences noted in the Washington State study between male and female officers were minimal with respect to ranking the primary job-related stressors. However, the literature supports the contention that family stress is more pronounced in female officers, as well as stress responses related to violent crimes involving children. On the other hand, male officers tend to be more stressed by critical incidents involving shooting. Gender differences discovered in Washington State officers with respect to duty death are discussed more fully in Chapter 8. A detailed examination of gender differences in law enforcement personnel also occurs in Chapter 7.

Geographical differences are also less prominent than similarities, although significant. These differences have important implications for training current and future law enforcement personnel. Across the globe, organizational stressors are perceived as most difficult, although duty death or injury is the most stressful (albeit rarer) event. Rural officers commonly experience more stress associated with obtaining continuing education as well as obtaining "off-time" due to the isolated nature and smaller police forces in rural areas. This suggests a variety of interventions to improve the quality of life for officers, which are discussed in the Afterword.

## REFERENCES

Aron, F. (1992). *An analysis of police stressors.* Unpublished, Russell Sage College, Albany, New York.

Berg, A. M. et al. Stress in the Norwegian Police Service. *Occupat. Med. 55* (2) 113-120, 2005.

Blum, L. N. (1998). *The impact of public safety work upon the health and life of those who serve: Disease, disturbance, disability and mortality in Washington State public safety personnel.*

Burke, R.J., & Mikkelsen, A. (2005). Burnout, job stress and attitudes towards the use of force by Norwegian police officers. *Policing–An International Journal of Police Strategies & Management, 28* (2): 269-278.

Carlier, I. V. E., Voerman, A. E., & Gersons, B. P. R. (2000). The influence of occupational debriefing on post-traumatic stress symptomatology in traumatized police officers. *Brit J of Medical Psychology, 73*: 87-98, Mar.

Emsley, R. A. et al. (2003). Post-traumatic stress disorder and occupational disability in South African Security Force members. *J Nerv Ment Disorders, 191*(4):237-241.

Franke, W.D., Ramey, S.L., & Shelley, M.C. Relationship between cardiovascular disease morbidity, risk factors, and stress in a law enforcement cohort. *J Occupat and Environ Med, 44* (12): 1182-1189.

Gershon, R. R. M, Lin, S., & Li, X. B. (2002). Work stress in aging police officers. *J of Occupat and Environmental Medicine, 44* (2): 160-167, Feb.

Madonna, J. M., & Kelly, R. E. (2002). Treating police stress: The work and the words of peer counselors. Springfield, IL: Charles C Thomas.

Newman, D.W., Rucker-Reed, M.L.Police stress, state-trait anxiety, and stressors among U.S. Marshals. *J of Crim Justice, 32* (6): 631-641, Nov-Dec.

Oliver, W. M., & Meier, C. A. (2004). Stress in small town and rural law enforcement: Testing the assumptions. *Am J Crim Justice, 29*(1):37-56.

Sorensen, L. et al. Physical activity, fitness and body composition of Finnish police officers: A 15-year follow-up study. *Occup Med, 50* (1): 3-10, Jan.

Spielberger, C. et al. (1981). *The police stress survey: Sources of stress in law enforcement.* Tampa, FL: Human Resources Institute.

Spielberger, C. D. et al. (1983). *State-trait anxiety inventory.* Palo Alto, CA: Consulting Psychologists Press.

Storch, J. E., & Panzarella, R. (1996). Police stress: State-trait anxiety in relation to occupational and personal stressors. *J of Crim Justice, 24*(2):99-107.

Thompson, B. M., Kirk, A., & Brown, D. F. (2005). Work based support, emotional exhaustion and spillover of work stress to the family environment: A study of policewomen. *Stress and Health, 21*:199-207.

Toch, H. (2002). *Stress in policing.* Washington, D.C.: American Psychological Association.

Tougas, F., et al. (2005) Policewomen acting in self-defense: Can psychological disengagement protect self-esteem from the negative outcomes of relative deprivation? *J Pers and Soc Psychol, 88*(5):790-800.

Violanti, J., Marshall, J., & Howe, B. (1983). Police occupational demands, psychological distress and the coping function of alcohol. *J Occupat Med, 25*(6):455-458.

Violanti, J. M. (1993). Coping strategies among police recruits in a high-stress training environment. *J Soc Psychol, 132*(6):717-729.

Violanti, J. M., & Aron, F. (1994). Ranking police stressors. *Psychol Reports, 75*:824-826.

Violanti, J. M., & Aron, F. (1995). Police stressors: Variation in perception among police personnel. *J Crim Justice, 23*(3): 287-294.

Violanti, J. M., & Gehrke, A. (2004). Police trauma encounters: Precursors of compassion fatigue. *Int J of Emerg Mental Health, 6*(2):75-80.

Violanti, J. M., & Paton, D. (1999). *Police Trauma: Psychological aftermath of civilian combat.* Springfield, IL: Charles C Thomas.

Violanti, J. M., Vena, J. E., & Petralia, S. (1998). Mortality of a police cohort: 1950-1990. *Am J of Indust Med, 33*:366-373.

# Chapter 3

# COMMON CAUSES OF "UNFIT" OFFICERS

Kathleen P. Decker

## I. MISCONDUCT VERSUS MENTAL ILLNESS

### 3.1 What Is Police Misconduct?

Police misconduct encompasses a wide variety of issues. Misconduct ranges from insubordination to violence, corruption, or misuse of police powers. At every level of police personnel from patrol officer to chief, a significant degree of discretion regarding the application of laws and the administration of force is exercised. As there are approximately 600,000 sworn officers in the United States, misbehavior of even 0.5 percent would amount to 3,000 cases a year. If 5 percent of officers had an incidence of some form of misconduct, this would rise to 30,000 officers potentially involved in illegal or improper activities. Thus, understanding misconduct and differentiating it from behavior of psychiatrically disturbed personnel is important.

### 3.2 Psychiatric Illness or Bad Behavior?

A major reason that evaluators need to understand the issue of police misconduct is that frequently there may be misconduct in the presence of various psychiatric impairments. Thus, an officer may have both misconduct issues AND a psychiatric impairment. For example, In Kelly v. Salt Lake City Civil Service Commission, 8 P.3d 1048 (Utah App. 2000), a police officer became intoxicated after taking a prescription sleep aid. It was held to be "voluntary intoxication."

The officer was held responsible for her conduct unbecoming an officer, which was committed while she was intoxicated. The officer exceeded the prescribed dosage voluntarily and with no medical supervision. The officer told her roommate that she was going to take enough medication to "feel good," thus indicating that her use of the medication was recreational rather than medicinal. The officer's conduct was also deemed "subversive to the operation" of the police department as she called police and fire dispatch centers while intoxicated and threatened to blow up buildings housing emergency services.

Imagine the circumstances if the case had been slightly different. If the officer had been sent for a FFD evaluation and subsequently found to have (chronic) prescription substance dependence, she would still have been subject to discipline, but the agency would also have had to examine reasonable accommodations and allowed her to seek treatment for the disorder, rather than immediate termination. The remainder of this chapter focuses on the underlying reasons law enforcement personnel may experience difficulty in the performance of their jobs.

It is particularly important to differentiate "simple misconduct" from bad behavior that is the result of mental illness. Thus, evaluators need to understand the concept of misconduct and have some awareness of the police disciplinary process as it relates to misconduct. The topics of misconduct and discipline are covered in detail in Chapter 11.

## II. PSYCHOLOGICAL CHARACTERISTICS OF UNFIT OFFICERS

### 3.3 Crystal Ball Performance

Does pre-employment psychological test data predict future unfit officers? A recent Australian study reviewed various psychological tests utilized in screening police candidates (Arrigo, 2003). The investigators postulated that certain traits such as conscientiousness are essential to good performance in officers. They recommended utilizing tools other than the MMPI to examine this trait. For example, the Inwald Personality Inventor (IPI) has been used to attempt to predict job performance (Cortina, 1992; Inwald, 1984). In one study, Inwald reported that the IPI correctly predicted 72 percent of male officers and 82 percent of female officers who were terminated. This contrasted with using the MMPI to predict termination in the same officers. The MMPI only correctly predicted 62 percent of male officers and 66 percent of female officers that were terminated. In another study several years later, similar data was obtained. In that study 69 officers were administered the IPI and the MMPI while in training (Scoggin, 1995). The IPI correctly classified 72 percent of officers who performed well within a year of hiring, whereas the MMPI correctly classified only 64 percent. In addition to termination issues, agencies are concerned with routine behavior. Specific job-relevant characteristics such as excess absence, tardiness, and disciplinary incidents were found to be predicted by the IPI.

A large study was conducted on a sample of police officers from both a metropolitan and a rural southern region (Weiss, 2005). The study utilized psychological testing with the Personality Assessment Inventory (PAI) during the pre-employment psychological evaluation and at one year after hiring. They used a number of variables associated with poor performance, including insubordination, excess citizen complaints, and neglect of duty. They found the trait "Antisocial-Egocentricity" correlated with negative job performance. They also found that traits of "Antisocial-Stimulus Seeking" and "Negative Impression" were correlated with neglect of duty. Finally, these investigators found that insubordination and excess citizen complaints correlated with "Antisocial-Egocentricity."

### 3.4 Testing the Effect of Treatment

Do psychological tests assist in determining improvement after treatment in unfit officers? One study on FFD evaluations studied the outcome of 376 officers who were referred for FFD Evaluation in a Midwestern metropolitan area (Schmitt, 1996). The demographics of the study included 148 African-American officers, 211 Caucasian officers and 17 officers from other ethnic groups. The study showed that African-American officers were more likely to be referred for FFD evaluations. There was no difference between the age or tenure on the job of officers referred versus those not referred. An examination of the job performance ratings showed that the officers referred for evaluation had lower ratings both in the 10-year period prior to referral as well as lower ratings close to the time of referral.

Of the officers referred for FFD evaluations, 18 declined any intervention and the remaining 171 underwent an Employee Assistance Program (EAP) intervention. All of the 171 officers had taken the MMPI-2 and 65 also had a CPI. Many of the officers (42%) referred had one or more elevations on subscales of the MMPI-2 and another 30 officers had a lower-grade elevation. There was no consistent pattern of dysfunction in those officers with subscale elevation on the MMPI-2, there was a consistent pattern of improvement or normalization of MMPI-2 scores after their EAP intervention. There was no change in scales associated with veracity (L or K) or in masculinity/femininity. In contrast, the group that declined EAP intervention had no significant improvement in their MMPI-2 scores. The CPI was less useful at defining change after the EAP. There were more subtle improvements in officers on this measure. The same pattern of lack of improvement in officers who declined EAP intervention was noted using the CPI.

The studies cited above highlight the importance for evaluators to compare pre-employment psychological data with that obtained during the course of a FFD evaluation. Wherever possible, follow-up testing after psychiatric intervention is also recommended.

## III. FITNESS FOR DUTY EVALUEES IN WASHINGTON STATE

### 3.5 Primary data from Washington State

This is apparently the first study to systematically examine psychiatric diagnoses of police officers subjected to FFD evaluations. The investigator is a psychiatrist, so she may have been sent evaluees who were deemed to be more disturbed than those sent to psychologists for FFD evaluations. It should be noted that this study represents data obtained by one investigator in one state. However, the data represents three types of geographical regions, as described below.

The following data was collected on 57 sequential FFD evaluations over a six-year period in Washington State. Of these, 36 were police officers and 21 were corrections officers. The sample was comprised of 17 female and 40 male officers. The majority were Caucasian (49), with five African-American and one Asian officer represented. The majority (34%) of the officers was still in their first marriage, another 12.5 percent were remarried, and 30 percent were divorced. Some officers had been divorced multiple times (10.7%). The mean age was 35 years among the female officers and 40 among the male officers, which was not statistically significantly different.

The officers were referred from three geographical regions: urban, suburban, and rural law enforcement agencies within a 250 mile radius of Seattle, Washington. Table 3.1 shows the distribution by geographic sub-region. Urban and suburban officers were evaluated in equal proportions and for many of the analyses described below, were considered as a single metropolitan group versus rural officers who were located approximately 150-200 miles from large metropolitan areas.

Table 3.1
GEOGRAPHIC DISTRIBUTION OF FFD EVALUEES

| Region | Number | % |
|---|---|---|
| Urban | 15 | 26.3 |
| Suburban | 15 | 26.3 |
| Rural | 27 | 47.4 |

### 3.6 Psychiatric Diagnoses

Table 3.2 shows the most common psychiatric diagnoses of officers referred for FFD evaluations in this study. A primary diagnosis is considered the most severe or important presenting problem and a secondary diagnosis is one which is clinically significant but not the primary problem. Axis I refers to the *Diagnostic and Statistical Manual for Mental Disorders (DSM-IV)* system which divides psychiatric conditions into multiple axes to describe different contributing factors to the individual's overall psychiatric makeup (APA, 1994). Axis I diagnoses are reserved for "Major Psychiatric Syndromes." These are more generally severe problems, often with a biological or genetic component. Axis II diagnoses and disorders are discussed below in Section 3.10.

As shown in the table, the most common diagnosis was major depression (42%) in all evaluees in this series. The second most common primary diagnosis was bipolar disorder (19%). The most common secondary diagnosis was substance use disorder. Posttraumatic stress disorder and attention deficit disorder were seen in a minority of cases as either a primary or secondary diagnosis.

Table 3.2
PSYCHIATRIC DIAGNOSES OF FITNESS FOR DUTY EVALUEES

|  | *Primary Axis I Diagnosis Number* | *Primary Axis I Diagnosis %* | *Primary Axis I Diagnosis Number* | *Primary Axis I Diagnosis %* |
|---|---|---|---|---|
| **None** | 11 | 19.3 | 42 | 73.7 |
| **Major Depression** | 24 | 42.1 | 1 | 1.8 |
| **Bipolar** | 11 | 19.3 | | |
| **Anxiety** | 2 | 3.5 | 2 | 3.5 |
| **Posttraumatic Stress Disorder** | 3 | 5.3 | 1 | 1.8 |
| **Psychosis** | 1 | 1.8 | 1 | 1.8 |
| **Substance Use** | 1 | 1.8 | 7 | 12.3 |
| **ADD** | 3 | 5.3 | 3 | 5.3 |
| **Developmentally Delayed** | 1 | 1.8 | | |

### 3.7 Comparison with Prior FFD Studies

There are very few published reports regarding psychiatric diagnoses of unfit police officers. To date, most studies concentrated on psychological test data, but not on *actual psychiatric diagnoses* of unfit officers. However, a previous study of 271 FFD cases of employees presenting for FFD evaluations from 32 federal agencies was performed by OSHA (Allen, 2000). The study summarized findings of diagnoses of employees from 1992 to 1997. There are major differences between the studies in that the study population of Allen was broader. It consisted of subjects presenting to Federal Occupational Health from a *variety* of federal, civilian, and military agencies. Therefore, it also included *civilian* employees as well as law enforcement personnel.

A comparison of the Allen study to the data obtained in the current Washington study is presented in Table 3.3. Also, the sample size in the Allen study was much larger (271 versus 57). However, their study also shows that the major diagnosis associated with unfit was depression. Bipolar disorder and substance use disorder were also frequently diagnosed in unfit evaluees in their study.

Table 3.3
DIAGNOSES ASSOCIATED WITH "UNFIT"

|  | % Unfit Decker 2006 | % Unfit Allen 2000 |
|---|---|---|
| None | *19.4 | |
| Major Depression | 36.1 | 70 |
| Bipolar | 22.2 | 9.5 |
| Anxiety Disorder | 2.8 | ** |
| Posttraumatic Stress Disorder | 2.8 | *** |
| Psychosis due to a Medical Condition | 2.8 | 5 |
| Substance Use Disorder | 2.8 | 9.5 |
| Attention Deficit Disorder | 8.3 | ****5 |
| Developmentally Delayed | 2.8 | **** |

\* Those officers were deemed "unfit" because of an Axis II Personality Disorder.
\*\* In Allen's study, Depression and Anxiety were combined as a single diagnostic category: DSM-IV was not used as the method of classification.
\*\*\* In Allen's study, PTSD was not listed as a diagnosis.
\*\*\*\* In Allen's study, Learning Disorders were combined with ADD.

## 3.8 Comparison of Psychiatric Diagnoses: "Fit" versus "Unfit"

The findings above lead to the question: Were there differences in the psychiatric diagnoses between officers who were unfit for duty and those that were fit for duty? One would expect that those who were "fit" had no psychiatric diagnosis or a less serious diagnosis. The most frequent diagnosis amongst those referred for a FFD evaluation but returned immediately to duty was major depression. Some officers found "fit" had no Axis I disorder as below. In those cases, the officers were found "fit" because the events precipitating the FFD evaluation were not attributed to a psychiatric diagnosis. The officers were then subject to disciplinary action. Twenty-one officers were found "Fit" for duty immediately. Of those found fit for duty immediately, 35 percent were male officers and 40 percent were female officers. In this sample,

60 percent of evaluees were found "unfit," of which 33 percent were deemed temporarily "unfit" for duty but returned to duty within two months and 29 percent were deemed "unfit" by the evaluator without foreseeable return to duty.

Another way to understand data in the current Washington State study is to examine the Axis I primary and secondary diagnoses to see if there are differences between fit and unfit officers. As shown below in Table 3.4, both officers deemed fit and unfit were most likely to be suffering from major depression, with the second most common diagnosis being bipolar. However, officers deemed fit were more likely to have anxiety disorder of posttraumatic stress disorder. The most common secondary diagnosis for both groups was substance use disorder, then attention deficit disorder. So different Axis I diagnoses did not explain the (immediate) return to fitness. Some other possible factors include the severity of the primary condition, presence or lack of treatment, or personality diagnosis contributing to unfitness.

Table 3.4
DSM-IV DIAGNOSES OF UNFIT AND FIT OFFICERS

| *DSM-IV Psychiatric Diagnosis* | *Primary Axis I Diagnosis UNFIT %* | *Primary Axis I Diagnosis FIT %* | *Secondary Axis IA Diagnosis UNFIT %* | *Secondary xis I Diagnosis FIT %* |
|---|---|---|---|---|
| None | 19.4 | 19.0 | 69.4 | 81.0 |
| Major Depression | 36.1 | 52.4 | 2.8 | 0 |
| Bipolar Disorder | 22.2 | 14.3 | 0 | 0 |
| Anxiety Disorder | 2.8 | 4.8 | 5.6 | 0 |
| Posttraumatic Stress Disorder | 2.8 | 9.5 | 2.8 | 0 |
| Psychosis (Due to a General Medical Condition) | 2.8 | 0.00 | 2.8 | |
| Substance Use Disorder | 2.8 | 0.0 | 11.11 | 4.3 |
| Attention Deficit Disorder | 8.3 | 0.0 | 5.6 | 4.8 |
| Developmentally Delayed | 2.8 | 0.0 | 0.0 | 0 |

## 3.9 Attention Deficit Disorder: A Frequent Diagnosis. Why?

Attention Deficit Disorder (ADD or ADHD) was seen frequently as a primary diagnosis in unfit officers but also was a frequent secondary diagnosis in *both* fit and unfit officers. Combining primary and secondary diagnoses, 15 percent of officers found to be "unfit" had a diagnosis of ADD. Almost 5 percent of the officers found "fit" had ADD (as a secondary diagnosis). This disorder affects approximately 3-5 percent of the adult population according to recent estimates (Faraone, 2004; Kessler, 2004). No systematic study has been undertaken to examine the incidence of ADHD either in police applicants or in officers referred for FFD evaluations to date. The only other known study describing specific psychiatric diagnoses in employees referred for FFD (Allen, 2000) was discussed in detail in Chapter 3. The investigators in that study combined learning disabilities with ADD, which is no longer be considered appropriate for diagnostic purposes, as they are separate disorders according to modern psychiatric research.

As with the diagnosis of bipolar disorder, the high percentage of evaluees diagnosed with ADD is not likely due to evaluator bias. The majority of the individuals so diagnosed by the evaluator had previously been diagnosed and treated for ADD by external physicians. One hypothesis for the high percentage of individuals in this series with ADD is that law enforcement and other paramilitary professions may attract individuals with ADD because of specific intrinsic work factors. For example, these professions include frequent movement (as opposed to "desk jobs") exciting situations, and relatively little paperwork or memorization.

In fact, the ability to avoid deskwork is frequently cited in interviews with pre-employment candidates for law enforcement as well as the ability to be mobile rather than in an office (Decker, unpublished observation). Additionally, many individuals with ADD state that they function best under pressure, and law enforcement or paramilitary professions offer an unlimited amount of stress. For individuals with *mild* symptoms of ADD the diagnosis is one which is potentially likely to be missed because of the superficial nature of cognitive testing involved in pre-employment testing.

The author proposes that rather than looking at ADD as purely an "illness," it may be more appropriate to consider the possibility that individuals with (**mild**) ADD may have a selective advantage in certain situations. Specifically, individual with low-grade symptoms of ADD may tolerate stressful events such as critical incidents better than "normal" individuals because they do respond with "blunted" stress responses. Physiologically, individuals with ADD may possess a selective advantage over "normal" individuals under stress as catecholamines, including epinephrine, norepinephrine, and dopamine, are released during stress along with other hormones (Sluiter, 2000). These neurotransmitters can produce agitation or anxiety in "normal" individuals. The principal chemical defect in ADD appears to be a relative imbalance or deficit of catecholoamine neurotransmitters: dopamine and norepinephrine (Biederman, 2005). A number of studies have shown that individuals with ADD have "blunted" responses with respect to the release of hormones, catecholamines, and other physiologic changes induced by stressful events (Konrad, 2003, King, 1998). This means that they do not mount as great a hormonal response in response to stressful events as do "normal" individuals. Some investigators have hypothesized that the evolutionary advantage of ADD was an adaptive response to highly urgent situations as in primitive hunting (Glickman, 1998). According to this theory, individuals with ADD had a selective advantage as they were able to respond quickly and calmly to intense, urgent situations.

In individuals with ADD, increased catecholamine release may result in improved concentration and focus while under stress. The higher levels of catecholamines may mimic the effects of stimulant or antidepressant treatment, which also enhances catecholamine release by different mechanisms. The converse finding has certainly been established, in that individuals with anxiety disorders experience panic attacks and decreased functioning associated with increased levels of catecholamines triggered by stress (Hoehn, 1997).

Additionally, individuals with PTSD have been found to have higher catecholamine levels than individuals exposed to trauma without posttraumatic stress disorder (Young, 2004). Interestingly, individuals exposed to trauma who did *not* develop PTSD demonstrated significantly lower urine catecholamine levels than either individuals who were not exposed to trauma and the PTSD groups. This supports the hypothesis that certain individuals who are resistant to negative effects of trauma have different catecholamine responses. Stress responses seen in "normal" individuals are associated with a variety of long-term negative physical effects when stress is either prolonged or repeated. Therefore, individuals with ADD might actually suffer *fewer* long-term consequences of stress than "normal" individuals.

***The reader is cautioned that the hypothesis presented above is novel and is untested.*** However, it suggests further research areas including more detailed research into the prevalence of ADD in law enforcement officers as well as prospective physiologic testing of officers under various types of stress. This hypothesis is in *no* way meant to suggest that individuals with ADD make better police officers than others–clearly moderate or severe symptoms of ADD including impulsivity and low frustration tolerance *would not be consistent* with the careful, considered judgments and responsible behavior of law enforcement personnel. But it may be that those with *mild* ADD symptoms should not be automatically disqualified from consideration from careers in law enforcement.

### 3.10 Personality Disorders in "Unfit" versus "Fit" Officers

Axis II refers to personality disorders, which are defined as enduring patterns of difficulties with interpersonal relations. A 2004 survey showed that nearly 14.8 percent of adult Americans met diagnostic criteria for personality disorders as defined by the American Psychiatric Association's DSM-IV. As of 2002, 7.9 percent of all adults had obsessive-compulsive personality disorder; 4.4 percent had paranoid personality disorder; 3.6 percent had antisocial personality disorder; 3.1 percent had schizoid personality disorder; 2.4 percent had avoidant personality disorder; and 0.5 percent had dependent personality disorder.

Cluster A is used to define a series of personality disorders which are associated with unusual behavior, perceptions or habits which do not meet the criteria for a more serious thought disorder or psychosis such as schizophrenia. The Cluster A disorders include paranoid, schizoid, and schizotypal. Occasionally, police officers manifest some paranoid traits, but it is rare for an officer to meet the criteria for these disorders as such individuals are usually removed during hiring process. It is clear that massive difficulty with interpersonal skills and avoidance of social interaction would be very problematic for officers. Police officers often joke about "becoming paranoid" as they become more experienced, but rarely does structured testing show overt trends toward paranoia, except in individuals who are actively under investigation or who have developed serious problems.

The second, frequent and most problematic set of disorders is called Cluster B. These disorders include: antisocial, borderline, histrionic, and narcissistic personality disorders. These disorders are generally associated with more "acting-out behavior" such as self-destructive, impulsive, and/or socially disruptive behaviors. Although they have different criteria, these four disorders share several characteristics: lack of empathy for others; avoidance of responsibility; extreme and often violent mood swings, anger, or self-destructiveness; and a sense of exaggerated personal entitlement. It is obvious that these characteristics would be undesirable in a police officer who needs to maintain a calm demeanor when dealing with agitated or violent individuals, and perform his/her job with the highest integrity.

Cluster C disorders are also frequent and are problematic in a different way. They tend to be more inwardly oriented and represent disorders characterized by ambivalence and introspection compared to the Cluster B disorders, and include avoidant, dependent, obsessive compulsive, and passive aggressive. Obsessive-compulsive *traits* are very frequently seen in law enforcement applicants (Decker, unpublished), but the full-blown disorder would be crippling for a police officer. For example, imagine a police officer who could not drive his/her patrol area without counting signs on the road! Similarly, passive-aggressive traits are a major hindrance to officers who need to communicate their reservations directly but respectfully to command staff. Avoidant traits are problematic for similar reasons–law enforcement requires a direct approach interpersonally.

The term "mixed personality disorder" is used when elements of multiple personality disorders are present. The remaining two axes of DSM-IV diagnosis include Axis III, IV, and V. Axis III is reserved for general medical conditions. Axis IV is used to rate the degree of psychosocial stressors, and Axis V is used as a global assessment of functioning of the individual.

A personality disorder was diagnosed in this study by a combination of three or four different psychological instruments combined with a thorough review of historical features suggestive of a disorder. The contribution of an Axis II or personality diagnosis to "unfitness" in this sample was statistically significant ($p < 0.05$). The vast majority (95%) of the officers returned immediately to duty were not diagnosed with a personality disorder, although the remaining 4.8 percent had a suspected personality disorder. However, 28 percent of officers found unfit for duty were found to have a personality disorder.

It is hardly surprising that a higher incidence of personality disorders was found in unfit officers, since pre-employment screening tends to prevent individuals with a personality disorder from law enforcement positions. This occupation is primarily a people-oriented occupation and with the increased emphasis on community policing, good interpersonal skills are a necessary prerequisite for success. However, agencies and departments have variable screening procedures which may be of varying sophistication with respect to detecting personality disorders. It is unlikely that these diagnoses represented changes in the officer's psychological makeup since hiring as these disorders are defined as fixed patterns of relating to others.

Thus, certain officers may have been hired with personality disorders. In a number of cases in the current study, the author was able to obtain pre-employment raw psychological test data. The pre-employment raw data was then compared to psychological test data obtained in the course of the evaluation. In several of these cases, the pre-employment evaluator's report basically ignored pre-employment test results suggestive of personality disturbances. In certain other cases, the pre-employment evaluator stated that other aspects of the applicant's psyche outweighed the potential interpersonal problems highlighted by the tests. The fact that these officers were subsequently referred for a FFD Evaluation and found unfit implies that pre-employment evaluators should use caution when overriding concerns raised by psychological testing in the pre-employment period.

Table 3.5
AXIS II DIAGNOSES OF UNFIT AND FIT OFFICERS

| Personality Disorder Diagnosis | Unfit Number | % | Fit Number | % |
|---|---|---|---|---|
| None | 23 | 63.9 | 20 | 95.2 |
| Cluster A | 1 | 2.8 | 0 | 0.0 |
| Cluster B | 1 | 2.8 | 0 | 0.0 |
| Mixed Personality Disorder | 7 | 19.4 | 0 | 0.0 |
| Probable Personality Disorder | 4 | 11.1 | 1 | 4.8 |

### 3.11 Geographic Differences

A comparison of officers' psychiatric diagnoses from different geographical regions was undertaken. As demonstrated in Table 3.5, primary and secondary diagnoses were quite similar between metropolitan and rural police officers in this sample. The most common diagnosis was major depression with bipolar disorder as the second most prevalent diagnosis. The most common secondary diagnosis was substance use disorder. Thirty percent of metropolitan officers were diagnosed with Axis II diagnoses versus 19 percent of rural officers. ADD was seen more than twice as often (7.4% vs. 3.3%) in rural vs. metropolitan officers as a primary diagnosis but was equally common as a secondary diagnosis. Further discussion and hypotheses regarding ADD were presented in Section 3.9 above.

Table 3.6
REGIONAL PRIMARY AND SECONDARY DIAGNOSES OF UNFIT OFFICERS

| *DSM-IV Axis I Diagnosis* | *Primary Diagnosis Metropolitan* % | *Primary Diagnosis Rural* % | *Primary Diagnosis Metropolitan* % | *Primary Diagnosis Rural* % |
|---|---|---|---|---|
| **None** | 13.3 | 25.9 | **73.3** | **74.1** |
| **Major Depression** | **46.7** | **37.0** | 0 | 3.7 |
| **Bipolar Disorder** | **20.0** | **18.5** | 0 | 0 |
| **Anxiety Disorder** | 3.3 | 3.7 | 3.3 | 3.7 |
| **Posttraumatic Stress Disorder** | **6.7** | 3.7 | 3.3 | 0 |
| **Psychosis** | 3.3 | 0.0 | 0 | 3.7 |
| **Substance Use** | 3.3 | 0.0 | **13.3** | **11.1** |
| **Attention Deficit Disorder** | 3.3 | **7.4** | 3.3 | 3.7 |
| **Developmentally Delayed** | 0.0 | 3.7 | 0 | 0 |

## 3.12 Regional Variations in Treatment and Treating Professionals

Although diagnoses between metropolitan and rural officers were similar, regional differences in use of psychiatrists prior to the evaluation were striking as shown in Table 3.7. The percentage of metropolitan police officers who were receiving medications from a psychiatrist was 33 percent but only 3.7 percent of rural police officers were receiving medications from a psychiatrist. Fifty-eight percent of the rural officers received medications from primary care practitioners versus 47 percent of metropolitan officers. More of the rural officers were not receiving medication compared to metropolitan officers (37% versus 20%).

Table 3.7
PRESCRIBING PRACTITIONER

| Type of Practitioner | Metropolitan % | Rural % |
|---|---|---|
| Psychiatrist | 33.3 | 3.7 |
| Primary care physician | 40.0 | 55.6 |
| Advanced registered nurse practitioner | 6.7 | 3.7 |
| No prescription | 20.0 | 37.0 |

## 3.13 Fictionalized Scenarios

The following scenarios are offered to illustrate common issues raised in the course of FFD Evaluations as well as several different potential outcomes depending on the officers' and agencies' responses to the evaluator's recommendations and/or to treatment. They are offered to illustrate many of the concepts discussed above as well as to illustrate that the outcome of FFD evaluations for both officer and agencies depends on the subsequent behavior of all involved.

### Case Scenario 1

A 32-year-old female officer had several documented episodes of inebriation on the job. Her overall job performance had deteriorated over a three-year period and she had been using excess sick leave. She had two citizen complaints regarding unprofessional conduct and other members of her squad indicated that they felt she was "not safe" on the job. She admitted she had been diagnosed with alcohol dependence but assured her primary provider (a nonpsychiatric nurse practitioner) that she would abstain from alcohol and take Disulfiram (Antabuse) to quit drinking. However, she was found to have alcohol on her breath on two subsequent occasions and was observed to be drinking alcohol in a bar while off duty by another officer. In the course of the FFD evaluation, the officer disclosed that she had been to three different alcohol treatment programs over the last five years at her own expense, without departmental knowledge. The evaluator discussed the officer's treatment to date with nurse practitioner who said "the officer was trying" to remain sober and reminded the evaluator that alcohol dependence is a difficult process to arrest. She stated that the officer had relapsed so many times that Antabuse was a last resort.

### Possible Outcome 1

The evaluator communicated her findings to the referring institution. She indicated that given the relapse history to date, the potential of the officer relapsing on the job was a great forensic liability risk to the department. The evaluator recommended a course of inpatient substance use treatment, but the evaluee declined stating she "had already been through programs and they don't work." She demanded to "do it herself." The employer then chose to implement a medical separation.

### Possible Outcome 2

The evaluator communicated her findings to the referring institution. She indicated that given the relapse history to date, the potential of the officer relapsing on the job was a great forensic liability risk to the department. The evaluator recommended a course of inpatient substance use treatment. The evaluee reluctantly agreed and was placed on medical leave. She completed a 30-day inpatient program and returned to work thereafter. The employer then chose to provisionally return her to duty with random urinalysis monitoring for a one-year period, proof of AA attendance once a week, and periodic letters from treatment professionals that she was complying with psychiatric (including substance use) treatment. The officer maintained sobriety and remained productively employed.

### Comments

The officer might not be regarded as disabled from many civilian occupations with this history. However, even such industries as construction or those that involve machinery operation might also view intoxication on the job as an unacceptable risk. Indeed, many corporations have a "zero-tolerance" for substance use in their employees. However, it should be clear that there are major differences between isolated episodes of alcohol abuse and chronic relapses. The incidence of alcohol abuse in law enforcement personnel may be higher than in the general population and it is a high-stress profession. However, chronic abuse or dependence, resistance to treatment, or repeated treatment failures are all serious problems which must be addressed by the employee and the employer. Not all agencies are able to implement random drug monitoring because of differences in local, state, or federal statutes or agreements made with collective bargaining units representing police officers. However, it is an essential mechanism clinically regarding

## Case Scenario 2

A twenty-year, veteran officer experienced a series of panic attacks. He did not advise his superiors that he was under treatment by his primary care physician until he was referred for a FFD evaluation. The incident that brought him to attention of the department occurred when he discharged his firearm accidentally in the course of a panic attack while on duty. Fortunately, no one was injured. The officer was put on administrative leave and sought treatment from a psychiatrist. He achieved partial relief of symptoms after a month's trial of a medication (Paxil) but continued to have episodic panic attacks. When he presented for the FFD evaluation, he was still having several episodes of panic per week but desired to return to work. Carrying a firearm was an essential part of his job and he was expected to both defend his weapon from inmates and to safely transfer it several times a week. The referring institution was advised that he would likely continue to suffer episodic panic attacks over several weeks or months in spite of overall improvement in his mood and that it was not possible to predict when they would cease entirely.

### *Possible Outcome 1*

The institution did not have a light duty, administrative position available and all officers were required to be armed at all times. He was placed on disability and the case was referred for re-review at a later date. However, he decided to pursue a civilian career after two months on disability. He became a successful businessman.

## Possible Outcome 2

The officer remained on leave for five weeks, then the institution allowed him to return to half-time, light duty (administrative and clerical duties) for another four weeks. At the end of that time, the officer reported that he had had no panic attacks in three weeks and felt his level of anxiety was reduced to normal levels. His treating psychiatrist concurred and he was returned to duty with the understanding that if there were any future incidents he would be terminated.

## Comments

This particular vignette by no means represents all the possible outcomes of treatment. Many officers who are treated for depression experience complete remission. If the above officer had had a swifter response to treatment and the Paxil had completely suppressed his panic attacks, the evaluator might well have recommended a return to unrestricted duty. As illustrated above, a different outcome may be possible in a larger institution which had more resources to provide light duty positions to its employees.

## Case Scenario 3

Officer Wilding was hospitalized after she exhibited bizarre behavior while off duty in a small town. Specifically, she was stopped by another officer while speeding at 120 miles per hour on the main road. When she was stopped in a shopping mall, she was hypersexual and agitated, saying "I'm God's messenger and the message is to make love, not war. The angels are singing my praise. Hey, Joe wanna have sex with me?" She then became incoherent. A crowd had gathered around the vehicles. The responding officer conducted her to a local hospital where she was admitted for emergency psychiatric treatment. She was diagnosed with bipolar disorder or manic depressive disorder (type I) and was treated with a mood-stabilizer and an anti-psychotic (ziprasidone). She requested a return to duty one month later. Officer Wilding's treating psychiatrist's note to the department stated, "the patient's moods have been stabilized on valproic Acid and she is fit for duty at this time."

## Possible Outcome 1

Officer Wilding was discharged with several medications including valproic Acid and ziprasidone. However, she elected to discontinue medications four weeks after her hospitalization. She had been to see her psychiatrist once for 15 minutes, during which the psychiatrist recommended she continue medications for a year. During the course of the FFD evaluation, she stated she thought that the "incident had been exaggerated." She refused to believe she had acted inappropriately (lack of insight) and stated she had simply been "kidding around." Given her non-compliance with her psychiatrist's treatment plan and lack of insight into her behavior, she was found unfit for duty and the department sought a medical separation.

## Possible Outcome 2

Officer Wilding presented after four weeks. She had seen her psychiatrist once a week for an hour and they had discussed the diagnosis, treatment plan, and risks of medication discontinuation several times. She also expressed her new-found awareness of possible precipitants for mood swings which included sleep deprivation due to shift changes or jet lag. It turned out that Officer Wilding had experienced jet lag of four hours after flying home for the holidays, one week prior to the episode. The evaluator discussed the situation with the agency and Officer Wilding was offered a position in an unarmed capacity with regular daytime hours, at a reduced pay rate. She accepted the offer.

## Comments

This case illustrates several issues. First, the officer's erratic behavior was in public in a small town. Thus, this department faced an immediate confidentiality breach as both the general public and other officers had witnessed a severe breakdown in her behavior. Second, her treating psychiatrist gave no specific indication of the likelihood of relapse (recurring mood swings) nor did he address the issue of firearms safety. One forensic difficulty with bipolar illness is that this condition is characterized by episodic lapses in judgment *and* by breakthrough episodes. In other words, an individual may be stable for months or even years and exhibit few or no symptoms of the disorder. However, they may also have mood swings even while taking their medicine properly due to the internal chemical imbalance.

Psychiatrists cannot predict these mood swings with precision, although they often occur in defined temporal cycles (such as certain times of the year etc.). However, no assurance could be given that she would not have another episode as it takes months to determine if a particular mood stabilizer is working and that breakthrough episodes can occur. The treating psychiatrist in this scenario was unfamiliar with forensic issues and did not view the risk of carrying firearms or of a higher standard of judgment as significant. When these issues were considered, the evaluator recommended that this individual might be a valued employee in a number of other occupations, but she was not fit for return to duty as an armed officer, even with mood stabilization. However, the difference between Outcomes 1 and 2 highlights that cooperation between the individual and the agency, as well as demonstrating that good insight and/or responsibility for one's behavior make the difference between a poor and good outcome.

### 3.14 Conclusions

Literature has shown that it is difficult to predict which officers will have performance issues necessitating a FFD evaluation. Certain personality inventories such as the IPI and PAI have some predictive value with respect to termination and excess use of force. So far, there are no tests which accurately predict the development of Axis I (major psychiatric) psychiatric disorders. This is hardly surprising since depression, the largest cause of "unfit" officers, is due to both environmental and genetic factors and represents the largest cause of disability in all professions, not just law enforcement. Measurable improvement of "unfit" officers' scores on the MMPI-2 was demonstrated after EAP intervention, although the CPI failed to demonstrate significant changes. In other words, personality inventories are of less utility in measuring improvement in treated officers than the MMPI-2. This is not surprising—major psychiatric syndromes are more likely to change with intervention than personality styles.

Primary data was presented in this chapter on FFD evaluations in law enforcement personnel from Washington State over a five-year period. The number of subjects did not permit a detailed analysis by gender. The most common causes of "unfit" officers were found to be major depression (36%), bipolar disorder (22%), personality disorder (19%), and ADD (8%). The fact that a significant number of evaluees were found to have personality disorders suggests that pre-employment testing (in these cases) was not entirely successful at "weeding out" applicants with personality disorders!

Major depression was also seen more frequently (36%) than in the general population, where its prevalence is 20 percent. This is hardly surprising, as it is well-known that major depression is a serious problem. However, although not the most frequent cause of "unfit" officers, the diagnosis of ADD was seen at twice the accepted rate in the general population. This is in contrast to bipolar disorder, which occurs in 15 percent of the general population, so it was only slightly overrepresented in "unfit" officers. Similarly, personality disorders were only diagnosed slightly more frequently in "unfit" officers than in the general population (19% versus 15%, respectively). Substance use disorders were seen almost equally frequently in both "fit" and "unfit" officers and were less frequent than in the general population.

A hypothesis is presented that there may be a self-selection process such that more people with ADD tend to seek out law enforcement positions than in the general population. They may have a biological selective advantage with respect to higher tolerance to traumatic situations such as critical incidents. The hypothesis has not been tested but suggests the need for further studies on ADD in law enforcement professionals. This should include an examination of whether the trend (overrepresentation of individuals with ADD) presented in this data set is supported by nationwide or international trends.

Primary and secondary diagnoses were quite similar between metropolitan and rural police officers in this sample. The only notable difference was the proportion of "unfit" officers with ADD was higher (7.7% vs. 3.3%) in rural officers than in metropolitan. As might be expected, poorer access and/or utilization of psychiatric care were demonstrated in the rural officers. Fewer rural officers took psychiatric medications, and the medications were more often prescribed by primary care providers. The percentage of metropolitan police officers who were receiving medications from a psychiatrist was 33 percent, but only 3.7 percent of rural police officers were receiving medications from a psychiatrist.

The data presented above highlight the need for continued research and intervention into stress management for law enforcement personnel. Major depression remains the most critical area for intervention.

# REFERENCES

Allen, M. G., & Hibler, N.S. (2000). Psychiatric evaluations by the federal occupational health procedures. *The Forensic Examiner,* Nov/Dec: 13-18.

American Psychiatric Association. (1994). *Diagnostic and statistical manual for mental disorders.* (4th ed.). Washington, D.C.

Arrigo, B. A., & Claussen, N. (2003). Police corruption and psychological testing: A strategy for preemployment screening. *Int J Offender Therapy and Comp Criminol, 47*(3):272-90.

Biederman, J. (2005). Attention-deficit/hyperactivity disorder: A selective overview. *Biol Psych, 57*:1215-1220.

Cortina, J. M. et al. The "Big Five" personality factors in the IPI and MMPI: Predictors of police performance. *Personnel Psychology, 45*:119-130.

Department of Justice, Civil Rights Division. (2005). *Addressing police misconduct: Laws enforced by the United States Department of Justice.*

Faraone, S.V., Biederman, J. & Monuteaux, M.C. (2001). Attention deficit hyperactivity disorder with bipolar disorder in girls: Further evidence for a familial subtype? *J Affect Disord,* Apr:64(1):19-26.

Faraone, S. V. (2004). *A family-genetic perspective.* Abstract, American Psychiatric Association. May 1-6.

Glickman, M. M., & Dodd, D. K. (1998). GUTI: A measure of urgent task involvement among adults with attention-deficit hyperactivity disorder. *Psychol Rep,* Apr:82(2):592-4.

Hoehn, T., Braune, S., Scheibe, G., & Albus, M. (1997). Physiological, biochemical and subjective parameters in anxiety patients with panic disorder during stress exposure as compared with healthy controls. *Eur Arch of Psych and Clin Neurosci, 247* (5): 264-274, Oct.

International Association of Chiefs of Police. (2005). Alexandria, Virginia.

Inwald, R. E. (1984). The Inwald Personality Inventory: An introduction and rationale. *Police Times, 4*:3-5.

Inwald, R. E., & Shusman, E. J. (1984). The IPI and the MMPI as predictors of academy performance for police recruits. *J of Police Sci and Admin, 12*:1-11.

Kelly v. Salt Lake City Civil Service Commission, 8 P.3d 1048 (Utah App. 2000).

Kessler. (2004). *Prevalence of adult ADHD in the U.S.: Results from the National Comorbidity Survey Replication.* Abstract, American Psychiatric Association. May 1-6.

King, J. A., Barkley, A., & Barrett, S. (1998). Attention deficit disorder and the stress response. *Biol Psych, 44*:72-74.

Konrad, K., Gauugel, S., & Schurek, J. (2003). Catecholamine functioning in children with traumatic brain injuries and attention-deficit/hyperactivity disorder. *Cognitive Brain Res, 16*:425-433.

Pliszka, S. R., et al. The Texas Children's Medication Algorithm Project: Report of the Texas Consensus Conference Panel on Medication Treatment of Childhood Attention-Deficit/Hyperactivity Disorder. Part II: Tactics. Attention-Deficit/Hyperactivity Disorder. *J Am Acad Child Adolesc Psychiatry*, Jul:39(7):920-7.

Schmitt, M. J., & Stanard, S. J. (1996). The utility of personality inventories in the employee assistance process: A study of EAP referred police officers. *Employ Assist Quarterly, 11*(4).

Sluiter, J. K, Frings-Dresen, M. H. W., Meijman,T. F., & van der Beek, A. (2000). Reactivity and recovery from different types of work measured by catecholamines and cortisol: A systematic literature overview. *J Occupat and Environ Med, 57* (5): 298-315 May.

Scoggin, F. et al. (1995). Predictive validity of psychological testing in law enforcement settings. *Prof Psychol: Res and Practice, 2*(1):68-71.

42 U.S.C. § 14141.

Young, E. A., & Breslau, N. (2004). Cortisol and catecholamines in posttraumatic stress disorder–An epidemiologic community study. *Arch of Gen Psych, 61* (4): 394-401 Apr.

Weiss, W. U. et al. (2005). Problematic police performance and he personality assessment inventory. *J Police Crim Psychology, 20*(1):16-21.

# Chapter 4

# PSYCHOLOGICAL TESTS FOR FITNESS IN LAW ENFORCEMENT PERSONNEL

KATHLEEN P. DECKER

## I. BACKGROUND

### 4.1 One Component of a Comprehensive Evaluation

Police chiefs and sheriffs often wonder, "What is THE BEST test to assist with choosing great law enforcement personnel?" Ideally, law enforcement personnel would be chosen perfectly and would perform perfectly after a brief and inexpensive selection process. Similarly, police managers often wish that fitness for duty evaluation would provide a clear answer with one or two simple tests. It is clear to forensic psychologists and psychiatrists that performing excellent pre-employment evaluations and fitness for duty evaluations requires a battery of tests which measure different areas. It would be convenient if a single psychological test could be used, but understanding the complexities of an individual requires a thorough assessment of various qualities. On the other hand, a recent estimate of the cost to train a police officer is $100,000 (Cochrane, 2003) so it seems reasonable to invest a few hundred dollars in a comprehensive assessment to ensure that fit officers are hired.

There is a wide range of tests available which measure psychological dysfunction, coping mechanisms, and personality styles. There is no standardized procedure or set of tests that is required, although pre-employment psychological testing is increasing. As of 2003, 37 states mandated a mental health standard for law enforcement officers and

23 states required a baseline psychological evaluation. This chapter will examine the role of psychological testing in both pre-employment evaluations and fitness for duty evaluations. Wherever possible the utility of tests will be contrasted in the two types of evaluations.

## *4.2 Legal Considerations*

There are legal considerations that have occasionally posed challenges to the use of psychological tests during evaluations of law enforcement personnel. Title VII Civil Rights Act of 1964 has been evoked in certain cases. Title VII states that it is unlawful for employers to use any pre-employment tool that has a substantially negative impact on a protected subgroup. However, to be successful, challenges based on this section of the Civil Rights Act must demonstrate a disparate impact of the application of these tests on the subgroup tested. The original goal of this Act was to protect specific subgroups from discrimination based on psychological testing.

Therefore, integrity tests and clinical personality tests have held up under multiple research and legal challenges. The Equal Employment Opportunity Commission (EEOC) has not found a disparate impact in most cases. The Americans with Disabilities Act (ADA) specifies that an employer must not discriminate based on employees' disabilities. In the pre-employment setting, psychological testing is administered after an offer of employment is made. In the case of a fitness for duty evaluation, it is administered after an employee has demonstrated suboptimal performance or has become impaired. It should only be one component of the overall evaluation and no specific cutoff levels on any particular test should be used.

Furthermore, personality testing constitutes a medical examination because it provides evidence about mental disorders or impairments. It can allow the evaluating professional to suggest recommendations to the employer regarding both initial fitness for duty and/or reasonable accommodations for temporarily or permanently impaired officers. Several years ago, studies concluded that certain personality characteristics, entitled "The Big Five," were of major predictive value in choosing police officers who were subsequently successful (Barrick, 1991; Tett, 1991). The "Big Five" are conscientiousness, extraversion, agreeableness, neuroticism, and openness to experience.

Legal challenges have been encountered because of privacy issues in applicants or evaluees. Personality testing is invasive and has been ruled that the use of such instruments must be justified by compelling interest of the employer. For example, employees who work in high-risk areas such as law enforcement or other fields involving critical incidents need specialized skills and personality characteristics. In McKenna v. Fargo (1979) it was found to be acceptable to test firefighters because of the high-risk nature of their work. In a U.S. Supreme Court case, psychological testing was ruled allowable in Treasury employees seeking promotion (National Treasury Employees Union v. von Raab, United States Supreme Court, 1989). In that case, the Court ruled that invasive tests could be used in screening U.S. Customs employees applying for promotion to jobs that required them to carry firearms or be involved in the interdiction of illegal drugs.

### 4.3 International Association of Chiefs of Police Guidelines

The International Association of Chiefs of Police (IACP) developed a set of assessment guidelines. As will be discussed in greater detail in Chapter 10, employers have a responsibility to exercise caution in hiring. In fact, an employer would be liable if adequate caution was NOT exercised in the hiring process. Briefly summarized, guidelines from the IACP include:

- Know law and ethics that guide the type of evaluation as well as your ethical standards of practice.
- Conduct a job analysis—what does the job require?
- Obtain informed consent from subject and organizational client (benefits and limitations of evaluation).

The first guideline is fairly self-evident. These standards are similar, but not identical between psychologists and psychiatrists. They include the concept of not harming the client or evaluee, of providing accurate information, of maintaining confidential records, and of maintaining certain ethical boundaries with evaluees. In the main, for the purposes of this book, they may be considered to be more similar than different.

As to the second guideline, it is extremely important both for pre-employment and fitness for duty evaluations to understand the specific job tasks and even the general profile of the agency. For example, one contributor routinely consults to urban, suburban, and rural departments and the type of personality profile and cognitive level of performance is significantly different. For example, a deputy who is highly autonomous and excels at handling dangerous situations in nearisolation may be a good fit for a rural department but a poor fit for a department based in the suburbs, which requires tact and frequent coordination with a variety of agencies. The third guideline refers to the issue first raised in Chapter 1. The limits of confidentiality need to be carefully explained to evaluees. The department or organizational client also needs to realize they may require specific information on which to make a decision, but other types of information collected by the evaluator are not critical to their decision.

The IACP guidelines continue with a series of comments on the conduct and range of information collected and reported on in the evaluation:

- Select appropriate testing materials to address the information obtained on the job analysis.
- Obtain relevant biographical data; conduct a structured interview.
- Report results in an informative and appropriate manner.

A detailed analysis of the limitations imposed by different states is beyond the scope of this chapter. However, IACP mandates that the focus of such evaluations be based on psycho-legal questions posed by state law. Detailed information on state restrictions may be found in state legal codes that address peace officer certification/decertification.

### 4.4 Test Objectivity

Fitness for duty evaluations and pre-employment evaluations are conducted for different reasons (Hainer, 1990). However, they are quite similar in that disqualification of applicants or rendering a verdict of "unfit for duty" in evaluees should be approached with objective data wherever possible. In some respects, they are similar with respect to the types of concerns raised by the evaluation process. An understanding of the grounds for disqualification of applicants is help-ful in understanding fitness for duty issues. A large scale survey of peace officer applicants placed the psychological disqualification rate at 16 percent (Bonacum & McCrery, 1985). Grounds for disqualifica-tion included issues appropriate to the referral question, responses to objective validated tests, personality traits undesirable in a police offi-cer, major psychopathology, cognitive difficulties, and inability to per-form specialized tasks necessary in law enforcement.

The IACP Guidelines state: "A test battery including objective, job-related, validated psychological instruments should be administered to the applicant. It is preferable that test results be available to the eval-uator before screening interviews are conducted." The IACP Guidelines also specify that "if mail-order or computerized tests are employed, the psychologist conducting the follow-up interview should verify and interpret individual results." The guidelines encourage the use of tests that have been validated for use with public safety officials and discourage the use of specific cut-off scores to determine suitabil-ity.

## II. TYPES OF TESTS

### 4.5 Assessment of Basic Skills

A written autobiography of one to two pages is fairly standard. It is often a first glimpse of the applicant's motivation for seeking a position in law enforcement but is also useful to psychiatrists and psychologists as it often reveals patterns of thought and emotion in an unstructured manner.

### 4.6 Integrity Tests

One characteristic that is considered paramount in law enforcement personnel is integrity. There are several ways in which this quality may be assessed. Most departments require pre-employment applicants to fill out an extremely detailed background packet. A polygrapher is often employed to explore and/or verify certain aspects of the back-ground information. In addition, certain questionnaires attempt to assess this characteristic. The Reid Public Safety Report (London House) measures attitudes and behaviors in the areas of integrity, anti-social history, drug use, public safety experience, and work history. This instrument is *not* a medical examination, but it has been shown to predict behavior. The Reid Report measures each applicant's attitudes and behaviors through a comprehensive analysis of integrity attitude, history of antisocial behavior, drug use, public safety experience, and employment history. It is comprised of 261 attitudinal and behavioral items and designed to be completed in 60 minutes.

The PsyQ (Johnson, 2001) is another test which utilizes a number of attitudinal and behavioral items in an effort to predict problematic employees. It is primarily a questionnaire which provides evaluators and background investigators detailed autobiographical information about a wide variety of historical psychological issues.

### 4.7 Brief Cognitive Testing

Most evaluations for pre-employment include various brief tests to yield a rough estimate of intelligence. Some of the measures used to assess basic skills include the Weschler Abbreviated Scale of Intelligence (WASI) (Stano, 2004) and the Wonderlic Intelligence Scale. The Wonderlic has established law enforcement norms. Fitness for duty evaluations generally do not require measurement of intelligence unless the case involves the possibility of dementia or other cognitive decline in the officer referred for the fitness for duty evaluation.

However, it should be noted that different departments and positions may have different requirements. For example the author is usually requested by departments to screen for a higher score in applicants for the position of deputy sheriff than that seen for line (patrol) police officers. However, it is important not to overvalue cognitive scores on brief intelligence tests. First, adequate degree of IQ is important, but at higher levels of intelligence there is a weak relationship with performance. Also, brief IQ testing may not be accurate. Comparison of brief IQ testing with actual educational attainment is particularly useful in cases of questionable results. Actual educational attainment of the evaluee may shed light on whether the brief IQ test is valid or if the applicant is sick, preoccupied with the evaluation process, or otherwise emotionally stressed.

## Case Scenario 1

A real-life example of the limits of IQ testing using the Wonderlic occurred during pre-employment testing of an applicant. Identifying data have been fictionalized here, but not the IQ numbers, which are just as she tested. A 28-year-old Hispanic applicant presented for her interview and was pleasant, personable, and prompt. She neither had inconsistencies in questions on her polygraph nor difficulties with prior issues regarding integrity. In fact, she was attempting to transfer from a northeastern police department where she had worked under-cover vice for three years as a rookie patrol officer. She had no diffi-culties with interpersonal relations and her MMPI-2, MCMI-III, and 16-PF were well within expected limits for police officers.

However, the applicant tested with a score of 18 on the Wonderlic. This score was considered too low for the sheriff's office for which she was applying, which preferred scores above 22 for the rank of deputy sheriff. The evaluator discussed her case with the referring agency. She (the evaluator) stated that there was also a discrepancy between the applicant's early (grade school) educational attainment and her later educational attainment. The applicant had been in gifted reading classes in early elementary school, but fell behind in high school and graduated as an average student. She had pursued only one year of college instruction in criminal justice, then sought employment as a police officer. The agency dug deeper on her background and found she had been an exemplary officer in the Northeast and had shown good judgment and independent thinking while undercover.

The evaluator offered to perform more sophisticated intelligence testing as well as a screen for cognitive difficulty (Gardner Test of Auditory-Perceptual skills). The agency agreed and the applicant was understandably nervous but complied. The test results showed that the applicant's Verbal ability was in the 85 percentile, Abstract ability was in the 85 percentile, and Memory was in the 88 percentile. Auditory-Perceptual abilities also fell within the 87 percentile across the board. The poor Wonderlic score was fully explained by her unique deficit–her Quantitative ability was in the 23 percentile. The evaluator noted that she took a long time to complete the math items, using good rea-soning but frequently making numeric errors which resulted in the wrong answer. Interestingly enough, she commented that she had been in advanced geometry but had never done well on story problems. She also explained that she had taken excess time on the Wonderlic on the math problems, checking and rechecking her math work. The evaluator and agency concluded that the officer possessed more than adequate cognitive skills to perform the duties required. The agency hired her and reported great satisfaction with her performance six months later.

This case clearly illustrates the danger of relying too heavily on brief intelligence tests. However, this case also highlights that sorting out questionable performance issues may take more time than an agency prefers for applicants. All told, the applicant's screening process took twice the usual time for applicants. Therefore the cost of the screening was significantly higher for this applicant. This evaluator has evaluated other applicants for whom the referring agency was not as keen to pay for more detailed testing.

Occasionally applicants may have the reverse problem. Although police officers are generally hired with above average IQ, a recent case illustrates that occasionally officers are rejected for being "too intelligent" for police work (Hughes, 2003). An applicant was told his IQ (according to the Wonderlic) was too high. He scored a 33 on the Wonderlic. He sued in the U.S. District of Connecticut because of denial of job opportunity. The court rejected the case because it ruled that the employer was relying on a body of literature and that overqualified applicants more frequently become dissatisfied, although the latter point has never specifically been proven. The author of that paper then undertook a survey of police officers to see whether they felt that intelligence was an important attribute of police work, that intelligent officers were more likely to perform better. Finally, the officers surveyed did not feel that the more intelligent officers were more likely to become bored. However, this was a survey. Primary data to test the hypothesis was not obtained in this study.

### III. MENTAL STATE TESTING

#### 4.8 The Minnesota Multiphasic Personality Inventory (MMPI-2)

Clinical tests of personality and psychopathology are useful for both pre-employment and fitness for duty evaluations. MMPI-2 remains the most widely used and researched forensic test. It is somewhat sensitive to pathology, but many of the questions are "transparent." It is therefore possible to answer questions on the test to minimize any evidence of psychopathology. The test is relatively long, with 567 items and utilizes a true-false structure. It has nongendered norms to comply with federal civil rights act and EEOC. It is essentially a newer version of the MMPI. There are several possible ways to score the MMPI-2. It can be scored against clinical norms, or a special personnel report based on 18,000 personnel cases of law enforcement officers. Like any test, there is some variability in individual scores, but there is an "average police officer profile."

This profile typically consists of a most scores on the subscales in the average range, but with low-level elevations on Scale K ($<$ T = 65). The K scale elevation basically indicates desirability and is only one of several ways in which law enforcement candidates attempt to minimize psychological dysfunction. This may be either through a somewhat "macho" attitude, also called "tough-mindedness" which is typical of law enforcement officers or through limited psychological mindedness. Low psychological mindedness means an individual is simply not in tune with psychological or emotional concerns and focuses on external events rather than on introspection. Obviously, an excessive amount of introspection is undesirable in law enforcement personnel so it is not surprising that they are often low in psychological mindedness. Other characteristics typically seen in law enforcement personnel include low-level elevations on Scale 4 (Hargrave & Berner, 1984; Hargrave & Hiatt, 1990).

## 4.9 Ethnic Variations on the MMPI-2

Variability in responses on the MMPI-2 is seen in certain subgroups. Some ethnic differences in testing with the MMPI-2 have been noted. In several studies, minority candidates scored significantly higher than white candidates on F and Depression but the T-value was less than 65, making the finding less statistically robust (Detrick, 2001). Other important findings on the MMPI include careful examination of the Immaturity Index. Elevations on this scale are often seen in individuals with hypomania (9) or personality disorders (4). These elevations have been shown to predict termination. Minor elevations in the L, K, and S scales are common in law enforcement applicants, but major elevations indicated high levels of defensiveness and/or attempts to present an unrealistically positive impression.

## 4.10 Performance Prediction with the MMPI-2

The MMPI-2 has been used for many years in law enforcement pre-employment evaluations and currently has "norms" of over 50,000 pre-employment applicants including several thousand female candidates. Certain scores predict positive supervisor ratings such as a conventional psychological profile and a moderately defensive approach to the MMPI-2 test as shown on the K Scale (Hiatt & Hargrave, 1988; Bartol, 1991).

Certain profiles on the MMPI-2 are likely to predict difficulties with disciplinary suspensions (Costello, Schneider & Schoenfield, 1996). Several MMPI-2 scales predict supervisor ratings. It contains an index regarding aggression. In addition to these areas, certain score elevations would be unacceptable in either an applicant or an evaluee in a fitness for duty evaluation. These include elevated scores on Psychopathic Deviate scale, Psychasthenia, Mania, Hypochondriasis, or Hysteria. As stated, the MMPI-2 is very long and at times its use has been criticized because of concerns that it is more oriented towards symptoms of psychiatric illness (for which it was first designed) than health. However, the author maintains it provides an excellent baseline in pre-employment candidates which may then be compared to their scores if they are subsequently sent for a fitness for duty evaluation.

## 4.11 Measurement of Personality Qualities

Several personality inventories yield data about how an individual interacts with others. The California Personality Inventory (CPI) is an instrument which was designed to provide a snapshot of various personality traits which may be considered desirable in law enforcement applicants. Unlike the MMPI, which was initially designed to measure clinical pathology, the CPI was designed to look for general personality traits which may or may not be desirable in certain personnel populations. These traits are not necessarily dysfunctional or traits of illness, but simply traits which are not as useful for employees performing certain jobs.

As early as 1971, certain trends were found on the CPI in law enforcement personnel. Results of one early study indicated that highly-rated police officers scored high on CPI scales that rated intellectual efficiency, self-confidence, and sociability (Hogan, 1971).

The second edition was published in1987 and contains 462 items. Norms have been generated for police officer, firefighters, EMT, juvenile probation, and public safety employees. The data base currently contains over 50,000 applicants. Investigation continues into its predictive value for both pre-employment and fitness for duty evaluations (Kostman, 2005). The CPI yields conclusions about a number of different personality styles which are labeled "norm-favoring" or "norm-doubting," which means that the applicant or evaluee's personality structure is similar to that of thousands of other law enforcement applicants or different. For example, one particular personality subtype, called "Gamma," is one in which the individual is described as innovative, insightful, and creative. These are not dysfunctional qualities, they are wonderful qualities. However, research using the CPI has determined that many individuals who test as "Gamma" may also be uninhibited, test limits, unable to delay gratification, and nonconforming. These latter qualities would clearly be problematic in law enforcement personnel (Consulting Psychologists Press, 1986, 1995, 2000).

A test entitled the 16-PF for 16 Personality Factors was developed toassess personality styles (Cattell, 1989). This test does not measure *any* form of pathology but rather addresses a number of general personality traits such as warmth, reasoning, emotional stability, dominance, liveliness, rule-consciousness, social boldness, sensitivity, vigilance, abstractedness, privateness, apprehension, openness to change, self-reliance, perfectionism, and tension. The scale contains 185 items. The 16-PF has been used for decades to attempt to predict police performance (Fabricatore, 1978). Several qualities have consistently been associated with success in law enforcement, of which the most important is tough-mindedness. The scale is also very useful in law enforcement populations as questions are not aimed at illness behaviors but at styles of viewing the world.

## 4.12 Performance Prediction with Personality Inventories

Several inventories measuring personality traits have been examined in law enforcement personnel who subsequently had review of their performance. Elevations on certain scales of the Personality Attitudes Inventory (PAI) have been associated with poor performance (Weiss, 2005). Specifically, antisocial-egocentricity was found to be a highly significant predictor of insubordination and excessive citizen complaints. Two subscales were found to correlate highly with neglect of duty (antisocial stimulus-seeking and negative impression).

An example of such a measure is the Inwald Personality Inventory (IPI). It was developed by Inwald for law enforcement on a rational basis after review of 2,500 pre-employment evaluations (Inwald, 1982, 1983). It contains 310 true-false items and has 26 scales. The Inwald test gives predictive equations that estimate several possible areas of dysfunction in prospective law enforcement personnel. These include:

- Likelihood of disciplinary action during the first year of employment
- Likelihood of $> 3$ absences during first year of employment
- Likelihood of being late $> 3$ times during first year
- Termination

Research on IPI has shown some robust results. For example, Mufson and Mufson (1998) followed 45 hired police officers given the IPI between 1991 to 1994. They were rated on a five-point scale by supervisors into three categories: successful, intermediate, problem officers. The IPI scores predicted 77 percent of successful officers and 67 percent of problem officers. In fact, the IPI was a better predictor than MMPI-2 in that study. The use of the IPI to predict performance is also discussed in Chapter 3.

## 4.13 The Millon Clinical Multiaxial Inventory (MCMI-III)

The Millon MCMI-III is a sensitive instrument which delineates potential problematic personality characteristics as well as certain major psychiatric syndromes. The MCMI-III makes an attempt to code problems in a manner consistent with the Diagnostic and Statistical Manual of Mental Disoders (DSM-IV) which is the major accepted coding system for psychiatric disorders. Thus, the MCMI-III produces a report with multiple subscales, some of which represent personality disorders (Axis II of the DSM-IV) and others for major psychiatric syndromes such as depression or posttraumatic stress disorder (coded on Axis I of the DSM-IV).

It was first published in 1969 as the MCMI (Millon, 1969) and is now in its third version (Millon, 1990). The current version was modified significantly from the original and is based on the theory that personality disorders are the result of attempts by an individual to adapt to the environment. The Millon MCMI-III is a true-false test of 175 items. It is thus quick to administer (20 minutes) and score. Additionally, it is widely recognized as an instrument which is sensitive at detection of deviant personality traits. It is usually used in clinical populations, but the questions are less "transparent" than the MMPI-2. Thus applicants or evaluees may reveal problems more thoroughly than on the MMPI-2. Investigations are in progress in a multitude of specific ethnic populations. There is an excellent textbook on the use of the MCMI-III in forensic assessments (McCann & Dyer, 1996), although the text focuses primarily on populations of disturbed individuals and felons.

The MCMI-III is useful in both pre-employment and fitness for duty evaluations as it suggests potential problematic personality characteristics that may be explored in depth during the interview. It may be thought of as a rapid screening tool to provide hypotheses for deeper examination of interpersonal relationship difficulties in an evaluee utilizing either standard unstructured questions or a structured approach, as discussed in Section 4.14 below.

# IV. SPECIAL CONSIDERATIONS

## *4.14 The Symptom Checklist (SCL-90)*

The SCL-90 was originally developed for use in psychiatric patients (Derogatis, 1976). It assesses the perceived severity of a number of psychological and physical symptoms associated with anxiety, depression, and other major psychiatric syndromes. It might be argued that this instrument's primary utility is in fitness for duty evaluations, as pre-employment applicants are (hopefully) unlikely to suffer from major psychiatric symptoms. However, the scale takes only a few moments to complete.

However, this instrument may provide additional value in a pre-employment battery as well as in fitness for duty evaluations, as it provides both information whether symptoms are present or absent. Imagine a police officer who describes posttraumatic stress disorder symptoms less than a year after being hired. It would be quite useful at that time to compare the pre-employment score with the postemployment score to ensure that symptoms of posttraumatic stress disorder were not present at entry.

### 4.15 Structured Clinical Interview (SCID)

The SCID for DSM-IV Personality Disorders was designed as a research instrument by psychiatrists. It utilizes standardized criteria for the diagnosis of personality disorders from the DSM-IV. The utility of this measure is that it consists of a highly structured approach to personality disorders rather than simple value judgment made by the evaluator. This instrument is primarily useful in Fitness for Duty Evaluations, as it consumes a fairly lengthy interview period. The interview may be shortened in some cases by conducting the structured interview based on preliminary indications of a personality disorder obtained from another instrument such as the certain Millon MCMI-III or MMPI-2 scale elevations.

### 4.16 Post-Traumatic Stress Disorder Rating Scale

There is an elegant rating scale for posttraumatic stress disorder, entitled the Clinician-Administered PTSD Scale (National Center for Post-Traumatic Stress Disorder, 2000). The rating scale is very detailed and provides a comprehensive assessment of the severity of each PTSD symptom and the degree of impairment. The disadvantage of this scale is that it takes almost an hour to administer and thus adds another hour of interview time. In any case, this measure is not likely to be utilized for the pre-employment purposes as candidates are unlikely to be selected if they are currently suffering from PTSD symptoms. Its use in fitness for duty evaluations depends on whether the issues encountered include PTSD, especially from multiple episodes. It can also be useful if certain types of malingering are suspected.

### 4.17 Rorschach Inkblot Test

The Roschach Ink Blot was used frequently in early batteries for pre-employment testing (Spielberger, 1979; Zacker 1997). It is a projective test in which the evaluee views abstract ink blot images and describes possible interpretations or images. This test is seldom used currently for pre-employment in favor of standardized tests that can be rapidly scored. However, it may still be used more for fitness for duty evaluations for assessing coping resources, ability to manage affect, thought disorder, cognitive processes, and interpersonal relatedness.

### 4.18 Measures to Detect Malingering

Malingering is seldom the chief concern in Fitness for Duty Evaluations. Most officers desire to return to work and if anything, attempt to minimize their difficulties and symptoms, not exaggerate symptoms or malinger. However, certain officers may seek an exit strategy from their job by presenting as unfit for duty on a psychiatric basis and then apply for disability. If an agency has concerns that an officer may be malingering or exaggerating symptoms, command staff should make the evaluator familiar with these concerns from the outset, so that a number of strategies can be employed to address such concerns.

In such rare cases, one useful indicator which may suggest malingering is the response style on psychological testing or during the interview. There are also specific tendencies during structured test-taking which can indicate malingering, as well. There are several specific validity scales on the MMPI-2. As above, they must be interpreted cautiously, as law enforcement applicants generally demonstrate a slightly elevated profile on certain of these subscales which could be mistaken for malingering by someone inexperienced in the interpretation of this test in law enforcement populations. Another approach to establishing malingering is to examine test-retest validity. The MMPI-2 may be repeated by different evaluators or at slightly different times and a detailed comparison of inconsistencies may reveal a pattern of malingering.

The Millon MCMI-III also can be used to test for certain types of malingering and has validity scales. There is a structured test which specifically assesses malingering involving memory, called the Test of Memory Malingering (TOMM). It may be a particularly useful tool in certain circumstances such as evaluation of an officer who claims industrial injury such as a head injury following an on-duty motor vehicle accident.

Evaluators need to recognize and remember that accusations of malingering are very serious and may have criminal repercussions for the officer as well as civil repercussions for both evaluee and evaluator. It is recommended that evaluators use extreme care in formulating language and discussing results which lead them to conclusions regarding potential malingering. The interpretation and scoring of these tests will not be discussed in further detail as this chapter might become a text for malingering rather than fitness for duty!

The issue of individuals who minimize psychological dysfunction is an important concern for both pre-employment testing and for fitness for duty. Clearly, law enforcement applicants have a vested interest in appearing "normal." However, some evaluees in Fitness for Duty evaluations may also try to suppress any characteristics they think are negative in order to resume employment when short-term disability benefits are exhausted. Unfortunately, there are few sophisticated psychological instruments that specialize in the diagnosis of psychopaths trying to pose as "normal."

The following case is a synthesis based on not one, but several examples encountered by the author in the course of fitness for duty evaluations!

## Case Scenario 2

Officer Jim Dandy presented for a Fitness for Duty after exhibiting unusual behavior on duty. Specifically, his agency stated he had been overly anxious and nearly "trigger-happy" for a period of several months. He had been almost belligerent with coworkers when he perceived they did not respond as quickly as he did to routine calls. He was seen traveling at high speeds in his patrol car as though on a car chase, but there was no other vehicle in sight to pursue. He pulled a gun on a coworker who drove near him while he was parked at a shopping center. Officer Dandy stated that he "wasn't sure who was driving" the other patrol vehicle, although the officer was on radio and there was no reason to suspect the vehicle was hijacked. The agency required him to report for a fitness for duty evaluation after the car incident.

Officer Dandy was polite and cooperative with the fitness for duty interview. He even laughed and joked once or twice. He completed all requisite paperwork. He denied any psychiatric symptoms but did endorse a mild amount of stress associated with recent marital problems. His MMPI-2 and MCMI-III scores were valid and unremarkable for Axis I pathology such as depression, anxiety or posttraumatic stress disorder. He did not score on any test as having an Axis II personality disorder. The psychological test data basically failed to illuminate *any* psychiatric difficulties. Nevertheless, on the basis of the observed behavior, including brandishing a weapon at another officer, the evaluator recommended he pursue counseling for stress management and that he be off-duty for two to four weeks. The evaluator explained to the agency that she suspected a psychiatric disorder but could not fully document one because of the lack of described symptoms. The officer maintained he was fit after a four-week vacation and was sent back for re-evaluation.

During the course of the re-evaluation, the evaluator pressed Officer Dandy to explain his behavior. She commented that she was puzzled because his psychological test data showed no problems, but his behavior indicated he was anxious and almost paranoid. She prolonged the interview (although according him a 20-minute break after one hour) and returned several times to the issue of why an officer would pull a gun on another officer. She also repeatedly asked him to comment on his fellow officers' lax response time and why that irritated him so much.

Finally, after two hours of interview time, the officer began crying. He stated he was much more stressed than he'd admitted in the original interview. He stated he had been concealing symptoms of posttraumatic stress disorder and depression for almost a year. In fact, he was having frequent flashbacks to war-time stress including guerilla warfare and had thought the other officer was an enemy in disguise. He was distressed by his colleagues' slow response time because he felt as though his city was an urban jungle and that each encounter with a civilian might be his last. He did not describe hallucinations, just a profound worry that his safety was constantly jeopardized. He was only sleeping four hours a night and had nightmares.

He then admitted that he had responded to each and every psychological test in the original evaluation so as to conceal these symptoms. He offered to "repeat the tests" and "answer the items correctly" for the evaluator. Repeat psychological testing was consistent with diagnosis posttraumatic stress disorder, major depression, and obsessive-compulsive personality disorder.

This worrisome scenario illustrates the need for further research on psychological instruments to develop better mechanisms for detecting evaluees who are attempting to mask symptoms of psychiatric symptoms or problematic personality characteristics.

### 4.19 Conclusions

The question posed in the beginning of the chapter has now been answered: **There is no single psychological test that provides a quick answer.** A wide variety of psychological tests measure everything from styles of relating to others to symptoms of psychiatric illness. Evaluators should be prepared to justify their choice of test instruments and have a thorough understanding of the limitations. Responsible evaluators should use multiple tests that provide complementary information whenever possible.

Evaluators should utilize both clinical interviewing techniques and psychological test data to provide agencies with a detailed picture of how the individual views herself and the world around her. A degree of skepticism regarding the potential for secondary gain must be maintained–the answers on most psychological tests were normed on individuals who were responding honestly and with no intention of concealing abnormal behaviors nor of maximizing psychological difficulties for purposes of disabilities etc.

### REFERENCES:

Barrick, M. R., & Mount, M.D. (1994). The big five personality elements and job performance: A meta-analysis. *Personnel Psychology, 44*:1-26.

Bartol, C.R. (1991). Police psychology: Then, now and beyond. *Criminal Justice and Behavior, 23*:70-89.

Cattell, H. B. (1989). The 16-PF: *Personality in depth.* Champaign, IL: Institute for Personality and Ability Testing, Inc.

Cochrane, R. E. et. al. (2003). Psychological testing and the selection of police officers: A national study. *Crim Justice and Behavior, 30*(5):511-537.

Consulting Psychologists Press, Inc. (2000). *California Psychological Inventory.* 1986, 1995.

Costello, R.M., Schneider, S.L., & Schoenfeld, L.S. (1996). Validation of a pre-employment MMPI Index correlated with disciplinary suspension days of police officers. *Psychol Crime & Law, 2* (4): 299-306.

Derrogatis, L., Rickels, K., & Rock, A. (1976). The SCL-90 and the MMPI: A step in the validation of a new self-report scale. *Brit J Psychiatry, 128*:280-289.

Detrick, P., Chibnall, J. T., & Rosso, M. (2001). *Professional Psychology: Research and Practice, 32*(5):484-490, October. Minnesota Multiphasic Personality Inventory–2 in Police Officer Selection: Normative Data and Relation to the Inwald Personality Inventory.

Fabricatore, J. et al. Predicting performance of police officers using the Sixteen Personality Factor Questionnaire. *American Journal of Community Psychology, 6*(1) Feb, 63-70.

First, M. B. et al. (1997). *Structured clinical interview for DSM-IV Axis II personality disorders (SCID-II).* Washington, D.C.: American Psychiatric Press.

Hainer, B. L. (1994). Preplacement evaluations. *Prim Care,* Jun;21(2):237-47, Review.

Hargrave, G. E., & Hiatt, D. (1989). Use of the California Psychological Inventory in law enforcement officer selection. *J Pers Assessment, 53*(2):267-277.

Hogan, R. (1971). Personality characteristics of highly rated policemen. *Personnel Psychology, 24*(4) Winter, 679-686.

Hughes, T. (2003). Jordan v. the City of New London, police hiring and IQ: When all the answers they don't amount to much. *Policing, 26*(2):296-312.

Inwald, R. E., Knatz, H., & Shusman, E. (1982). *Inwald Personality Inventory Manual.* Kew Gardens, NY: Hilson Research.

Inwald, R. E. (1983). *Issues and guidelines for mental health professionals conducting pre-employment psychological screening programs in law enforcement agencies.* Washington, D.C.: U.S. Department of Justice.

International Association of Chiefs of Police. *IACP Guidelines.* Alexandria, VA.

Johnson, Roberts and Associates, Inc. (2001). *PsyQ: Psychological History Form,* 1992.

Kostman, S. (2005). An examination of the "Job Suitability Snapshot" on the PAI and the CPI law enforcement, corrections, and public safety selection report, and its usefulness in predicting "Fitness for Duty." *Dissert Abs Intl:* Section B: The Sciences and Engineering. Vol 65(9-B), pp. 4886.

McCann, J. T., & Dyer, F. J. (1996). Forensic assessment with the Millon Inventories. New York: Guilford Press.

McKenna v. Fargo, 601 F.2d 575 (3rd Cir. 1979).

Millon, T. (1969). *Modern psychopathology: A biosocial approach to maladaptive learning and functioning.* Philadelphia: W.B. Saunders.

Millon, T. (1990). *Toward a new personology.* New York: John Wiley.

National Center for Post-Traumatic Stress Disorder. (2000). *Clinician administered post-traumatic stress disorder scale.* Boston: West Haven.

Mufson, D., & Mufson, M. A. (1998). Predicting police officer performance using the Inwald Personality Inventory: An illustration. *Professional Psychology: Research and Practice, 29*(1):59-62.

National Treasury Employees Union v. von Raab (United States Supreme Court, 1989).

Reid. *Public safety report.* London House Publications.

Speilberger, C. D. (1979). *Police selection and evaluation: Issues and techniques.* Washington, D.C.: Hemisphere.

Stano, J. F. (2004). Wechsler Abbreviated Scale of Intelligence. *Rehab Counseling Bulletin, 48*(1):52-57.

Tett, et al. Personality measures as predictors of job performance: A meta-analytic review. *Personnel Psychology, 44*:703-740.

Weiss, W. U. et al. (2005). Problematic Police Performance and the Personality Assessment Inventory. *J Police Crim Psychology, 20*(1):16-21.

Zacker, J. (1997). Rorschach responses of police applicants. *Psychol Reports, 80* (2): 523-528 Apr.

# Chapter 5

# MEDICATION ISSUES IN FITNESS FOR DUTY EVALUATIONS

KATHLEEN P. DECKER

## I. SELF-TREATMENT ISSUES

### 5.1 Why Are Medication Issues Important?

This chapter focuses on effects of psychotropic medications in law enforcement personnel. A variety of medications used for common medical and psychiatric disorders have powerful effects on essential elements of law enforcement personnel's fitness for duty (Decker, 2006). These effects include both physical and cognitive components.

The most important considerations which are specific to the use of psychotropic medications include: reaction time, judgment, mood, and interpersonal effects. Various agents may have side effects which are merely annoying or mildly disruptive to civilians but may be deleterious to the performance of a police officer's duty. The following acronym may assist with understanding the concepts presented in this chapter: CAPI. The acronym represents: **CHRONIC, ACUTE, PREVENTION, and IMPROVEMENT of various medical or psychiatric conditions.**

- **Chronic** psychiatric problems not only benefit from medication treatment, but require it. Certain chronic medical problems are frequently treated with medications that can affect fitness for duty.
- **Acute** symptoms of psychiatric problems may be reduced or abolished by treatment with psychiatric medications. Acute treatment

of problems such as orthopedic pain conditions, certain transient sleep disorders, or migraine may be necessary to avoid longer-term disability.

- **Prevention** of relapse or future episodes of certain psychiatric disorders is an excellent reason for long-term psychiatric medication use.
- **Improvement** above the pretreatment baseline is common in people who begin taking many psychiatric medications during a crisis. Medications may not only restore function but result in improved self-confidence, less worrying, and decreased interpersonal anxiety so that individuals may actually function better than they imagined after treatment.

## 5.2 Insomnia

Sleep disorder symptoms may motivate law enforcement personnel to take medications. Many law enforcement personnel work on rotating shifts during the course of their career. There is data to support that shift work and sleep deprivation due to changes in work routine can result in impairment in some individuals (Drake, 2004). They found that 10 percent of a cohort of 2,700 subjects from a sample of the general population of metropolitan Detroit had symptoms of shift work sleep disorder. In their study, some of the consequences of perturbed sleep patterns due to difficulty with shift work included ulcers, sleepiness-related accidents, absenteeism, depression, and missed family and social activities. It is often tempting for law enforcement professionals to take medication to assist with changing sleep routines or to combat insomnia.

Perturbed sleep is often associated with psychiatric conditions such as major depression, posttraumatic stress disorder, or bipolar disorder, so that the use of sedative/hypnotic medications by law enforcement personnel may be masking a more serious psychiatric syndrome as well.

The agents to treat insomnia are reviewed below in Section 5.14.

## 5.3 Chronic Pain

Chronic pain conditions result in medication use. Chronic pain from orthopedic injuries and back strain are another major reason law enforcement professionals utilize prescription medications as well as "natural remedies." Chronic pain is a psychiatric disorder which affects much of the general population, and is also highly relevant in law enforcement personnel. The nature of law enforcement which results in frequent contact with violent suspects or detainees results in a significant number of physical struggles in which law enforcement personnel may suffer either acute or chronic, additive damage or stress to joints, bones, and musculature.

Chronic pain from injuries is the most common medical cause of retirement of police officers in some studies (Blum, 1996). This is hardly surprising as back pain is reported in 70-85 percent of people at some point in their lives (Scnitzer, 2004). Another researcher found that the most common physical problem associated with stress in older officers was chronic back pain (Gershon, 2002). The routine of slouching in a patrol car, tackling violent subjects, and/or prolonged desk work between incidents involving rapid physical force provides a fertile field for chronic back problems in law enforcement professionals. In a study performed on British police officers, the effect of different types of assignments was studied (Gyi, 1998). As a one would expect, they found that officers whose job mainly involved driving also experienced more low back trouble than those whose job primarily involved sitting at desks, standing, and lifting tasks.

Police motorcyclists may have significantly higher prevalence figures for shoulder trouble than police who drive patrol cars. According to a study on Japanese police officers, motorcycle officers have significantly higher prevalence of shoulder problems and other orthopedic difficulties (Mirbod, 1997). In their series, the rates of finger numbness (19.3%), finger stiffness (16.0%), shoulder pain (13.3%), and shoulder stiffness (45.4%) were significantly higher among police motorcyclists as compared with controls.

Another large study on Canadian police officers appears to contradict the findings of Gyi (Brown, 1998). They found that the incidence of back pain was not significantly different in police officers than in the general population. They also found that only about half of the officers who replied drove for more than half the working day or wore a duty belt. Officers endorsed the belief that they experienced more back pain when driving or wearing a duty belt. However, the officers who drove or wore a duty belt had the same prevalence of low back pain as those who did not drive nor wear the duty belt. They concluded that there was no effect of driving or wearing duty belts on back pain. The results must be interpreted with caution as they did not utilize any physician's assessment of the conditions such as objective severity of the back conditions. It was also a short-term study (12 months).

In conclusion, further studies with more objective data are necessary to ascertain the exact correlation between driving, wearing duty belts, and back pain. However, there is clearly a perceived problem with driving and wearing of duty belts in police officers. Perception of a problem by officers which may lead to self-treatment for chronic pain makes this an important issue whether or not there really is more medical or objective difficulty with back problems in police officers.

An additional variable that may need to be examined in future studies is the different forms of physical activities in which law enforcement personnel engage. Law enforcement professionals must pass stringent physical fitness tests when they enter the profession. Also, the author has noted that the average exercise regimen *outside* the workplace is significantly higher in entering law enforcement applicants (Decker, unpublished). Furthermore, law enforcement applicants typically endorse using physical exercise to control stress, as discussed in Chapter 2. A recent study on Swedish police officers showed that both work-related injuries but also off-duty physical activities resulted in sick-leave use in both male and female officers (de Loes, 2002). The percentage of injuries from self-defense training was twice as high in women as it was in men (29%, 15% respectively). In 1995, 42 of the 72 injuries in males and six of the 21 injuries in females caused more than 14 days of sick-leave. The major part, 32 of 48 injuries, came from team or contact sports (mainly floorball and soccer).

A variety of agents are utilized for treatment of chronic pain. Prescription medications commonly used to treat chronic pain are reviewed below in Section 5.13. A recent, comprehensive review utilizing the technique of meta-analysis focused on efficacy and safety of various agents to treat acute and chronic low back pain (Schnitzer, 2004). The major categories of agents used to treat low back pain and other forms of chronic (noncancer) pain include: nonsteroidal anti-inflammatory medications (NSAIDs), antidepressants, muscle relaxants, and opioid analgesics. An examination of the efficacy of these agents shows that all of these agents have been demonstrated to have efficacy in chronic pain, although opioid analgesics were not found to have efficacy in one study of acute back pain.

Common side effects of NSAIDs include gastrointestinal upset (most common), nosebleeds, nausea, and occasionally bruising. The side effects of antidepressants will be considered below and are similar to the side effects seen in patients treated for depression (5.12). Frequently, they are seen to a lesser extent in chronic pain patients as the doses used to treat pain are often significantly below those used for treatment of depression. The common side effects of muscle relaxants and opioid analgesics include sleepiness, dizziness, nausea, and headaches (Olson, 2004). Side effects of these classes of medication are presented in Table 5.2 below and reviewed in Section 5.11.

### 5.4 Over-the-Counter Medications for Chronic Pain and Insomnia

Other categories of medications used for acute and chronic pain that may also be important to consider include health food supplements such as St. John's wort, willow bark, chondroitin sulfate, and glycosaminoglycan. Their efficacy will not be reviewed here, but the reader is advised that the literature is varied and complex with respect to these and other "natural product" agents. Because they are labeled as health food substances and not medications, they are exempt from the rigorous quality control and dosage measurement to which prescription medications are subject. They may thus have a variety of unpredictable side effects depending on the purity and composition of the particular batch or source. Many of these agents such as St. John's wort or willow bark contain components also present in prescription medications and may interfere with prescription medications or cause increased side effects.

People have been attempting to treat themselves for insomnia for centuries. Another good example of a "health food" substance that may pose significant risks is Valerian root, a non-prescription treatment for insomnia. This root is a naturally occurring plant which contains high levels of benzodiazepine compounds (Leuschner, 1993). One study purported to demonstrate the lack of cognitive effects of Valerian root but assumed a specific low dose, when in fact the preparations sold in health food stores usually contain widely variable concentrations of the active compounds (Kuhlmann, 1999).

The prescription forms of benzodiazepines are reviewed in Section 5.14. In general, they cause cognitive and psychomotor impairment, similar to alcohol intoxication at higher doses. Valerian root, as a non-prescription form of a benzodiazepine, may be habit-forming and result in significant cognitive impairment as well as pose serious medical consequences during withdrawal (Garges, 1998). Another recent addition to over-the-counter sleep remedies is melatonin. It is a naturally occurring peptide which confers sedation, if used at a precise time and dosage. The difficulty is that other dosages and different administration times may lead to aggravation of insomnia, even within the same individual. Therefore, it is extremely difficult to ascertain the precise time and dosage for this medication without a fair amount of trial and error. It is not habit forming.

Two other important classes of common over-the-counter medications are the anti-histamines and preparations containing ephedrine. Antihistamines are often used to induce sleep but may produce psychomotor slowing, general sedation, and rebound agitation the next day. Ephedrine compounds are low-potency stimulants and are found in a wide variety of cough, cold, and allergy preparations. In some of these preparations, the stimulants are then combined with the antihistamines. Consequently, individuals may react to the stimulant, the antihistamine, or the combination in unpredictable ways. Serious psychiatric symptoms have resulted from use of ephedrine compounds. Psychosis, mania or severe agitation, severe depressions, hallucinations, delusions, suicide attempts, paranoia, and violent behavior have all been described (Maglione, 2005). For a review of common over-the-counter psychotropic medications, the reader is referred elsewhere (Heiligenstein 1998).

## II. PSYCHIATRIC CONDITIONS AND TREATMENT

### *5.5 Psychiatric Medications*

Common psychiatric syndromes account for major use of prescription medications in law enforcement personnel. The most common cause of psychiatric difficulty in law enforcement personnel is depression, as with the general population. Over 20 percent of the population at large will suffer from at least one episode at some point in their lives and 12 percent of the population has recurrent problems with depression. Law enforcement is a particularly stressful profession and much has been written about depression, often minimized and euphemized as "burnout" (a nonspecific lay term not usually utilized by psychiatrists).

The second most common major psychiatric problem in the general population is bipolar disorder, which affects 15 percent of the population. Mood stablizers are prescribed for the treatment of bipolar disorder. However, in some individuals, they are also used in the treatment of seizures, chronic headaches, or chronic pain. Mood stablizers, although prescribed less commonly than antidepressants, may also present problems for law enforcement personnel.

The third common type of psychiatric problem in the general population is anxiety disorder, which affects over 15 percent of the population. It is likely that most law enforcement professionals are eliminated during pre-employment evaluations because anxiety disorders tend to present earlier. Also officers are specifically selected to demonstrate low anxiety levels. Similarly, obsessive-compulsive disorder, which is also classified as an anxiety disorder, is relatively rare in the general population (2-5%). Interestingly, many individuals who apply for law enforcement positions possess obsessive-compulsive *traits* (Decker, unpublished observations). Obsessive-compulsive traits represent a much less severe form than the disorder and are not usually treated with medication. Such traits are potentially useful in officers pursuing white-collar crime or paperwork investigations as opposed to those primarily involved in tactical (street) operations.

Attention deficit (hyperactivity) disorder (ADHD or ADD) is a disorder that affects approximately 10 percent of children and at least 3-5 percent of the adult population (Faraone, 2004; Kessler, 2004). It is important to consider this disorder for several reasons. First, although there are a number of nonstimulant medications that are useful in the treatment of this disorder, stimulants remain the treatment of choice (Popper, 2000). This potentially raises problems in law enforcement personnel—many police departments and most federal agencies will not hire or retain officers who require controlled substances for treatment of psychiatric problems. Second, moderate or severe symptoms of ADD may be associated with judgment problems, impulsivity, and violence connected with low frustration tolerance. Third, it is frequently associated with comorbid psychiatric conditions, notably depression and substance dependence (Bierderman, 1993). Thus, both the treatment of ADD and the untreated condition may pose problems.

However, mild symptoms of ADD are frequently seen in law enforcement applicants (Decker, unpublished observation). There may even be a selective advantage to mild symptoms of ADD, as individuals often function best under pressure or in crisis. This hypothesis is presented in more detail in Chapter Three. Whether or not there is a selective advantage to law enforcement professionals, the brief cognitive testing utilized during most pre-employment testing does not currently provide an adequate screen to eliminate officers with mild symptoms of ADD.

Antipsychotic medications are sometimes used to reduce anxiety and on rare occasions to treat chronic pain. They have increasingly been used as a treatment for individuals with bipolar disorder in crises because of their sedative effects, as well as some documented efficacy in mood-stablization. They will not be reviewed in detail here, but the most common, newer antipsychotic medications which are commonly used to treat bipolar disorder are olanzepine (Zyprexa) and ziprasidone (Geodon). Thus it is critical for a psychiatrist to assess the nature, dosage, and function of medications in order to determine whether the use is appropriate or safe in law enforcement professionals. Primary care providers do not possess sufficient expertise with the range of either psychiatric disorders nor the psychological or medical effects of psychiatric treatment to analyze these issues.

Posttraumatic stress disorder (PTSD) is a frequent problem in law enforcement professionals. It is discussed in Chapter 2. For the purposes of this chapter, the importance of PTSD is largely in its untreated manifestations. This is because there is no specific medication that treats the symptoms of PTSD, although antidepressants have been utilized to reduce symptoms of concomitant depression. The treatment of choice for PTSD remains psychotherapy. Eye movement densititation and reprocessing (EMDR) is a very popular treatment for PTSD among law enforcement professionals because it does not involve medications and is usually restricted to a few sessions. A recent article compares its use in police officers to other treatments for PTSD (Wilson, 2001). EMDR does not have any effect on cognition or psychomotor parameters, but resolution of PTSD by any technique may result in restoration of proper reaction times and reduction of hyperarousal as shown in Table 5.1 below.

## 5.6 Drug-free Policies

Why not just exclude people with psychiatric disorders or medical problems from careers in law enforcement so that medication issues don't have to be considered? This was the traditional approach taken for decades by both the military and a variety of paramilitary organizations. The mistaken assumptions that underlie this question are:

- One can detect all pre-employment candidates with psychiatric problems and weed them out. FALSE!
- Officers who are "free" of psychiatric problems at age 20 or 25 or 30 at hiring will remain so for the rest of their lives. FALSE!
- People who take psychiatric medications are never as healthy as those who've never needed them. FALSE!

Complete exclusion of officers with psychiatric disorders is not only illegal, it is short-sighted. The parity or equality of treatment of psychiatric illness with medical illnesses is still an evolving concept. For example, it is obvious when an individual has a broken leg to others that the injury is significant, results in significant loss of functioning (walking) for a period of time, and yet does not negate the ability of the individual to perform a variety of useful tasks nor return to full functioning. However, in the case of depression or mood swings, individuals were historically thought to be possessed by evil forces, morally decrepit, or even lazy. The fact is that it will *always* be more difficult for people to understand illnesses they can't see or touch, in spite of the increasing sophistication of psychiatric diagnosis and treatment. The author often asks skeptics of the chemical or genetic basis of psychiatry, "Which specific gene causes high blood pressure?" The answer is that in spite of a much higher research budget and many more personnel attempting to answer that question for decades, the genes governing hypertension are less well understood than a psychiatric diagnosis that went unrecognized and was not even treated as a medical problem until the last few decades, attention deficit disorder. Researchers have identified several specific genes involved in this disorder, and strong biochemical and functional evidence highlights the fact that this disorder is primarily mediated by difficulties with catecholamine neurotransmission.

Furthermore, police departments invest a significant amount of time, personnel, and money fostering the development of applicants into officers. A "good" officer who undergoes treatment for an episode of major depression may return not only with improved energy for her/his job, but an improved understanding of subjects who may be suicidal, socially withdrawn, etc.

Finally, the psychiatric profession has data from long-term studies which shows that the rate of relapse or recurrence of psychiatric disorders can be dramatically lowered by long-term medication treatment. In fact, after successful treatment with medications, or during long-term maintenance treatment, such individuals may tolerate stress *better* than their colleagues. Antidepressant medications actually cause increased synaptic connections as well as improved transmission of nerve impulses in the brain which result in improved functioning.

### 5.7 Pre-existing, Undetected Psychiatric Problems

Even with a battery of psychiatric tests, with clinical interviews, with detailed and comprehensive background investigations, and with polygraph, the selection system is not infallible. There will always be a few applicants who are adept at lying and hide negative factors in their background or who manage to conceal weaknesses from evaluators such that they are accepted for a career in law enforcement. Therefore, a small percentage of police officers may be hired with pre-existing personality disorders *or* untreated major psychiatric syndromes. Over time, the symptoms of these disorders may become more obvious to coworkers who see them daily for extended periods. Specifically, disturbed interpersonal interactions, which are the hallmark of personality disorders, may be concealed for a few hours or days, but will likely be demonstrated after a few months on the job. (The reader is referred to Chapter 4 for further discussion of instruments to attempt to detect personality disorders and to Chapter 12 for a discussion of the management of such individuals in the context of fitness for duty evaluations.)

Similarly, if a new officer is frequently moody, agitated, or despondent even during routine police work, supervisors or colleagues may clearly note aberrant reactions to the job. They may note an increased startle response, trembling hands, or reluctance to go to dangerous calls. Colleagues may not be able to differentiate from which major psychiatric disorder the officer is suffering, but they may realize a referral to a mental health professional is indicated and should do so.

An example of this occurred during the course of a fitness for duty evaluation when a corrections officer was referred with anxiety symptoms. During the course of the evaluation she disclosed she had suffered from low-grade anxiety her whole life, but the day-to-day reality of violent and foul-mouthed inmates had precipitated full-fledged panic attacks. She had simply not understood what the reality of working with inmates was like and became discontented and acutely anxious within the first several months of employment. The panic attacks subsided with antidepressant treatment, but she requested transfer to a lower-paying desk job which involved less frequent contact with inmates where she performed admirably.

## 5.8 Development of New Psychiatric Disorders

Many psychiatric disorders may first appear in childhood, but a number of the most common ones may have onset later on, in adulthood. For example, Bipolar Disorder is a disorder which may appear in early childhood, but the peak age of onset is 35 years. Thus individuals may present later in adulthood with bipolar disorder, and remain undiagnosed in their twenties.

Major depression is only 50 percent genetic, so that individuals develop this disorder just as frequently as a result of stressful life events as those who have a predisposition to it. Law enforcement provides a fertile environment for disappointment, exposure to human suffering, and corruption and disaster. These events take their toll. Bipolar disorder has a genetic component but is also exacerbated by stress, inadequate sleep, or rotating shift work. Posttraumatic stress disorder (PTSD) is basically a wholly environmental disorder (although there may be some genetic vulnerability to its development that will not be explored in this discussion).

Furthermore, there is a tremendous body of evidence to demonstrate its development as officers are exposed to incident after incident throughout their careers. There is no specific medication that treats PTSD; in fact, its treatment is usually composed of psychotherapy or counseling and/or interventions such as EMDR (Wilson, 2001). However, PTSD is often comorbid, meaning it occurs at the same time with major depression, so medications are often used in officers with this diagnosis.

### 5.9 Is It the Medication or the Condition?

*Either* underlying psychiatric conditions *or* psychotropic medications may have undesirable effects on key attributes of law enforcement personnel. Therefore, we will begin with a consideration of some of the effects of untreated psychiatric conditions which are of particular concern in law enforcement personnel. These special issues include:

- **Reaction time**
- **Judgment**
- **Forensic Risk**

Reaction time is particularly important in law enforcement personnel as they must drive for much of their workday and are commonly operating in a multitasking setting. Typically, they are driving while listening to the radio and monitoring a laptop computer which is permanently mounted in between the driver's seat and passenger seat. They may be typing on the computer to identify license plates of other cars in traffic that they find suspicious. Second, reaction time is critical when law enforcement professionals become first responders to a critical incident such as a high-speed pursuit, shooting, or struggle with an armed suspect. Even a small impairment in reaction time can lead to lethal outcomes (ADD shooting book).

Law enforcement personnel frequently deal with life and death situations. Their response to hostile or dangerous civilians requires tact and a balance between authority and deference to public sensitivities. Split-second decisions are required in which threats are assessed and the police officer must judge how best to defuse situations. In other circumstances, they must be able to treat harmless but annoying civilians with respect, and not abuse their authority. Finally, with the advent of community policing, it is more important than ever for officers to not only defuse tension during civil unrest, but to improve the image of the police force on a daily basis. It is clear that impairment of judgment can result in either overreaction or escalation of violence and danger, or in inadequate vigilance and thus greater danger to the community.

The issue of forensic risk is covered in more detail in Chapter 10. However, the specific forensic risk that is particularly relevant to this discussion relates to both the perception and the reality that the requirement for both physical and mental stability for police officers is higher than that of the general public. Officers frequently testify in court and they are thus held to the highest standard of truthfulness and health. If it is demonstrated that an officer was impaired by substances (or an underlying psychiatric condition) at the time of an arrest, search, or critical incident, both the officer's and the department's credibility are immediately at risk during all subsequent proceedings. The assessment of the severity of the risk may be somewhat subjective and may also be different between a medical professional and an attorney. Therefore, evaluators should be aware of this constraint but state findings factually and avoid all but the clearest of discussions of forensic risk. Data provided by the evaluator may be used by the agency or department in discussions with their risk management staff and/or attorneys. The evaluator may need to clarify potential consequences of either an untreated condition or medication treatment for the agency, but ultimately, judging the least forensic risk to the agency is the province of the agency and its representatives. They must decide how to proceed with the evaluator's data and medical opinion.

### 5.10 Untreated Conditions: Effects on Reaction Time

Untreated psychiatric or medical conditions may cause overreaction or underreaction physically and mentally. In both depression and anxiety disorders, there is typically increased fear and tension in the affected individual. Along with negativity comes decreased confidence and often ambivalence or indecision. Finally, physical reactions including tremor and altered motor reactions are common. Paradoxically, either anxiety or depression can be associated with increased or decreased agitation so that one individual who is depressed or anxious may be hyperactive and react excessively quickly and another may show signs of motor retardation and react more slowly.

Another common condition which affects law enforcement professionals (and increases with increasing experience on the job) is chronic pain. Individuals suffering from chronic pain may have a "shorter fuse," exhibit intolerance to others, and suffer from irritability or anger outbursts during moments of increased pain. Similarly, individuals suffering from posttraumatic stress disorder typically have a shorter fuse and are hyper-vigilant. However, during critical incidents, they may "freeze" or experience tunnel-vision so that their perception of events is altered. The last condition that is typically associated with hyper-arousal and agitation is bipolar disorder. In the manic phase, individuals may also demonstrate a shorter fuse and be more irritable. Their energy and mood may be labile or changeable. In the depressed phase, they may show psychomotor retardation and increased time to react. The effect of these untreated conditions is shown in Table 5.1.

Table 5.1
EFFECTS OF UNTREATED CONDITIONS ON REACTION TIME

| *Increased Reaction Time* *("Slow on the Draw")* | *Decreased Reaction Time* *("Trigger-happy")* |
|---|---|
| Retarded Depression | Agitated Depression |
| Anxiety | Anxiety |
| Bipolar Depression | Bipolar Mania |
| Chronic Pain | Posttraumatic Stress Disorder |

## II. MEDICATION EFFECTS

### 5.11 Are There "Safe" Medications?

Which psychoactive medications are safe for law enforcement personnel? It's not that simple! The phrasing was specifically chosen to illustrate that the answer is complex. ***There is no perfectly safe medication or dosage for all officers.*** The answer highlights why law enforcement agencies need to work closely with psychiatrists to answer this question on a case-by-case basis. There is a wide individual variability in the tolerance and metabolism of all medications such that one individual might tolerate or require a dose tenfold higher than another. Additionally, some people have idiosyncratic effects from various medications. Idiosyncratic means that they may respond to a medication in an unexpected and often opposite way to that experienced by most other individuals.

There are some general statements that may be made about certain families or classes of medications prior to discussing specific effects.

For example, the antidepressants are generally safe, well-tolerated, and some specific studies have been conducted that suggest these medications may safely be used in individuals in law enforcement.

The use of a class of medications called mood stabilizers in law enforcement personnel is more controversial. There is no question that this class has been extraordinarily useful at improving function in individuals with bipolar disorder in the general population. There are really two issues with use of mood stabilizers in law enforcement personnel. The more important one has more to do with the underlying issue of the whether individuals with this disorder may be subject to significant lapses in judgment *even* when successfully treated. The second issue will be explored below in terms of specific side effects of mood stabilizers.

The use of some classes of medication in law enforcement personnel is basically undesirable, but frequent anyway. Examples of these classes include "anti-anxiety" medications and "sedative-hypnotic" medications. The anti-anxiety medications were originally developed for use in anxiety disorders, but this term is nearly a misnomer, as it implies that this is the preferred type of treatment for these issues. In fact, antidepressants are currently used more frequently as they treat many anxiety disorders better and with fewer long-term side effects than the medications termed "anti-anxiety."

The "anti-anxiety" medications most frequently belong to a chemical family called benzodiazepines. They are approved for short-term usage rather than as maintenance agents by recommendation of the Food and Drug Administration. Both doctors and patients frequently ignore these recommendations and attempt to utilize these medications as long-term agents for the treatment of anxiety in spite of frequent warnings regarding side effects, tolerance, dependence, and potentially dangerous withdrawal from these medications. A rebound increase in anxiety may occur in the course of chronic treatment when a dose is missed. Finally, judgment may be impaired due to lack of vigilance in individuals taking anti-anxiety medications. Clearly, vigilance in law enforcement personnel is an absolute must, so this may present particular problems.

Sedative-hypnotic medications have been used for almost a century to improve sleep and calm severe agitation. Unfortunately, that is exactly what they do. Therefore misuse and at times, even routine use may result in decreased vigilance as well. Literature addressing this issue is presented below in Section 5.13.

## 5.12 *Typical Medication Effects on Judgment*

All medications have primary effects and side effects. Psychotropic medications may restore an individual with one of the psychiatric conditions listed above to a normal state, or they may induce problems of their own. Table 5.2 is a comparison of the relative likelihood of negative effects on physical and cognitive parameters according to class of medication.

Table 5.2
POTENTIAL NEGATIVE EFFECTS OF MEDICATIONS

| Medication Class | Decreased Vigilance | Decreased Motor Skills | Balance Problems | Sedation | Memory Difficulties | Muscle Weakness | Concentration Difficulties |
|---|---|---|---|---|---|---|---|
| Anti-depressants | | | | X | | | |
| "Anti-Anxiety" | X | X | X | X | X | X | X |
| Sedative-Hypnotics | X | X | X | X | X | X | X |
| Opioid-Analgesics | X | X | X | X | X | X | X |
| Muscle Relaxants | X | X | X | X | X | X | X |

## 5.13 *"Pain" Medications*

A wide variety of substances have been used to treat acute or chronic pain conditions (Schnitzer, 2004). As discussed in Section 5.3 above, the anti-inflammatories NSAIDs are the preferred first-line treatment for pain. They have few negative effects on cognition or reaction time, are not habit-forming, and attack the most frequent cause of pain conditions–inflammation. However, many individuals resort to other substances, a small sample of which is presented in Table 5.3. This table merely represents a window into the multitude of medications used for the treatment of pain. These substances may produce cognitive slowing, increased reaction time ("too slow on the draw"), and physical dependence. The potential for harm to law enforcement personnel is clear. These effects are summarized in Table 5.2.

Cognitive slowing may impact officers in several ways: first, law enforcement professionals make life and death decisions. If they are unable to decide upon a course of action within a short time (seconds to minutes), lives may be lost. One example of such a situation would be to decide whether to initiate or terminate a high-speed pursuit in a residential neighborhood. Another might be to determine within a few seconds whether to shoot at a suspect. A final example includes approaching a vehicle the officer has stopped to issue a citation. In many instances, such "routine" traffic stops prove to be associated with violence and may become a critical incident. If the officer's vigilance is impaired, he/she may run the risk of being fatally wounded.

The effects of narcotic pain medications on reaction time are similarly negative–if reaction time is slowed, an officer may not draw his/her weapon fast enough to terminate the threat. In a routine event such as a physical struggle with an individual who is resisting arrest, an officer under the influence of narcotics may be subdued due to slowed physical responses. During an incident of domestic violence, an officer under the influence of these medications might not focus on potential danger from *both* parties in the dispute simultaneously.

Hence, although commonly prescribed and commonly used, these medications may be quite problematic. In a meta-analysis or statistical comparison of previously published data, Chou et al. found that although both long and short-acting opioid medications have been touted by various authors as having fewer side effects, the literature to date does not support the conclusion that *either* type is associated with fewer symptoms or better effect (Chou, 2003). One thing is clear: the current street favorite is Oxycodone or Oxycontin. It is the most commonly abused opiate at the current time. Apparently, it is somewhat preferred over other drugs as it has a short, intense duration of action and has become more accessible than a number of the long-acting opiates.

There are a number of solutions to deal with acute or chronic pain other than opioid medications. These include: NSAID medications, antidepressants, physical therapy, relaxation therapy, and exercise. In order to reduce dependence upon opioids, society needs decreased pharamceutical industry pressure (to prescribe these medications), improved patient and doctor eduation regarding NSAIDs, and other nonmedication approaches to treat pain. An additional dimension of concern is that chronic pain patients have a higher rate of suidical ideation and other psychiatric disorders (Sharp, 2005). Thus a supervisor or chief who discovers an officer is taking chronic medication for chronic pain should have a higher index of concern that the officer may have a psychiatric condition. Also, just as with alcohol, opiates reduce inhibitions, making it more likely that an individual contemplating suicide may actually make an attempt. The issue of whether chronic pain itself causes suicidal ideation is complex and unresolved, so the reader is referred to a recent review of this area (Fishbain, 1999). Finally, if an officer becomes dependent on a narcotic medication and is "cut off" by physicians who decline to continue prescribing it, the officer may enagage in illegal behavior to obtain it. Thus, the risk of dependence creates both a medical risk, a psychological risk, and a forensic risk.

Table 5.3
COMMON "PAIN" MEDICATIONS AND MUSCLE RELAXANTS[1]

| Generic Name | Trade Name[2] | Class | Dose # or (mg/day) |
|---|---|---|---|
| Pentazocine/Naloxone | Talwin | Combination Opiate | 2-6 tabs |
| Oxycodone/Aspirin | Percodan | Combination Opiate | 2-6 tabs |
| Oxycodone/Acetominophen | Percocet | Combination Opiate | 2-6 tabs |
| Acetaminophen/Codeine | Tylenol III | Combination Opiate | 2-6 tabs |
| Propoxyphene/Acetominophen | Darvoset | Combination Opiate | 2-6 tabs |
| Hydrocodone/Acetominophen | Lorcet | Combination Opiate | 2-6 tabs |
| Hydrocodone/Acetominophen | Vicodin | Combination Opiate | <5 tabs |
| Hydromorphone | Dilaudid | Opiate | 2-8 mg |
| Codeine | Hydrocodone | Opiate | 30-90 mg |
| Morphine Sulfate | MSContin | Opiate | 15-200 mg |
| Stadol | Butorphanol | Partial Opiate Agonist | IV[3]: 0.5-6 mg |
| Tramadol | Ultram | Opioid Receptor binding | 25-300 mg |
| Tizanidine | Zanaflex | ∝ 2-Adrenergic Receptor Agonist | 8-36 mg |
| Lioresal | Baclofen | Muscle Relaxant | 10-80 mg |
| Cyclobenzaprine | Flexaril | Muscle Relaxant | 5-10 mg |
| Methocarbamol | Robaxin | Muscle Relaxant | 500-1500 mg |

[1]See Table 5.5 for Benzodiazepine class muscle relaxants.
[2]Each of these drugs is sold under a number of brand names; only one is listed.
[3]IV: intravenous, IM: intramuscular method of administration.

## Case Scenario 1

Officer Pain O'Neck is a 49-year-old veteran who has been employed as an officer for 18 years. He comes to the attention of his department because he presented for work one day with slurred speech, staggered a bit, and made "weird jokes." Upon questioning, he stated he had consumed no alcohol or other substances but had "been taking a pill for my back" for a "few days." However, the chief is concerned because he recently had a citizen complaint about Officer O'Neck for unprofessional conduct after he insulted a civilian. He has missed six days of work this month, putting him over the limit for sick days. In fact, he had missed four days of work last month and has been "borrowing" sick leave from the pooled sick leave of other police officers in the department, as well. He was referred for a FFD evaluation based on both his unusual behavior, abuse of sick leave, and because he declined to produce a note from his doctor explaining his medical condition.

**Possible Diagnoses:** Chronic pain, prescription medication dependence, depression, malingering.

**Further Information:** During the FFD interview, Officer O'Neck revealed he had been having back pain of increasing severity for almost a year. He had tried a variety of substances (including Chondroitin Sulfate, Glycosaminogly,can and willow bark) on his own. A few months prior to evaluation, he went to his primary care doctor for prescription medications. They tried NSAIDs such as Ibuprofen, but he had little result. He had declined to take two weeks off work to rest his back and lay flat, as his primary care provider suggested. Finally, the pain worsened and his provider gave him a prescription for Flexaril and Valium "to relax the back muscles." Officer O'Neck had taken exactly the prescribed dose for three days prior to exhibiting unusual behavior, but on the fourth, he took triple the dose because "it wasn't working good enough."

**Final Diagnoses: Axis I: No major psychiatric disorder, Axis II: No personality disorder, Axis III: Chronic back pain.**

## *Comments*

Officer O'Neck's case is typical of that of many law enforcement officers. Chronic pain is the most common cause of retirement, as discussed in Section 5.3 above. It is often exacerbated when patients do not comply with "conservative treatment" such as bedrest and simple back exercises, or when they are unable to change the stresses, such as sitting in a patrol car. However, Officer O'Neck might have experienced relief from his back problem if he had tackled it properly early on. His use of higher than the prescribed dose was based partly on his rationalization that he was a "big, tough guy." However, it resulted in significant cognitive impairment. He was subsequently required to utilize proper medical procedures for management of back pain, and he remained off work for two weeks continuously, on bed rest. He followed the new regimen of back exercises prescribed by a chronic back pain specialist and a year later he was back at work with significant improvement.

## 5.14 Sedative Medications

Many of the sedative-hypnotic medications are listed in Table 5.4. They may have many potential negative effects on both physical and cognitive skills even in moderate dosages. These include decreased vigilance or awareness, higher risk-taking behavior which may result in an apparent "insensitivity" to dangerous situations or to subtle interpersonal cues and an increased forensic risk of "impairment." As some of these deleterious effects on cognition or judgment can occur at typical therapeutic dosages, their use should be reported to the employer as they may impair performance in law enforcement professionals.

As detailed in Table 5.4, individuals using these substances may have increased reaction time, decreased fine motor skills (dexterity), dizziness or balance problems, muscle weakness, or sedation (sleepiness). Other potential side effects of these agents include constipation, nausea, and vomiting (Walsh, 2004).

The degree of impairment depends on individual tolerance and it is not possible to predict a specific dose that will result in impairment. Some individuals may become impaired even with low doses of these medications; others may be able to perform their duties without evidence of impairment on much higher doses. The following scenario illustrates a common presentation of this issue in law enforcement personnel.

Table 5.4
COMMON SEDATIVE/HYPNOTIC MEDICATIONS

| Generic Name | Trade Name | Class | Usual Dose |
|---|---|---|---|
| Amobarbital | Sodium Amytal | Barbiturate | 65 mg[1] |
| Phenobarbital | | Barbiturate | 100 mg[1] |
| Pentobarbital | Nembutal | Barbiturate | 100 mg[1] |
| Butalbital | Fiorinal | Barbiturate | 1-2 tabs/day[2] |
| Secobarbital | Seconal | Barbiturate | 100 mg[2] |
| Sodium thiopental | Sodium Pentothal | Barbiturate | Anesthesia, IV |
| Thiobarbital | | Barbiturate | Anesthesia, IV |
| **Zaleplon** | **Sonata** | Pyrazolopyrimidine Hypnotic | 15-30 mg[3] |
| **Zolpidem** | **Ambien** | Imidazopyridine Hypnotic | 10 mg[3] |
| **Eszopiclone** | **Lunesta** | Pyrrolopyrazine Hypnotic | 1 mg[3] |

[1]These medications are no longer commonly used for sleep induction by the general public but may still be used in some cases of epilepsy or anesthesia induction by physicians.
[2]These medication are commonly used in chronic pain and headache patients.
[3]These medications have rapidly become "best-sellers" for sleep induction in the general public.

## 5.15 "Antianxiety" Medications

Although used for a wide variety of reasons including the treatment of anxiety, insomnia, muscle tension, and chronic pain, the "antianxiety" medications may have a variety of effects that directly relate to the safe performance of key law enforcement personnel duties. The medications called "antianxiety" agents primarily belong to a chemical class or family called the benzodiazepines. Many of the possible negative effects are similar to those described above for sedative/analgesics. These include short-term memory difficulty, decreased fine motor skills, muscle weakness, and impaired reaction time or judgment. These effects may occur from either use or from withdrawal. The magnitude of these effects depends on dose, potency of the agent, and timing of the dose compared to the situation demanding performance.

Table 5.5
COMMON BENZODIAZEPINE ("ANTI-ANXIETY") MEDICATIONS

| Generic Name | Trade Name | Half-Life | Usual Dose (mg/day) |
|---|---|---|---|
| Chlorodiazepoxide | Librium, Librax | Long | 10-40 |
| Diazepam | Valium | Long | 5-20 |
| Flurazepam | Dalmane | Long | 15-30 |
| Nitrazepam | Mogadon | Long | 5-10 |
| Flunitrazepam | Rophynol (date rape) | Long | 10x > potent than valium |
| Temazepam | Restoril | Long | 20 |
| Clonazepam | Klonapin | Intermediate | 0.5-2.0 |
| Alprazolam | Xanax | Intermediate | 1-3 |
| Oxazepam | Serax | Intermediate | 50 |
| Triazolam | Halcion | Short | 0.25-1 |
| Lorazepam | Ativan | Short | 0.5-2 |
| Zolpidem | Ambien | Short | 15 |

* Time it takes for 1/2 drug dose to leave the body

There are no randomized, prospective trials of benzodiazepines that directly address side effects in law enforcement personnel. However, driving is an activity that is central to job performance in police officers. Data regarding impairment of driving ability in civilians may shed some light on potential issues in law enforcement personnel, but the data presented in these studies is likely to represent an *underestimate* of the demands required of an officer driving a police vehicle. An officer driving while listening to the radio, monitoring a laptop computer, and typing in data in response to radio questions is clearly performing far more complex tasks than were required of the participants of the studies presented below.

A number of studies have been based on a standardized method developed to test driving ability and/or impairment after benzodiazepines (O'Hanlon, 1984). More recent studies, as summarized in a recent review (Vermeeren, 2004), show that benzodiazepine drugs can cause significant impairment in driving the day after a typical dose. The impairment is dose-related and also related to the half-life (time it takes for half the drug to disapper from the body). Benzodiazepines that were associated with significant impairment in driving ability the next morning included flurazepam and oxazepam. Some of these effects persisted even later in the day for those with longer half-lives including flunitrazepam and nitrazepam. However, even certain drugs with short half-lives such as opiclone had moderate to severe residual effects, so the agents that have short half-lives are not necessarily free of these effects.

Some investigators endorse the view that certain individuals with chronic anxiety may need long-term benzodiazepine treatment to maintain function. For example, one investigaor writes that "due to the chronic nature of anxiety, long-term low-dose benzodiazepine treatment may be necessary for some patients; this continuation of treatment should not be considered abuse or addiction" (O'Brien, 2005). However, other investigators point to studies that indicate that long-term treatment with benzodiazepines has been associated with impairment in several cognitive sub-domains, such as visuospatial ability, speed of processing, and verbal learning.

In a meta-analysis of multiple peer-reviewed studies, it was found that cognitive dysfunction occurred in patients treated long term with benzodiazepines (Stewart, 2005). Although cognitive dysfunction improved after benzodiazepines were withdrawn, patients did not return to levels of functioning that matched benzodiazepine-free controls. The meta-analysis also examined data from neuro-imaging studies. Those studies showed that although transient changes were seen in the brain after benzodiazepine administration, no brain abnormalities were documented in patients treated long term with benzodiazepines.

One study examining the dosage of benzodiazepines in proven impaired drivers casts some light on doses necessary to cause impairment. The study comprised all impaired drivers who had toxicology submitted to the Washington State Toxicology Lab bewtween 1998 and 2003 (Clarkson, 2004). They examined medications detected in drivers who were found to be impaired. They found that many of the drivers had several substances besides lorazepam, which is a short-acting benzodiazepine. However, they concluded that significant impairment of drivers who had only lorazepam in their system was found, independent of dosage.

In another study of volunteer drivers, dosages of ethanol (alcohol) or various sedative drugs was administered and subsequent effects on driving ability, memory, and psychomotor performance were measured (Verster, 2002). A single dose of alcohol had significant effects on driving performance, cognitive tests, and memory, even when it only produced a blood alcohol level of 0.03-0.05 percent. They found that low doses such as 10 mg of the two newest nonbenzodiazepine sedatives, zaleplon (Sonata) and zolpidem (Ambien) did not cause impairment in memory or psychomotor skills. However, simply raising the dose to 20 mg resulted in measurable deterioration of performance as well as memory the next day. Also, if the dose of either sleep medicine was taken in the middle of the night, there was measurable impairment the next morning; whereas, if it was taken at bedtime, most of the effects had worn off by the morning.

## Case Scenario 2

Officer Merry Nomore is a 35-year-old who has been employed as an officer for six years. Her department is notified that she has been arrested by the Highway Patrol for a DUI. In addition to being intoxicated, she stated to the arresting officers, "I have no reason to live, my life's a shambles. I can't take it anymore." She was taken to a local hospital and admitted, then released after 24 hours. She was then referred for a FFD evaluation. She presents claiming "this whole thing has been a mistake."

**Possible Diagnoses:** Depression, alcoholism, personality disorder, Posttraumatic stress disorder, prescription drug abuse and bipolar disorder.

**Further Information:** She was found to have a BAL of 0.9 and a toxicology screen reveals levels of eszopiclone which are far higher than would be consistent with the purported dosage of 10 mg she states she had almost 16 hours prior to being stopped. She swore she was telling the truth. She was evaluated and held at a local hospital overnight and released the next morning. The next morning, she revealed she had recently broken up with her boyfriend, a corrections officer, and had "had a couple drinks" to help her sleep. They "didn't work" so she added two tablets of eszopiclone at a spacing of three hours apart. Officer Nomore then became more despondent than she had been prior to taking *any* of the substances and drove on the highway with the intention of committing suicide. She stated at the time of hospital discharge that she regretted using both the alcohol and the eszopiclone and vows she won't use either again, especially when she's upset. Intensive psychological testing is consistent with her contention that she is fundamentally mentally healthy but made poor choices in her management of the acute stress of breakup.

**Final Diagnoses: Axis I: Primary psychiatric disorder: Adjustment disorder, with depressed mood. Secondary psychiatric disorder: Alcohol and prescription drug abuse.**

This case illustrates several points. First, it is often impossible to assess the severity of suicidal ideation and/or psychiatric syndromes in the setting of intoxication by alcohol and/or prescription drugs. These substances cause "disinhibition," meaning individuals do a number of things they wouldn't do otherwise if they were not under the influence of the substance. Second, the practice of people who are agitated using various substances to "calm down," which actually may contribute to *increased* agitation, is quite common. Lay people frequently perceive alcohol and sedatives as "calming" whereas they are actually central nervous system depressants and result in increased depressive symptoms as well as general sedation or "numbing." Last, individuals frequently lose track of their consumption of alcohol and other substances when they are agitated and may overdose accidentally in the process, or at least cause inebriation.

### 5.16 Antidepressant Medications

The category of "antidepressant" medications is comprised of a number of different families or chemical classes of drugs. Anti-depressant medications are used not just for the treatment of depression, as their name implies, but for the treatment of chronic pain, headaches, and for anxiety disorders. They have been used for multiple indications as there are relatively few negative effects reported for many of them. The oldest family of antidepressant medications is the tricylic antidepressants and although they are efficacious, they have more minor, more major side effects, and are much more toxic in overdose than the newer antidepressants. More sedating antidepressant medications are more likely to cause side effects important to law enforcement professionals. All medications have some side effects including the antidepressants.

Possible negative effects of antidepressant medications include increased reaction time, decreased memory, and decreased dexterity. The presence or absence of side effects depends very much on the individual's pharmacology. There are **NO COOKBOOK ANSWERS** even for this class of medications. In general, one principle of choosing an antidepressant is to use a sedating antidepressant in an agitated (nervous) depression. Similarly, a stimulating antidepressant in an individual with a "retarded" (slowed down) depression is preferred. This strategy also applies to the potential for weight gain. Some individuals gain weight when they are depressed and agents such as mirtazepine (Remiron) are to be avoided when weight gain is undesirable. On the other hand, this same side effect of weight gain is used to advantage in individuals with anorexia and depression.

Table 5.6
COMMON ANTIDEPRESSANTS

| Generic Name | Trade Name | Class | Usual Dose (mg/day) |
|---|---|---|---|
| Bupropion* | Wellbutrin | DRI[1] | 100-400 |
| Reboxetine* | Vestra, Edronax | SSNRI[2] | |
| Maprotiline | Ludiomil | NRI[4] | 25-75 |
| Effexor | Venlafaxine | BICYCLIC | 75-300 |
| Remiron* | Mirtazepine | ALPH-ADRENERGIC | |
| Paroxetine | Paxil | SSRI[3] | 20-40 |
| Sertraline | Zoloft | SSRI[3] | 50-200 |
| Fluoxetine* | Prozac | SSRI[3] | 10-60 |
| Fluvoxamine | Luvox | SSRI[3] | 100-300 |
| Tranylcypromine | Parnate | MAO[5] | 25-75 |
| Phenylzine | Nardil | MAOI[5] | 15-90 |
| Desipramine | Norpramin | TRICYCLIC | 100-300 |
| Imipramine | Tofranil | TRICYCLIC | 100-300 |
| Nortriptyline | Pamelor | TRICYCLIC | 100-300 |
| Amitriptyline* | Elavil | TRICYCLIC | 100-300 |
| Doxepin | Sinequan | TRICYCLIC | 100-300 |
| Trazodone* | Deseryl | HETEROCYCLIC | 100-300 |
| Nefazodone | Serzone | SRI-NRI[6] | 100-300 |
| Duloxetine | Cymbalta | SRI-NRI[6] | 20-60 |
| Mirtazepine | Remiron | HETEROCYCLIC | 15-60 |

*Frequently used to treat chronic pain conditions
[1]Dopamine Reuptake Inhibitor
[2]Selective Norepinephrine Reuptake Inhibitor
[3]Selective Serotonin Reuptake Inhibitor
[4]Noradrenergic Reuptake Inhibitor
[5]Monoamine Oxidase Inhibitor
[6]Combined Serotonin-Norepinephrine Reuptake Inhibitor

There are several important risks in the administration of antidepressants to individuals who have bipolar disorder and whose condition has been not yet been diagnosed. The use of these medications in such patients can result in increased irritability and can "unmask" or precipitate symptoms such as mania or suicide due to rapid cycling. This is another reason that psychiatrists should be consulted to arrive at a proper diagnosis during the course of a fitness for duty evaluation of law enforcement personnel. If a primary care provider mistakes signs of irritability or agitation in an individual with bipolar disorder and begins an antidepressant, the individual may become **more** impaired.

Used properly, antidepressant medications *do not impair judgment* and are legally defensible when the individual has been stabilized with them. There is no absolute guideline, but in general, the time necessary for adjustments to reduce or eliminate side effects and achieve a therapeutic dose is three to four weeks.

### 5.17 Mood-Stabilizing Medications

As discussed in Section 5.5, bipolar disorder is a common problem in the general population. In Chapter 3, evidence was presented that it is also a common problem in officers presenting for FFD evaluations. A complete review of its treatment is beyond the scope of this chapter, but a few concepts are essential. First, the peak age of onset for bipolar disorder is mid-thirties. Therefore, pre-employment testing will not "weed out" individuals who may have low-grade, prodromal symptoms of mood swings in their twenties, but who have not yet had major mood-swing episodes. Second, denial and lack of insight into the severity of mood swings is a hallmark of the disorder, so prospective law enforcement candidates will hardly complain of these issues during pre-employment evaluations, instead attributing their mood swings to external events. If the symptoms are not flagrant, it is possible that an evaluator will also miss them. In fact, primary care providers frequently misdiagnose bipolar disorder and treat it as depression (Ghaemi, 2000). Therefore, it is likely that even with stringent attempts to hire "psychologically healthy" individuals in law enforcement, a number of officers will manifest this condition as they age.

The treatment of bipolar disorder is complex–for a review see the American Psychiatric Association guidelines (APA, 2002). Basically, type I bipolar disorder is treated with **high** doses of "mood stabilizers," which are listed in Table 5.7. Classically, "mood stabilizers" were developed as anticonvulsants (medications to treat epilepsy or seizures), which were found to have the property of stabilizing moods as well. Table 5.7 also lists three antipsychotic medications which were developed for use in schizophrenia and other thought disorders. However, these three medications are often used to treat acute mania and sometimes used as adjunctive maintenance treatment in bipolar disorder.

Table 5.7
COMMON MOOD-STABILIZER MEDICATIONS

| *Generic Name* | *Trade Name* | *Class* | *Usual Dose (mg/day)* |
|---|---|---|---|
| Lithium<br>Lithium Carbonate | Lithobid, ithonate,<br>Eskalith | Cationic<br>Mood-stabilizer | 300-2,000 |
| Carbamazepine | Tegretol,<br>Carbatrol | Heterocyclic<br>Anticonvulsant | 200-2,000 |
| Depakene<br>Valproic Acid | Depakote,<br>Valproate | Dicarboxylic Acid<br>Anticonvulsant[1] | 250-2,000 |
| Lamotrigine | Lamictal | Phenyltriazine<br>Anticonvulsant | 25-500 |
| Topiramate | Topamax | Monosaccharide<br>Anticonvulsant | 100-500 |
| Olanzepine | Zyprexa | Antipsychotic | 5-15 |
| Quetiapine | Seroquel | Antipsychotic | 300-600 |
| Ziprasidone | Geodon | Antipsychotic | 20-80 |

[1]Most "mood-stabilizer" medications were initially developed as anticonvulsants.

There are two major subtypes (and several others have been postulated but will not be discussed here): Bipolar I and Bipolar II. Bipolar I disorder is comprised of episodes of very high energy or mood termed "mania" alternating with brief periods of normal mood or energy followed by periods of low energy or severe depression. Type II bipolar disorder is characterized by periods of slightly elevated energy or mood which are not severe or destructive, interspersed with periods of depression. The course of these disorders is shown below in Figure 5.1. The filled curve demonstrates that we *all* have mood swings. The thin solid line shows the course for individuals with bipolar I disorder and the dotted line shows the course of Bipolar II Disorder. The thick grey line and the thick dark line show the potential effect of antidepressants on individuals who are unprotected by mood stabilizers—it often results in high energy/mood states such as mania or a mixed mood state. The filled-in dark area shows the quantitative difference between the "dangerously" high energy/mood of mania and the lesser elevation in individuals with Bipolar II, termed hypomania.

The treatment of bipolar I disorder utilizes high doses of mood stabilizers to protect against both up and down-swings. The treatment of bipolar II disorder is qualitatively similar but quantitatively different. Usually, individuals with bipolar II disorder are treated with antidepressants and *low* doses of mood stabilizers. This is for two reasons: high doses of mood stabilizers are not needed to "buffer" mania in these individuals as their high-energy state by definition is not as severe, and at least some dose of a mood stabilizer appears to be necessary to fully treat the depression (as opposed to individuals with major depression where antidepressants alone treat depression).

FIGURE 5.1.
THE COURSE OF BIPOLAR DISORDER

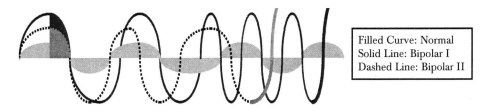

Filled Curve: Normal
Solid Line: Bipolar I
Dashed Line: Bipolar II

The major issues of most significance with respect to Bipolar Disorder in law enforcement professionals are:

a. Potential emergence of mood swing symptoms even after years of mental health and productive service in officers who experience onset of these symptoms in their mid-thirties.
b. Bipolar disorder becomes more severe with age if untreated.

c. Episodes of mania are usually associated with poor judgment, impulsivity, and reckless behavior which are inconsistent with police procedure.

d. Individuals with undiagnosed bipolar disorder may become manic or experience "rapid cycling" when prescribed antidepressants, with attendant problems.

e. In some instances, either mania or depression is associated with psychosis (loss of touch with reality).

f. Individuals with bipolar disorder frequently utilize a variety of nonprescription substances to attempt to self-treat mood swing symptoms and have a high rate of substance abuse.

g. Low-grade irritability is common even in between mood swings, which is a highly undesirable trait in law enforcement professionals who confront agitated or violent individuals daily.

A complete discussion of the pros and cons of retaining law enforcement personnel who have been diagnosed with bipolar disorder is beyond the scope of this book, and is controversial. The major concern is that although individuals with bipolar disorder may experience normal functioning for long periods in between episodes of mood swings, they exhibit significant impairment during such episodes (Judd, 2005). Impaired judgment and/or psychosis is unacceptable in law enforcement professionals. Evidence has shown repeatedly that functioning is impaired in a variety of ways in individuals during certain phases of the disorder. Even though hypomanic symptoms in individuals with bipolar II may even result in higher productivity, the functioning of individuals with bipolar disorder is usually mildly impaired at baseline. Thus, an argument could be made that those individuals with bipolar II disorder, but not bipolar I disorder, may be retained at lower risk. However, many departments are not willing to run the forensic risk of such a decision. Also, the difference between bipolar I and bipolar II often depends on accurate history and insight is limited in individuals with bipolar disorder, so that an officer might inadvertently or deliberately omit description of prior manic episodes.

Secondary concerns include the fact that the medications to treat bipolar disorder can be toxic at high levels, and need to be regularly monitored. If an individual accidentally takes too much of a mood stabilizer, it can have negative effects on reaction time and other motor skills. At times, the internal chemical imbalance that causes bipolar symptoms may result in mood swings even when the individual takes his/her medications as prescribed ("breakthrough" episodes).

The other concern is the forensic risk to agencies and departments: how can an officer and/or an agency *prove* that the individual was "between mood swings" after a critical incident in which a bystander was shot accidentally? In court, attorneys may successfully argue that because bipolar disorder is a relapsing/remitting illness, the individual may have suffered a brief lapse in judgment which was over by the time they presented for a postcritical incident FFD evaluation. The use of antipsychotic medications to treat bipolar disorder is increasing (Calabrese, 2005; Keck, 2003). However, it is difficult to prove that an individual on antipsychotic medication does not have nor ever had psychosis. Clearly, psychosis is unacceptable in law enforcement personnel.

The bottom line is that law enforcement personnel carry and use lethal weapons. They make life and death decisions under high stress daily. Therefore the standard of mental health in such personnel *must* be higher than that in civilians to ensure that such decisions as well as the application of force, *especially* lethal force, is applied using the highest standards of judgment.

### 5.18 Conclusions

The preceding chapter illustrates the tip of the iceberg with respect to the complexity of medications to treat medical and psychiatric conditions and their effects on law enforcement personnel. The most important concept is that *either* untreated conditions, *or* medication treatment can pose safety problems. It is clear that it takes a skilled clinician to ascertain whether and how the untreated condition is likely to be affecting an officer, as the same psychiatric condition may have different effects at different stages. Therefore, it is advisable to employ psychiatrists to evaluate the underlying condition and to evaluate medication effects on a case-by-case basis as part of a fitness for duty evaluation. Evaluation of these effects may include toxicology screens and/or measurement of blood levels. It is unwise to assume that blanket assertions can be made about the safety of any specific medication, as both their primary and side effects may be different in different individuals.

The second important concept is that many common medications or health food substances can have major effects on everything from physical reaction time to judgment to emotional stability. Thus, the assumption that law enforcement personnel are "safe" if they use "natural remedies" is unwarranted. The third important concept is that treating an underlying medical or psychiatric condition may result in *greater* officer safety.

**There is no perfectly safe medication or dosage for all officers. Both controlled experiments and real-life cases illustrate that a precise "safe dosage" is not predictable for many medications due to differences in individual metabolism.**

**Common over-the-counter medications may contain potent psychoactive substances. Although a variety of primary care providers may prescribe psychotropic medications, they are not trained to handle the complexities of psychiatric conditions and medication interactions. Therefore, the use of medications in law enforcement personnel can be problematic. A psychiatrist is best able to evaluate the potential or actual impairment in an individual.**

## REFERENCES

Allen, M. G., & Hibler, N.S. (2002). Psychiatric evaluations by the Federal Occupational Health Procedures. *The Forensic Examiner*, Nov/Dec: 13-18.

American Psychiatric Association. (2002). Practice guidelines for the treatment of patients with bipolar disorder. *Am J Psych, 159* (supplement).

Biederman, J., Faraone, S.V., Spencer et al. (1993). Patterns of psychiatric comorbidity, cognition, and psychosocial functioning in adults with ADHD. *Am J Psych*, Dec. 150(12) p. 1792-8.

Blum, L. N. (1998). *The impact of public safety work upon the health and life of those who serve: Disease, disturbance, disability and mortality in Washington State public safety personnel.*

Brown, J. J., Wells, G. A., Trottier, A. J., Bonneau, J., & Ferris, B. (1998). Back pain in a large Canadian police force. *SPINE, 23* (7): 821-827, Apr.

Calabrese, J. R. et al. (2005). A randomized, double-blind, placebo-controlled trial of quetiapine in the treatment of bipolar I or II depression. *Am J Psych, 162*(7):1351-1360.

Chou, R., Clark, E., & Helfland, M. (2003). Comparative efficacy and safety of long-acting oral opiods for chronic non-cancer pain: A systematic review. *J of Pain and Symptom Management, 26*(5), Nov.

Clarkson, J. E. et al. (2004). Lorazepam and driving impairment. *Journal of Analytical Toxicology, 28*(6):475-480.

Decker, K. P. (2006). Medications affecting fitness for duty in law enforcement professionals. *FBI Bulletin,* submittted.

de Loes, M., & Jansson, B. (2002). Work-related acute injuries from mandatory fitness training in the Swedish Police Force. *Int J of Sports Med, 23*(3): 212-217, Apr.

Drake, C.L., et al. (2004). Shift work sleep disorder: Prevalence and consequences beyond that of symptomatic day workers. *Sleep, 27*(8):1453-62.

Fishbain, D. A. (1999). The association of chronic pain and suicide. *Semin Clin Neuropsychiatry, 4:*221-227, 1999.

Garges, H. P., Varia, I., Doraiswamy, P., & Murali. (1998). Cardiac complications and delirium associated with valerian root withdrawal. *JAMA, 280*(18): 1566-1567, Nov.

Gershon, R. R. M, Lin, S., & Li, X. B. (2002). Work stress in aging police officers. *J of Occupat and Environmental Medicine, 44* (2): 160-167 Feb.

Ghaemi, N., Sachs, G. S., & Goodwin, F. K. (2000). What is to be done? Controversies in the diagnosis and treatment of manic-depressive illness. *World J Biol Psychiatry,* Apr;1(2):65-74.

Gyi, D. E, & Porter, J. M. (1998). Musculoskeletal problems and driving in police officers. *Occupat Med-Oxford, 48* (3): 153-160 APR.

Heiligenstein, E. & Guenther, G. (1998). Over-the-counter psychotropics: A review of melatonin, St John's wort, valerian, and kava-kava. *J Am Coll Health, 32:*680-691.

Judd, L. L. et al. (2005). Psychosocial disability in the course of bipolar I and II disorders: A prospective, comparative, longitudinal study. *Arch Gen Psychiatry, 62*(12):1322-30.

Keck, P. E. Jr. (2003). The management of acute mania. *B Med J, 327:*1002-1003.

Kuhlmann, J., Berger,W., Podzuweit, H.,& Schmidt, U. (1999). The influence of valerian treatment on "Reaction time, alertness and concentration" in volunteers. *Pharmacopsychiatry, 32* (6): 235-241, Nov.

Leuschner, J., Muller, J., & Rudmann, M. (1993). Characterization of the central nervous depressant activity of a commercially available valerian root extract. *Arzneimittel-Forschung/Drug Research, 43*-1 (6): 638-641, Jun.

Maglione, M., Miotto, K., Iguchi, M, Hilton, L, & Shekelle, P. (2005). Psychiatric symptoms associated with Ephedra use. *Expert Opin Drug Saf, 4*(5):879-884.

Mirbod, S. M., Yoshida, H., Jamali, M., Masamura, K., Inaba, R., & Iwata, H. (1997). Assessment of hand-arm vibration exposure among traffic police motorcyclists. *Int Archives of Occ and Environ Health, 70* (1): 22-28 Jul.

O'Brien, C.P. (2005). Benzodiazepine use, abuse, and dependence. *J Clin Psychiatry, 66*(Suppl 2):28-33.

O'Hanlon, J.F. (1984). Driving performance under the influence of drugs: Rationale for and application of a new test. *Brit J Clin. Pharmacol, 18* (Suppl. 1):121-9.

Olson, Y., & Daumit, G. L. (2004). Opioid prescribing for chronic nonmalignant pain in primary care: Challenges and solutions. In M.R. Clark & G. J. Treisman (Eds.). Pain and depression. An interdisciplinary patient-centered approach. *Adv Psychosom Med, 25:*138-150.

Popper, C.W. (2000). Pharmacologic alternatives to psychostimulants for the treatment of attention-deficit/hyperactivity disorder. *Child Adolesc Psychiatr Clin N Am*, Jul;9(3):605-646.

Schnitzer, T. J. et al. (2004). A comprehensive review of clinical trials on the efficacy and safety of drugs for the treatment of low back pain. *J Pain Symptom Management, 28*(1):72-95.

Sharp, J., & Keefe, B. (2005). Psychiatry in chronic pain: A review and update. *Curr Psychiatry Reports, 7*:213-219.

Stewart, S.A. (2005). The effects of benzodiazepines on cognition. *J Clin Psychiatry, 66*(Suppl 2):9-13.

Vermeeren, A. (2004). Residual effects of hypnotics: Epidemiology and clinical implications. *CNS Drugs, 18*(5):297-328.

Walsh, J. K. (2004). Pharmocologic management of insomnia. *J Clin Psych, 65*(16);41-45.

Wilson S. A., Tinker R. H., Becker L. A., Logan, C. R. (2001). Stress management with law enforcement personnel: A controlled outcome study of EMDR versus a traditional stress management program. *Int J of Stress Management, 8*(3):179-200, Jul.

# Chapter 6

# POLICE OFFICERS' EXPECTATIONS OF MENTAL HEALTH PROFESSIONALS

KATHLEEN P. DECKER

## I. THE OBSTACLES

### 6.1 General Misconceptions

There are a number of misconceptions about mental health issues in the general public. It has long been established that the lay public has a limited understanding of mental health treatment and mental health professionals. Many articles have been written about the social stigma that accompanies a diagnosis of mental illness, in spite of massive strides made in mental health research and treatment.

In a prospective study in New Zealand (Coverdale, 2002), a professional clipping bureau was used to identify all articles published in a four-week period that made any mention of mental health or mental illness. They found that of 600 pieces, which were primarily news articles or editorials, 61 percent of the articles focused on dangerousness and 47 percent focused on criminality. Only 27 percent of the articles featured positive themes such as human rights, leadership, and educational accomplishments. In 47 percent of the articles, generic mention of mental health topics was featured without a specific negative or positive bias.

Even individuals with chronic mental illness commonly have misconceptions about treatment and mental health professionals (Ryan, 2001). A unique study on a population of 21 individuals with chronic mental illness and 30 mental health providers examined stereotypes each group had about their own group (ill or provider) as well as the opposite group.

The patients' diagnoses included bipolar (48%), major depression (14%), schizophrenia (24%), and other (14%). The patients had an average of 13 years of education and the mental health providers (who ranged in qualifications from social workers to psychiatrists and psychologists) had 18 years of education. They found that almost half of *both* patients and mental health professionals held the stereotype that mental health professionals are "too busy to get to know my client," or were "controlling" or "mean." Positive attitudes toward mental health professionals included the fact that more than three-quarters of patients rated mental health professionals as well-educated and self-assured.

The limitations of the study include the fact that this group of individuals represents the most severely mentally ill population in the country, with the poorest functioning and generally indigent. Therefore, the opinions that those patients with more resources and who function effectively in the community, such as middle-class patients with a single episode of mental illness, might be substantially more positive. But this study highlights that both mentally ill patients and even mental health professionals have certain negative stereotypes of mental health providers.

There are also different attitudes towards mental health diagnosis, treatment, and mental health professionals amongst different American ethnic groups. For example, an early study examined attitudes of Mexican-American and Caucasian-American college students towards therapy and therapists. The Mexican-American students tended to be more positive about therapy than Caucasian-Americans (Acosta, 1976). On the other hand, in that early study, both Mexican-Americans and Caucasian-Americans demonstrated a preference for a therapist who was presented as Caucasian compared to one who was presented as being of Mexican-American ethnicity. Of course, much has changed since 1976.

In a follow-up study in 1983, the same authors found that low-income Caucasian-Americans were more knowledgeable than Hispanic patients or African-American patients (Acosta, 1983). There was no gender difference between knowledge of therapy. They then undertook an intervention to improve understanding of therapy and expectations of therapists. After merely being exposed to a 12-minute slide-cassette program of "orientation" of minority outpatients to therapy, improved attitudes toward psychotherapy resulted. Specifically, oriented patients were more likely to be self-disclosing with therapists, more willing to be assertive about disagreements and more willing to be assertive about the number of sessions.

## 6.2 Police Misconceptions

Many police officers also subscribe to stereotypes of violence and misconceptions about mental health that are commonly held by lay public (Patch, 1999). A study was undertaken to examine police officer's stereotypes of mental health and mental health treatment in England (Pinfold, 2003). The investigators surveyed officers prior to and after delivering an educational intervention designed to improve police officers' understanding of mental health issues and treatment. In the pre-intervention arm of the study, they found that 60 percent of police officers endorsed the belief that "we all have mental health needs." Only 57 percent believed that mental health treatment could return people to normal lives. Only 32 percent were aware that one in four people experience some form of mental health problems in their lives. Finally, 61 percent believed that individuals with mental health problems are likely to be violent.

The study intervention consisted of training focused on communication skills and on awareness of mental health diagnoses and treatment options. The workshop attempted to teach officers to assess each individual with mental illness the officers' encounter as a potentially different situation. After the educational intervention, they found that 80 percent of officers responded that we all have mental health needs and that 91 percent endorsed the belief that most people can get better with treatment. Thus, there was a statistically significant improvement in the attitudes of police officers towards the general concepts of mental illness and mental health. However, 32 percent still believed that individuals with mental health problems are more dangerous than people believe.

In contrast to the perception of police officers that mentally ill individuals are likely to be violent, only 20 percent of mental health professionals held that notion in a study performed on chronically mentally ill individuals and mental health professionals (Ryan, 2001).

The study above did not address police officers' attitudes toward mental health professionals, but it does lead to conclusions about the views of officers towards mental health in general. The results of the study indicate that police officers have a limited understanding of both incidence of mental illness, treatment options, and benefits. However, this study suggests that education of officers can lead to improved understanding of these issues. The study also highlights that the area of dangerousness is one in which police officers have unrealistic stereotypes which are somewhat resistant to educational interventions designed to improve understanding. This is likely based on their experience with violent subjects who represent a small subgroup of individuals with mental illness but one that is frequently encountered by police.

### 6.3 Primary Data: Washington State

A survey was undertaken to identify potential improvements in delivery of FFD evaluations and other interactions between mental health professionals and law enforcement professionals. The survey was conducted on current police officers in a variety 14 different police departments and sheriff's offices in Washington State. A total of 250 questionnaires were distributed to 12 police departments with 75 responses. Of the 75 responses, 18 were from urban police departments (Seattle and Tacoma), 28 were from suburbs of those two cities, and the 19 were from rural areas of Washington within a 250 mile radius of those cities (rural central Washington and rural northern Oregon). Sixty-five percent of the officers were male, 24 percent were female, and 11 percent declined to identify their gender. As shown in Figure 6.1, 29 percent of survey respondents were line police officers. Another 33 percent of respondents were of intermediate rank (detective, lieutenant, or sergeant) and the remaining 17 percent were command staff. Four individuals who identified themselves as support staff also responded. Certain analyses excluded these four individuals.

No ethnic or age demographics were obtained, as officers were concerned about confidentiality and over 80 percent declined to identify their ethnicity in the study. Survey results support that current law enforcement personnel maintain a number of negative perceptions about mental health professionals, as well as some positive perceptions.

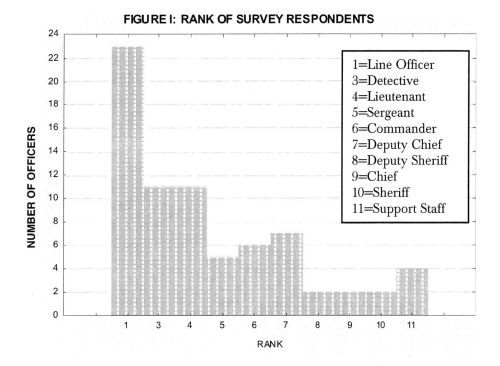

FIGURE I: RANK OF SURVEY RESPONDENTS

1=Line Officer
3=Detective
4=Lieutenant
5=Sergeant
6=Commander
7=Deputy Chief
8=Deputy Sheriff
9=Chief
10=Sheriff
11=Support Staff

The survey posed the following question of officers.

**Would you say that psychiatrists/psychologists are generally perceived to be positively/negatively/neutrally oriented by law enforcement professionals?**
**If negative, why?**

____ *They're hired by the department and therefore biased.*

____ *They like to diagnose illness.*

____ *The department will use it as an excuse for discipline/firing.*

____ *They're crazy themselves.*

____ *Other—specify.*

### 6.4 Negative Attitudes Predominate

Negative views of mental health professionals predominated. As shown in Table 6.1, 45 percent of officers surveyed had negative perceptions about mental health professionals and, 14 percent had a mixture of positive and negative perceptions. A minority (20%) felt that mental health professionals are neutral and only 17 percent had positive perceptions of mental health professionals. There was neither a difference by gender nor by geographical subregion in the primarily negative view of mental health professionals held by law enforcement professionals responding to the Washington survey. There were a number or different reasons for negative perception of mental health professionals by law enforcement professionals. Fifty-seven percent felt that perceptions of mental health professionals are negative. Of these, the most common response was that 21 percent felt the psychiatrists or psychologists are biased, and 27 percent felt there were multiple negative perceptions of mental health professionals by law enforcement professionals and most often included a citation of bias as well as other concerns. The perception that "they're crazy themselves" was felt to be a possible response. It was phrased that way because, although it is a painful misconception to contemplate by mental health professionals, it exists widely in lay population. Not surprisingly, a few individuals *did* endorse this view–5 percent of officers (4/75).

The comments from specific officers printed below reflect typical statements made in the comment section of this item. The results indicate that there were several categories. The categories of negative perceptions included:

- Fear of job loss due to contact with mental health professionals
- The department would use contact for a political agenda
- The stigma of mental health treatment
- The impact to advancement of being seen by mental health professionals
- Mental health professionals "just can't understand law enforcement personnel."

Table 6.1
POLICE OFFICERS' EXPECTATIONS OF
MENTAL HEALTH PROFESSIONALS

| View endorsed on survey | Number | % |
|---|---|---|
| Positive | 12 | 17 |
| Negative | 43 | 45 |
| Neutral1 | 5 | 20 |
| Mixture positive and negative | 10 | 14 |
| "No contact or no opinion" | 3 | 4 |

Examples of specific negative remarks include:

*"There is a negative connotation that because you went to see a psychologist there is something wrong with you."*
*"The mental health professionals located in headquarters are viewed as a pipeline to the chief."*
*"The only one available may not fit for all officers."*
*"Officers may have had negative contacts in the courtroom setting where the mental health professional is defending the bad guy."*
*"Law enforcement professionals by their nature do not trust outsiders."*
*"Law enforcement professionals would like to see mental health professionals be more active to detain disturbed persons."*
*"There is a lack of response of mental health professionals to dealing with disturbed persons who are intoxicated."*

Overwhelmingly, officers felt that the contact with mental health professionals was more negative during FFD evaluations. This is logical because the circumstances of the FFD evaluation are themselves stressful to officers and one potential outcome is job loss.

Specific negative comments made by police officers regarding their view of mental health professionals encountered in FFD evaluations frequently referred to the possibility of job loss. Typical comments included:

*"They are looking for a defect in you. They are biased to diagnose."*
*"The officer's job is on the line."*
*"They are perceived to work to confirm management's preconceived opinions."*

Table 6.2
EXPECTATIONS OF MENTAL HEALTH PROFESSIONALS
IN FFD EVALUATIONS

| View endorsed on survey | Number | % |
| --- | --- | --- |
| Positive | 3 | 4 |
| Negative | 47 | 63 |
| Neutral | 8 | 12 |
| Mixed positive and negative | 2 | 3 |
| "No contact or no opinion" | 13 | 17 |

Examples of neutral comments regarding perceptions during FFD Evaluations:

> *"Everyone recognizes the need for only high quality, stable officers to make it through the hiring process and get back on active duty after a critical incident. Nobody wants unstable officers."*
> *"FFD evaluations may be required by policy."*
> *"If the FFD evaluation is for officer-involved shooting or critical incident it is viewed as positive.*

### 6.5 Expectations Vary by Rank

Negative views of mental health professionals predominated among both low and high-ranking officers (62%, 68% respectively). However, higher ranking officers were more likely to view mental health professionals positively as 21 percent of high-ranking officers versus 4 percent of low-ranking officers stated positive views. Similarly, 16 percent of higher-ranking officers voiced neutral views of mental health professionals versus only 4 percent of lower-ranking officers. The difference in views of mental health professionals is likely multifactorial. Possible explanations include a higher educational level of higher-ranking officers and the fact that higher-ranking officers may have greater administrative involvement in cases with mental health professionals. Also, the primary contact that lower-ranking officers has with mental health professionals usually centers on street issues involving "emotionally disturbed persons" (EDPs) and such contact is usually frustrating, as discussed below in section 6.8. The fact that lower-ranking officers have less contact with mental health professionals was confirmed in this study by the large percentage (29%) that stated they had "no experience" with mental health professionals versus only 6 percent of higher-ranking officers.

Table 6.3
PERCEPTIONS OF MENTAL HEALTH PROFESSIONALS BY RANK

| View endorsed on survey | Low Rank (<Commander) | | High Rank (≥Commander) | |
|---|---|---|---|---|
| | Count | Percent | Count | Percent |
| Negative | 31 | 62 | 13 | 68 |
| Positive | 2 | 4 | 4 | 21 |
| Neutral | 1 | 5 | 8 | 16 |
| Mixed positive and negative | 0 | 0 | 1 | 6 |
| "No contact" | 12 | 29 | 1 | 6 |

Not surprisingly, both lower and higher-ranking officers had primarily negative expectations of mental health professionals during FFD evaluations. As shown in Table 6.4, higher-ranking officers had overwhelmingly negative sentiments (73%) versus only 45 percent of lower-ranking officers. Interestingly, although 27 percent of lower-ranking officers endorsed no contact, 15 percent expressed expectations of neutrality versus only 6 percent of higher-ranking officers. Is this because higher-ranking officers expect consultants to be biased towards the agency? Or is it because they encounter case after case of officers referred for FFD evaluations who have negative expectations? Further research is needed to clarify these issues.

Table 6.4
EXPECTATIONS OF MENTAL HEALTH PROFESSIONALS
BY RANK IN FFD EVALUATIONS

| *View endorsed on survey* | *Low Rank (<Commander)* | | *High Rank (≥Commander)* | |
|---|---|---|---|---|
| | *Count* | *Percent* | *Count* | *Percent* |
| Negative | 34 | 45 | 12 | 75 |
| Positive | 1 | 2 | 2 | 13 |
| Neutral | 6 | 15 | 1 | 6 |
| Mixed positive and negative | 0 | 0 | 1 | 6 |
| "No contact" | 11 | 27 | 1 | 6 |

## 6.6 Desire for Change!

There were a number of specific comments indicating that although the minority of officers perceives mental health professionals in a positive light, they also believe this is improving. The categories of positive remarks included:

• The useful role mental health professionals play in critical incident debriefing and management
• Their help with management of "disturbed persons" on the street
• Appreciation that mental health professionals "weed out bad applicants" during pre-employment evaluations
• A belief that mental health professionals can assist with "personal stress management"

• A belief that contact with mental health professionals can improve personal insight

The following statements represent some of the specific positive comments made by law enforcement personnel regarding mental health professionals.

*"It's scientific and there is documentation specifically for law enforcement."*
*"They provide a valuable and difficult service to the community."*
*"Some law enforcement personnel need to learn how to manage stress and maintain healthy long-term relationships with spouses, family, etc."*
*"I believe law enforcement personnel realize that mental health professionals are there to assist them in time of crisis."*
*"Having the ability to speak and gain ideas or thoughts in treatment is nothing but positive."*
*"They help the hiring process and when necessary help law enforcement personnel who may be experiencing stress in their lives."*

The last two categories of remarks indicate a more sophisticated view of mental health professionals than one might expect. It indicates either prior positive contact with mental health professionals on the part of these officers, or an increasing awareness that mental health treatment can prevent problems, not just manage crises. The survey did not request information on whether the officers surveyed had been in mental health treatment. However, one lieutenant specifically commented on the survey that negative views of mental health professionals predominate among line officers. This is consistent with the results above, as well. It may be partially due to education and partially due to increased collaboration and exposure to mental health professionals in higher-ranking officers. Another officer's comment may also explain the difference between low-ranking and higher-ranking officers. The officer, a sergeant, stated, "I believe that for a new person in law enforcement, contact with mental health professionals is negative due to the unknown of what they are or can do for them. It later becomes a useful tool for officers with more experience who know how to use them."
**A resounding 98 percent of officers surveyed stated that it is important to improve relations between the two disciplines!**

## II. THE BARRIERS

### *6.6 Barrier One: Lack of Formal Mental Health Training*

There are several ways in which differential formal training is an obstacle to healthy professional respect between the two disciplines of mental health and law enforcement. The first is that the educational background is markedly different. Police officers' educational level is rising, but for many departments, the median educational level is an AA degree or two years of education following high school, or 14 years total. This is in stark contrast to the average mental health professional at the level of psychologist who may have four years of college, and four years of doctoral work with a one-year internship which results in 21 years of education. A psychiatrist undergoes four years of college, four years of medical school, a year of internship, and then three additional years of residency. A postdoctoral fellowship in forensic psychiatry adds another year, so the total years of training for a psychiatrist in forensic psychiatry is typically 24. Thus the educational gap is profound between most police officers and most mental health professionals. There are ancillary mental health professionals who may have a degree in social work or nursing such that their total educational experience is intermediate between these two extremes (approximately 17 years for a Master's in social work or an ARNP) and there is also a significant difference in the complexity of the curriculum for these intermediate disciplines. These statistics do not necessarily reflect a difference in intelligence as intelligence is not necessarily reflected solely by years of education. However, the difference does reflect a wide discrepancy between educational attainments as measured by diplomas. This gap can lead to different views in a number of respects.

So quite literally, law enforcement personnel and psychiatrists or psychologists do not speak the same language. Psychiatrists and psychologists are taught impressive verbiage to use as expert witness to impress the court, whereas police officers use concrete descriptions of observed behavior in legal proceedings to avoid drawing conclusions about mental health areas in which they have no expertise. In a humorous moment, the author had explained the psychodynamics of an individual with great care in a large critical incident debriefing, explaining the difference between major psychiatric symptoms, the personality disorder from which the individual suffered, and how each might contribute to difficulties in the future. Near the close of the explanation, one officer impatiently raised his hand. "Listen, doc, if I read you right, what you're really sayin' is that this whack job is gonna do the same thing tomorrow and the next day and the next. . . ." Hence, mental health professionals have to constantly gauge our contacts with law enforcement personnel to communicate information effectively but in a way that remains useful to the audience.

Another dynamic is that most physicians are not chosen to be particularly physically fit; most law enforcement professionals are. So the two disciplines are not separated merely by differences in classroom education. This reflects another fundamental differences between action-oriented law enforcement professionals who may be either naturally or deliberately athletic and physicians or psychologists who have spent more years in a library than in any sports pursuit. This is reflected in core values as well as in differences in coping strategies between the two professions. The contribution of physical exercise to the fitness of law enforcement personnel was explored further in Chapter 2.

In brief, law enforcement personnel are more likely to utilize physical exercise to reduce stress, psychiatrists or psychologists to utilize verbal or written means of "working through" problems. In addition, those who have sought extensive postdoctoral education are highly likely to engage in psychological defense mechanisms such as rationalization or intellectualization, whereas police officers are more likely to utilize more concrete methods of coping.

In a recent study on Massachusetts' police officers, investigators surveyed 126 officers who attended a mental health training program (Vermette, 2005). The survey was designed to determine which topics are of interest to police officers. The results of the study indicate that dangerousness was rated as the most important topic. This is interesting because it echoes the British study cited above. Namely, although dangerousness or violence is not the most frequent mental health issue for mental health professionals, police viewed it as the most important topic. Other topics for future education, which were endorsed as important by police officers, included suicide by cop, potential liability, suicide risk, mental health law, and how to recognize mental illness, in that order. Interestingly, the topics of *least* interest to police officers were overview of types of mental illness, understanding of personality disorders, and types of medications and their side effects. There was no dominant preference in terms of training modality preferred; approximately a third of officers preferred each of the following methods of education: video, handouts, or lecture.

This study highlights one of the differences between law enforcement professionals and mental health providers: law enforcement professionals are more interested in understanding specific *behaviors* associated with mental illness, whereas mental health professionals are focused on the underlying *cause* for the behavior. It suggests that educational interventions designed to educate law enforcement professionals should be tailored to "nuts and bolts" and pay careful attention to behavioral management of subjects, not just theoretical concepts.

However, taken together, both the studies of Acosta regarding low-income patients and the studies presented on law enforcement personnel suggest that even very brief interventions designed to improve understanding of therapy can result in significant changes in the perception of therapeutic process and mental health professionals. As described in section 6.5, a variety of interventions other than just formal education may be important to change perceptions of mental health issues, treatment, and mental health professionals held by police officers (Gillig, 1990).

### 6.7 Barrier Two: Lack of Contact Between Disciplines

There are two ways in which police officers and mental health professionals suffer from lack of informal contact. The selection process for most law enforcement positions is long, arduous, and contains unstructured clinical interviews, structured psychological testing, and polygraph to ensure that successful candidates do not have mental illness when they are hired. This is clearly desirable but has the unintended consequence that police officers' *only* contact with mental health professionals occurs during the course of a critical incident or if they are sent for a FFD evaluation. Hence, they tend to think of psychiatrists and psychologists as skilled at dealing with severely disturbed persons or as evaluators who may cause them to lose their job. The same lack of contact is true of general medical providers, of course, but there are more mitigating factors. First, many normal people go in for medical checkups. Second, general medical physicians are seen by law enforcement personnel as people who save lives, as they do. Even though educated people may agree that psychiatrists not only change lives, but save them, this distinction is often lost upon law enforcement personnel with lesser education.

## 6.8 Barrier Three: Negative Formal Contact

Finally, formal contact between law enforcement personnel and mental health personnel is restricted. Specifically, the most frequent form of formal contact occurs during critical incidents, as opposed to that which might occur in a more leisurely, informative setting. Consider a typical hypothetical critical incident presented below.

### Case Scenario 1

Officer Jones is dispatched to the home of a DP (disturbed person). Neighbors state that they saw the person walking around her house, waving a gun, and yelling loudly. En route to the scene Officer Jones is informed that the DP has made threats against a neighbor in the last week, although she was unarmed at the time. Arriving at the house, Officer Jones checks with headquarters to see if any further information is available. The computer network has no record of prior arrests but notes ten 911 calls from the individual's house in the last month regarding domestic disturbance. Officer Jones calls for backup and a second unit arrives nearly immediately. They place a call to the subject's house and the DP (whom we'll call Mary Q. Contrary) answers. Ms. Contrary is nearly incoherent and labile, ranging from angry invective to tears within a three minute call. "I'm gonna do it," she grimly announces, "*this* time I'm *really* gonna do it. That crummy doc won't return my calls and Mean Hospital turned me away last week, so I'm gonna do it." Ms. Contrary hangs up before specifying what she's going to do so the officers are left to speculate about whether she is contemplating suicide, homicide, or both. They relay the information to headquarters and immediately a call is placed to Dr. Not-There. Dr. Not-There's voicemail informs them that he is out of town at a meeting and Dr. Not-Either is covering. The police next call Dr. Not-Either who does not return the call for an hour.

Meanwhile, the police call the County-designated Mental Health Providers (CD-MHPs). The CD-MHPs are mental health professionals who become involved in involuntary psychiatric commitment in the state of Washington. In Washington, an individual may not be committed by any physician, not *even* a psychiatrist, *only* by CD-MHPs. The police inquire as to whether a report has been made about Ms. Contrary or if she is the subject of an involuntary psychiatric order. The CD-MHPs state that they have no information on the individual.

Officer Jones and her newly arrived colleague Sgt. Smith try to reach Ms. Contrary on the phone again. Ms. Contrary is more willing to talk to Sgt. Smith as he is male and a higher rank and she bursts into tears again. "I don't *really* want to do it; he just left me and I can't take it no more. An' my doc don't care no more neither." Sgt. Smith persuades Ms. Contrary to put down the weapon, come out with her hands up, and they will help her "get in touch with your doctor." Ms. Contrary is taken into custody without much further protest and transported to a local psychiatric emergency facility for evaluation. The police officers wait for 30 minutes to speak with a CD-MHP regarding Ms. Contrary's behavior and make statements. The CD-MHP conducts an evaluation in concert with psychiatric emergency room staff including the on-call psychiatrist for the hospital.

The on-call psychiatrist recommends Involuntary Commitment for 72 hours on grounds of Danger to Self and Danger to Others, but the CD-MHP declines to pursue involuntary commitment of Ms. Contrary. He states that Ms. Contrary has not actually injured herself, or anyone else. Second, she is primarily suffering from a personality disorder, not major depression and she desires to return home. Finally, he points out that Ms. Contrary claims she has exaggerated her desperation because she had "three drinks" and indeed her blood alcohol was found to be 0.9. Ms. Contrary states she will see her psychiatrist in two days when he returns to town and vows to call the covering psychiatrist first in the morning. She is thus released after a few more hours of observation in the emergency room after she declines hospital admission on a voluntary basis. Meanwhile, Dr. Not-Either calls the ER to state that she is not fully aware of Ms. Contrary's treatment plan but was warned that this individual frequently voices suicidal ideation and has never made a serious attempt. She expresses willingness to speak to the patient, who has already been discharged and whose phone rings as busy.

The next evening, Officer Jones is again called to Ms. Contrary's residence where her neighbor has found her unconscious. He noticed an open door and feared some sort of foul play, so he entered. An ambulance arrives at the scene nearly simultaneously with Officer Jones and the determination is made that Ms. Contrary is not a threat to anyone else. The police officer deduces she has overdosed on anti-depressant pills, acetaminophen, and a half-liter of alcohol. A gun lies nearby, with a "stovepipe" (a misfired round which is partially stuck in the chamber). As she is taken back to the Mean Hospital where she is admitted to the intensive care unit, she mutters, "that'll show Dr. Not-There to go on vacation."

What messages does Officer Smith take away from the above scenario?

- High-priced psychiatrists are unavailable in a crisis.
- Their back-up physician may not be available in a timely way either.
- Hospitals won't admit psychiatrically disturbed people unless the state says they have to, and doesn't convince them to stay if the state won't force them.
- The mental health system won't take care of suicidal people unless they've actually hurt themselves.
- Basically, mental health treatment doesn't work.

In contrast, the messages that a psychiatrist might receive from the scenario above are:

- It is critical to arrange backup coverage including setting up specific appointments for patients who are known to decompensate when their doctor is unavailable, such as those with personality disorders or abandonment issues.
- Leave a detailed message for the covering psychiatrist with specific instructions on complex patients, including past history of parasuicidal or suicidal behavior.
- The civil commitment system won't take care of suicidal people unless they have actually made an imminent significant attempt.
- Even patients with a history of low-level threats or gestures may someday make a near-lethal or lethal suicide attempt.

The commonly occurring scenario above highlights that we need to continue to work on a variety of medical, social, and educational issues. We need to educate police officers about the importance of reporting critical information to civil commitment personnel to assist them in making better decisions. We need to develop liaison systems for dealing with habitually disturbed (and disturbing) patients.

## III. THE SILVER LINING

### 6.9 Breaking the Barriers!

The Washington survey also asked in which roles mental health professionals are useful to law enforcement personnel. Police officers were asked to check which strategies would be most useful to improve the relationship between mental health professionals and law enforcement personnel. The choices included formal education, "ride-alongs" (where a mental health professional rides with police officers while they pursue their normal routine), informal consultations, or to suggest other methods.

According to the officers participating in this survey, "ride-alongs" was listed as the most useful method to improve relations (59%). The approach of utilizing structured workshops or seminars was a closes second, with 56 percent of officers endorsing this item. The majority of officers (62%) endorsed that informal meetings to discuss mental health issues as they occur during police work (a "curbside consult") was not a useful strategy.

Table 6.5
GEOGRAPHIC DIFFERENCES IN PERCEIVED
USEFULNESS OF INTERVENTIONS

| Intervention | % of Urban Officers | % of Suburban Officers | % of Rural Officers |
|---|---|---|---|
| Formal training | 68 | 54 | 42 |
| Ride-along | 47 | 57 | 68 |
| Informal | 26 | 37 | 47 |

As shown in Table 6.6, there were statistically significant differences between the percentage of female and male officers regarding these interventions. Female officers were more likely to find ride-alongs useful than male officers (61% vs. 54%, Levene test of variance [p=.05]).

The seven officers who declined to identify their gender had a strong preference for informal mechanism and ride-alongs.

Table 6.6
GENDER DIFFERENCES IN PERCEIVED
USEFULNESS OF INTERVENTIONS

| Intervention | % of Female Officers | % of Male Officers |
|---|---|---|
| Formal training | 60.0 | 56.2 |
| Ride-alongs | 60.0 | 54.2 |
| Informal | 40.0 | 31.2 |

## 6.10 System Changes

Improving collaborative relationships requires not just correcting individual misconceptions but a re-examination of the system. In the following scenario, highlighting flaws in the current system and re-examining the roles of various professionals led to an improved outcome.

## Case Scenario 2

The following scenario represented a creative attempt by Dr. Yes to assist police, emergency dispatch personnel, and a psychiatric hospital with an extremely difficult patient. Ms. Nelly Nervous was a middle-aged, single woman who had been admitted to a variety of inpatient and outpatient treatment centers over 100 times. In fact, she had been admitted so many times that several local hospitals had a ban on read-mitting her (although the practice of banning a patient's admission is illegal, there are ways that hospital staff sometimes implement such a policy unofficially). The police, who had detained Ms. Nervous, called Dr. Yes at 2:00 a.m. The officer begged Dr. Yes to intervene. Ms. Nervous had called 911 over 50 times that week alone and had been taken into custody by police. She had already had one prior arrest for misuse of emergency service (911) and the jail didn't want her back either. The police disliked her multiple physical complaints of anxiety, whiny behavior, and constant near-delusional (but not actually delusional) fear of various illnesses. In jail, she was not violent but was so needy they could hardly wait to release, and even her jailors worried she would get severely injured by some of the "real criminals."

The police officer asked Dr. Yes if she could "do something to get her in the hospital so they wouldn't' have to arrest her again." Dr. Yes consulted with the charge nurse of the involuntary unit at the hospital and stated she intended to hospitalize Ms. Nervous. The charge nurse was furious and quoted the unofficial ban on Ms. Nervous to Dr. Yes. The ban was in place because Ms. Nervous was noncompliant and often left against medical advice (AMA) within 48 hours of admission. In between hospitalizations, she would alternately call with rage or tears asking why the staff "wouldn't help her." Both nursing staff, and medical and psychiatric attending physicians felt she "did not benefit" from hospital stays as a result. Dr. Yes offered to personally supervise the care of Ms. Nervous and to draw up a new behavioral contract. Dr. Yes spent the next day and a half pouring over Ms. Nervous' chart and discussing Ms. Nervous' fears. Dr. Yes came to a final diagnosis of:

**Axis I.** Generalized Anxiety Disorder, Somatization Disorder
**Axis II:** Mixed Personality Disorder with Borderline and Histrionic Features
**Axis III:** Recurrent Urinary Tract Infections and Asthma

Dr. Yes reviewed Ms. Nervous' medical treatment plan as well as her psychiatric treatment plan. She found the same difficulty with Ms. Nervous' medical care (not surprisingly): that her primary care providers were similarly "burnt out" and having difficulty sorting out her physical complaints. So they took twice as long to return her many phone calls, tried not to prescribe medicine unless her pulmonary function was truly marginal, etc. Unfortunately this approach had doubled her crisis calls to the medical service and appearances in the emergency room with primarily imaginary crises.

Dr. Yes pondered and pondered. What does a system do with someone who cries "wolf" all the time and then refuses assistance? Finally, she approached the police department first. "I know this is really radical, but I would like to discharge Ms. Nervous in a day or two. I have a new treatment plan this time." The nursing staff laughed at the plan (and Dr. Yes wondered about her professional reputation). The police were skeptical but agreed to try the new plan. "It can't get much worse than it is now!" they exclaimed. Ms. Nervous left AMA the next morning, to the vast relief of the nursing staff, but Dr. Yes already had the plan in place. Upon discharge, Ms. Nervous was *given* a pager to use by the police. She was notified that she would be paged "randomly" at intervals by the police or emergency dispatchers to "check on her." Ms. Nervous was confused but delighted.

Dr. Yes advised the police to page Ms. Nervous two or three times a week at different times of day and inquire how she was doing. They specifically were to ask if she was in distress and to reassure her they would call again later, randomly, each time. They began the random phone calls and to their surprise Ms. Nervous was almost polite and thanked them for their concern. At first the police were concerned that she would escalate use of emergency services, but Dr. Yes explained that this patient was terrified of abandonment and had unrealistic (although not psychotic) fears regarding her medical conditions. Once she believed that "professionals" were watching over her to make sure she did not die precipitously of any of her ailments, the patient settled down.

The new treatment plan worked to a large extent. Of course, Ms. Nervous did not cease her use of emergency services overnight, nor did she turn into a model patient. However, subsequent to the intervention her behavior stabilized enough that she was able to remain in the community, out of jail, and the frequency of hospital admissions decreased by half.

Of course, the case above is an extreme (but true) one. Neither emergency dispatchers nor the police can randomly call everyone to "check on them" and the scenario also raises some professional liability concerns as it shifts the burden for seeking care away from the patient. Such an unorthodox approach cannot be used all the time, but the concept might assist with the development of more formal consultative pathways for dealing with intransigent patients who abuse both emergency and medical personnel. The above case also illustrates that when law enforcement and mental health personnel view each other as members of a team not just to treat "sick people" or "put away bad guys," but to *restore* functioning to the most problematic of their charges, many strides can be made.

Indeed, a recent study of three southern U.S. cities was conducted that supports specialized systems for individuals like Ms. Nervous

(Steadman, 2000). It showed that when police and mental health agencies collaborated to develop a specialized response to police-referred persons with mental illness, the arrest rate was lowered significantly and the treatment rate rose correspondingly. The three cities utilized different approaches and major differences were found across sites in the proportion of calls that resulted in a specialized response—28 percent for Birmingham, 40 percent for Knoxville, and 95 percent for Memphis. Memphis utilized a crisis drop-off center for persons with mental illness that had a *no-refusal* policy for police cases, which accounts for its substantially higher rate. All three programs had relatively low arrest rates when a collaborative response was implemented. The arrest rate was 13 percent for Birmingham, 5 percent for Knoxville, and 2 percent for Memphis. Birmingham's program was most likely to resolve an incident on the scene, whereas Knoxville's program predominantly referred individuals to mental health specialists.

## 6.11 Conclusions

Further studies need to be pursued to address more obstacles to productive relationships between law enforcement professionals and mental health professionals. Specifically, further surveys of the stereotypes held by each profession about the other may illuminate specific "action items" to be improved. Subsequently, specific interventions may be designed to improve this. Some communities now have monthly or quarterly meetings between the directors of various emergency services. In these forums, ambulance, police, fire, and mental health service directors meet to educate each other regarding the services they provide and to communicate the current difficulties. Some of the limitations of the Washington State study include the fact that it was a one-armed study, meaning no corresponding survey of the attitudes toward law enforcement professionals by mental health professionals was undertaken. Such a complementary study would clearly be quite useful to improve relations as well. The current study only examines misconceptions of police officers, but the author has listened to a number of comments from mental health professionals indicating that stereotypes such as "authoritarian, poorly-educated officer who uses violence to solve problems" may adversely affect relations between the two disciplines. However, as this survey indicates, a "grass-roots" approach will also be beneficial. The author has found the relatively simple mechanism of riding along with police officers serves multiple functions. It allows the psychiatrist or psychologist (who has been stuck in classrooms for decades!) to get out into the community instead of relating to people in the safety of his/her office. It demonstrates the high degree of variability in the day of a police officer. It also demonstrates that mental health professionals are willing to learn something about the practice of police work, which is certainly different from any abstract concept taught in medical or graduate school.

For law enforcement personnel, it demonstrates that mental health professionals are not just bookish folk who are afraid of life. Finally, it turns out that many police officers are more comfortable talking about their work while doing it. Thus, they may "open up" to a mental health professional in the car, in between calls in a way they never would in an office setting. This is as one might expect from the psychological selection process for primarily concrete, rule-conscious, tough-minded extroverts who are more physically oriented.

Thus, a combination of formal training for both sets of professionals and specific action-oriented or hands-on learning approaches for mental health professionals seeking to relate better with law enforcement professionals is needed. This may ultimately provide not only improved relationships between the two professions, but better management of the most problematic of individuals, those who live somewhere in the territory between the "clearly criminal" and the "merely mentally ill."

## REFERENCES

Acosta, F. X., & Sheehan, J. G. (1976). Preferences toward Mexican-American and Anglo-American psychotherapists. *J Clin Consul Psychol, 44*(2):272-279.

Acosta, F. X. et al. (1983). Preparing low-income Hispanic, black and white patients for psychotherapy: Evaluatoin of a new orientation program. *J Clin Psychol, 39*(6):872-876.

Coverdale, J., Nairn, R., & Claasen, D. (2002). Depictions of mental illness in print media: A prospective national sample. *Austrl N Zealand J Psychiatry, 36*:697-700.

Gillig, P. M. , Dumaine, M., Stammer, J. W., Hillard, J. R., & Grubb, P. (1990). What do police officers really want from the mental health system? *Hosp Comm Psychiatry, 41*(6):663-665 Jun.

Patch, P. C., & Arrigo, B. A. (1999). Police officer attitudes and use of discretion in situations involving the mentally ill–The need to narrow the focus. *Intl J of Law and Psychiatr, 22* (1): 23-35, Jan-Feb.

Pinfold et al. (2003). Reducing psychiatric stigma and discrimination: Evaluating and educational intervention with the police force in England. *Soc Psychiatry Psychiatr Epidemiol, 38*:337-344.

Ryan, C.S., Robinson, D.R., & Hausman, L. R. M. (2001). Stereotyping among providers and consumers of mental health services. *Behav Mod, 25*(3):406-442.

Steadman, H. J., Deane, M. W., Borum, R, & Morrissey, J. P. (2000). Comparing outcomes of major models of police responses to mental health emergencies. *Psych Services, 51*(5):645-649, May.

Vermette, H.S., Pinals, D. A., & Appelbaum, P. S. (2005). Mental health training for law enforcement professionals. *J Am Acad Psychiatry Law, 33*:42-6.

## Chapter 7

# GENDER AND ETHNIC ISSUES IN POLICE HIRING, STRESS AND FITNESS FOR DUTY EVALUATIONS

KATHLEEN P. DECKER, ANNE E. KIRKPATRICK, BRIAN J. WILSON, AND FABIENNE BROOKS

### 7.1 Ethnic Differences in Police Hiring

American society has progressed towards equal gender and ethnic representation in many fields, and police work is no exception to this trend. The data presented below attempt to address current findings and attitudes as of the writing of this book. The author reminds the reader that this information will swiftly become dated as attitudes and structures of police forces change. Thus, this chapter serves as both a snapshot of current attitudes and as a springboard for consideration of future policies.

The total number of law enforcement personnel has grown steadily. As of June 2000, state and local law enforcement agencies had 11 percent more personnel than in 1996. From 1996 to 2000, the number of full-time sworn personnel increased by 7 percent. Of these, the increase in sworn police officers was 7 percent and the increase in the number of sworn sheriff's officers was 8 percent.

Table 7.1
LAW ENFORCEMENT OFFICERS

| Year | 1996 | 2000 |
|---|---|---|
| Total, State and Local Departments | 921,978 | 1,019,496 |
| Total Sworn Officers | 663,535 | 708,022 |
| Police Departments | 521,985 | 565,915 |
| Sworn Police Officers | 410,956 | 441,000 |
| Sheriff's Offices | 257,712 | 293,823 |
| Sworn Sheriff's Officers | 152,922 | 165,000 |

As shown in Table 7.2, from 1987 to 2000, minority representation among local police officers increased from 14.5 to 22.7 percent. In sheriffs' offices, minorities accounted for 17.1% of sworn personnel in 2000 compared to 13.4 percent in 1987. Representation of African American officers in large police agencies (with greater than one hundred sworn officers) increased from 9.5 percent in 1990 to 10.38 percent in 2000 (U.S. Department of Justice, Bureau of Justice Statistics 1990 and U.S. Department of Justice, Bureau of Justice Statistics 2000). The employment of Latino police officers grew more rapidly during the past decade, growing from 5.4 percent in 1990 to 7.7 percent in 2000. By 2002, 27 percent of recruits completing training were members of an ethnic minority. Thus, significant gains have been made in developing a representative police force. However, issues with respect to promotion of minority officers may still exist.

Unequivocally, there have been increases of minority members among sworn officers in law enforcement agencies since the 1968 report of the National Advisory Commission on Civil Disorders (Stokes, 1996). Many people have expressed concerns that the future of equal representation has been "clouded" by the recent decision in Adarand Constructors v. Pena (115 S.Ct. 1841, 1995), the 1991 Civil Rights Act, and the attempts to abolish affirmative action. Allen performed a study on three police departments (Phoenix, Mesa, and Tempe, Arizona) and found that affirmative action was a useful mechanism to assist departments with enhancing representation (Allen, 2003).

In a study by Lott, he undertook the ambitious task of attempting to analyze the quality of law enforcement in regions using aggressive affirmative action. People have hypothesized that "lowering the standards" of physical and other fitness to include women and minorities may result in either improved or impaired law enforcement. The results of his study are complex and will not be discussed in detail, but he found that enforcement of certain types of laws improved and others appeared to decrease when analyzed by both gender and ethnicity. Clearly, further research is needed in this area.

Table 7.2
REPRESENTATION OF MINORITY OFFICERS

| Year | 1987 (%) | 2000 (%) |
| --- | --- | --- |
| Police Departments | 14.5 | 22.7 |
| Sheriff's Offices | 13.4 | 17.1 |

## 7.2 Gender Differences in Police Hiring

Women still represent a minority of police officers. Although 17 percent of recruits who completed training in 2002 were female, they are still underrepresented at higher rank levels. Only 5 percent of police chiefs nationwide are female and only 1 percent sheriffs are female. As the numbers grow, attitudes towards women in police work continue to change. However, it is inevitable that there are gender differences both in the approach to work and in the individual's response to stress. An awareness of these gender issues may further help in management of police personnel during critical incidents. It is also important to determine whether there may be gender differences with respect to fitness for duty issues.

There are relatively minor factors that have made changes which can lead to either increased or decreased hiring of women in police forces. The San Jose Police Department is an example of the power of minor changes. From 1999 to 2000, the percentage of females in the academy had jumped from 8 percent to 50 percent, and the only change in recruitment practices was the department's creation of a "Women in Policing" section on its website (Milgram, 2002). Other departments that also produced large increases in female recruits to their respective police academies include:

• Albuquerque, New Mexico, Police Department (10 to 33 percent)
• Tucson, Arizona, Police Department (10 to 29 percent)
• Delaware State Police Department (11 to 23 percent)
• San Jose, California, Police Department (8 to 50 percent)

On the other hand, increasing the educational requirements of recruits has paradoxically had a negative effect on hiring of women. The minimum acceptable educational level for police officers has been rising for years. As of 2000, 15 percent of local police departments and 11 percent of sheriffs' offices had some type of college education requirement for new officers. Continuing training course requirements for police officers has also been rising steadily. There are differences in these requirements depending on the size of the department. In 2000, new local police recruits were required to complete an average of about 1,600 hours of academy and field training in departments serving 100,000 or more residents, compared to about 800 hours in those serving a population of less than 2,500. New deputy recruits in sheriffs' offices serving 100,000 or more residents were required to complete an average of 1,400 hours of training compared to about 780 hours in those serving a population of less than 10,000. It was found that by requiring a higher level of education, the proportion of women who were eligible for hiring decreased.

Another factor that used to result in lower numbers of successful female applicants was the issue of physical fitness for police recruits. In previous decades, such as the 1970s, police officers had to be six feet tall and pass physical fitness tests which precluded most women's success. In the 1970s with EEOC policies, the physical testing changed. Currently there are still discussions about the appropriate level of fitness to be hired versus that at the end of academy training. Current policy is to accept a lower level of physical fitness at hire but require increased physical fitness by the end of police academy training.

It is useful to examine gender-based differences in law enforcement hiring attitudes prior to considering the differences in stress response and fitness for duty. The New York Police Department (NYPD) has 40,000 sworn officers and is the largest department in the country. A study performed on the NYPD examined the views of officers regarding their motivation for becoming police officers.

The results of the NYPD study confirmed those of previous studies and extended gender-specific findings. They found that female and male police officers both ranked the opportunity to help people, job security, job benefits, and opportunity for advancement as the major factors motivating hiring in both male and female applicants. However, there were some gender differences, with females ranking the opportunity for advancement more slightly important than did males. Also, males were more likely to rank comradeship with colleagues as an important factor than did the female officers (Raganella, 2004).

## 7.3 Ethnic Differences in Police Stress

In an early study, occupational stressors of African-American police officers were surveyed and examined (Rodichok, 1995). Forty-three African-American police officers (25 male and 18 female) completed a standardized occupational stress index, an open-ended questionnaire, and a personal interview. The results of the standardized occupational stress index indicated that this sample of African-American police officers reported only moderate levels of overall job stress. There was a gender difference in that female officers reported a higher level of stress than males. Both male and female subjects indicated that organizational stressors, as opposed to significant life event stressors, were principal sources of job stress.

Principal sources of job stress identified on the standardized stress index included organizational issues such as departmental politics, lack of human resource development opportunities, lack of performance rewards, lack of participation in departmental decision making, perceptions of underutilization, and problems with supervision. Female police officers also identified time pressure as an additional source of job stress.

Sources of job stress identified on the open-ended questionnaire included fraternal police relations, shift work, and danger on the streets. Interviews indicated that significant progress has been attained by African-American police officers in ameliorating issues which were major sources of job stress in previous studies.

Advancements cited included an increased number of African-Americans represented in the police department, continued movement towards equality in job assignments, the advancement of African-American police officers into high-ranking supervisory level positions and, most importantly, the appointment of an African-American as police commissioner in that locality. Improvements in job appraisal and promotional testing were also noted.

A recent dissertation (Morton, 2004) explored the stressors that affect African American police officers in contemporary law enforcement. Fifty officers, 25 males and 25 females in urban Michigan, were surveyed with two novel instruments. African American policemen and policewomen in this small study experienced similar sources of stress, including those associated with conditions on the job: job assignment, tasks, or roles; interpersonal conflict with peers; and interpersonal relationships with managers and supervisors. Even though critical stressors were identified in each category, the greatest number of critical stressors for males and females were associated with organizational and management processes and procedures. The results of this study reproduce findings from other studies cited in Chapter 2 on police stress and indicate that organization factors are more stressful to police officers than inherent work risks.

Several studies have found that Hispanic Americans have higher rates of posttraumatic stress disorder (PTSD) than non-Hispanic officers including Caucasians and African-Americans. Predictors of PTSD symptom severity that distinguished Hispanic police officers (n= 189) from their non-Hispanic Caucasian (n= 317) and black (n= 162) counterparts were modeled to explain the elevated Hispanic risk for posttraumatic stress disorder (Pole, 2001). Greater peri-traumatic dissociation, greater wishful thinking and self-blame coping, lower social support, and greater perceived racism were important variables in explaining the elevated PTSD symptoms among Hispanics. Results suggest that both perceiving discrimination and anxiety regarding discrimination can serve as risk factors for the mental health of Puerto Rican individuals (Szalacha, 2003). Both the perception of discrimination and concern about discrimination were negatively associated with certain aspects of self-esteem and positively associated with more depression and stress (Pole, 2005).

Another issue is that different ethnic subcultural values may affect the presentation or the perception of professional stereotypes. An example encountered by one contributor (FB) was that of a prehiring interview in which an African-American male was judged as unprofessional and "not serious" because he presented for the interview in a suit that was brightly colored, and with manicured nails. He was judged flamboyant by the Caucasians interviewing him but "well-dressed" by African-American peers.

The issue of prioritization of family life versus professional commitments may be different in different subcultural groups, with effects on fitness for duty issues. For example, some Hispanic officers might be more likely to take time off work because of the prime importance of family commitments. On the other hand, some individuals may be less likely to take time off work because of their concern that they must "outperform" their Caucasian counterparts in order to be viewed as "serious" employees.

### 7.4 Gender Differences in Police Stress

While there are clearly benefits to the different approaches and roles of male and female police officers, there are clearly still areas in which gender differences create difficulties. For example, certain negative aspects of being female in a male-dominated profession are still seen. Both female Caucasian and African-American police officers report feeling excluded and at times alienated from their peers because of difficulties with bonding to fellow officers. In a recent study of suburban Colorado police officers (Pogrebin, 2000), several negative aspects of being a minority female were described by police officers, including discrimination, police subculture exclusion (meaning exclusion from informal bonding over coffee or free gym activities), and hiring and promotion issues. The difficulties with bonding were reported as more severe with African-American females than with their Caucasian female colleagues.

The Norwegian force was composed of 17 percent female officers as of 2000. Survey results presented by Berg were representative of the gender demographic (18% female) (Berg, 2005). They noted that female officers were more stressed than their male counterparts, although they ranked the frequency of stressful events lower than the males. The higher stress level among female police officers in Norway compared to male police officers was reflected in slightly higher levels of history of suicidal ideation in female officers compared to males (Berg, 2003). Although 28 percent of female officers compared to 23 percent of male officers, 1.9 percent of female officers had a previous history of a suicide attempt versus 0.5 percent of male officers. The major stressors associated with suicidal ideation were personal issues in 83 percent of female officers versus 52 percent of male officers. Females also quoted family stressors as more frequent than male officers (63% versus 48%, respectively). Male officers cited work problems as more likely to be associated with suicidal ideation than female officers.

In a comprehensive survey of female Australian police officers, some significant gender differences were noted in both stressors and coping mechanisms (Thompson, 2005). They surveyed all 1081 female police officers in the Australian state police force. The Australian police force is comprised of 15 percent female officers. They received responses from 421 officers, or 39 percent of the total females in the police force. In their study, female police officers reported that "role overload" and "role ambiguity" were important stressors. The most effective factor for stress reduction was supervisor support. They hypothesized that supervisors may be perceived as able to decrease stress by providing more resources and to decrease role ambiguity. Interestingly, they found that peer support was NOT an important method to decrease stress.

A study conducted in urban New England indicates that for police officers of both genders, work-family conflict and maladaptive coping mechanisms are among the strongest and most consistent stressors (He, 2002). They did find gender differences in the impact of exposures to negative work environment, camaraderie, and positive coping mechanisms on several measures of work related stressors.

### 7.5 *Critical Incident Stress*

The perception of various interventions to reduce stress after critical incidents was similar between genders. A survey was conducted on police officers in 2004 in Washington State (Decker, 2006). A survey was distributed to 20 police departments in different geographic regions of Washington state. The survey was returned by 50 percent of officers from 12 different departments in Washington State. Of the 75 respondents, 18 were from urban police departments (Seattle and Tacoma), 28 were from suburbs of those cities, and the 19 were from rural areas of Washington within a 250-mile radius of those cities. Of these, 26 percent of those responding to the survey question on stress reduction mechanisms were female.

No ethnic demographics were obtained as officers were concerned about confidentiality. However, the composition of western Washington's police force is approximately 95 percent Caucasian, so the majority of responses in this study were certainly from Caucasian officers.

The Washington survey asked respondents to rank the helpfulness of various interventions after a critical incident to reduce stress. The results are shown in Table 7.3 and Table 7.4. Both female and male police officers in this sample ranked immediate debriefing by a supervisor as the most effective mechanism for reducing stress after a critical incident. Both male and female officers ranked peer discussions as the next most useful stress reduction mechanism. Female officers also ranked discussions with their spouse as a more useful intervention than did males.

Although both males and females ranked immediate debriefing by supervisor as the most useful intervention, females ranked this intervention more highly than males ($p<0.005$). This is consistent with the Australian data presented above and suggests that female officers are either more likely to look to guidance from supervisors or to seek reassurance from them after critical incidents.

Table 7.3
USEFUL INTERVENTIONS AFTER CRITICAL INCIDENTS (FEMALES)

| Intervention | Mean Rank | Standard Deviation |
|---|---|---|
| Immediate debriefing by supervisor | 1.8 | 1.6 |
| Peer discussion | 3.6 | 2.5 |
| Discussion with spouse | 3.7 | 1.9 |
| Immediate debriefing by mental health professional | 4.1 | 3.4 |
| Delayed debriefing by mental health professional | 5.2 | 3.3 |

Table 7.4
USEFUL INTERVENTIONS AFTER CRITICAL INCIDENTS (MALES)

| Intervention | Mean Rank | Standard Deviation |
|---|---|---|
| Immediate debriefing by supervisor | 3.0 | 3.2 |
| Peer discussion | 3.8 | 1.9 |
| Immediate debriefing by mental health professional | 4.0 | 2.9 |
| Discussion with spouse | 4.4 | 2.7 |
| Delayed debriefing by supervisor | 4.4 | 2.7 |

Important limitations to this study include the fact that this survey did not address *chronic* stress reduction mechanisms, only specific interventions immediately following exposure to critical incidents. Also, physical exercise was not included as a specific intervention. The experience of the author with exercise levels in officers presenting for pre-employment evaluations as well as that of officers referred for fitness for duty evaluations suggests that exercise may be a particularly important coping mechanism for many police officers compared to most civilians (Decker, unpublished observation). Subsequent studies will be constructed to include this variable.

### 7.6 Gender Differences in Handling Violent Subjects

There is empirical evidence to support gender differences in handling of violent suspects which parallels these observations. In a study by Brandl, it was found that complaints of use of excess force were statistically significantly lower for female officers than male officers (Brandl, 2001). This finding has been recently replicated in another jurisdiction (McElvain, 2004). In the study by McElvain, he found gender differences, but that the clearest determinant to the use of excess force was inexperience. Officers with less than five years service were 4.4 times as likely to be investigated for excess force utilization. Brandl's results also suggest that the most important determinants to the use of excess force are officer gender and officer age as well as arrest activity.

Others have found few gender differences in overall values but that female police officers have in some departments less desire to have their self-image be based on physical force (Worden, 1993). In a report including seven major police agencies, it was found that complaints for the use of excess force against civilians by female officers were only 5 percent with only 2 percent sustained. However, the overall composition of the U.S. police force during the same time period was 12.7 percent in large cities.

In one phase of the current Washington survey (demographics described above in Section 7.5), officers were asked whether they felt male and female officers handled specific law enforcement situations differently. This survey did not request value judgments on whether there are gender differences in how well jobs are done; it only explored whether there are perceived differences in the manner in which work is performed between genders. Officers were asked to rank from one to five the ability of officers to handle various tasks.

As in Table 7.5, statistically significant findings included; both male and female officers felt that there are gender differences in the handling of critical incidents involving hostages, domestic violence, and suicide. Officers felt that the most pronounced gender difference was in how females and males handled violent suspects. A number of officers surveyed commented that they did not perceive women as handling such incidents better or worse, "just differently." For most other tasks, officers felt that there were not significant differences in the ability to handle tasks. Interestingly, male officers but not female officers felt that women handle "nonpaperwork" administrative tasks differently than men.

Table 7.5
PERCEPTION OF GENDER DIFFERENCES BY OFFICERS

| Ability to Handle | Males Mean Rank | Females Mean Rank | t-value | p |
|---|---|---|---|---|
| **Violent suspects** | **3.00** | **2.58** | 1.15 | 0.25 |
| Traffic violators | 1.53 | 1.38 | 0.65 | 0.52 |
| **Critical incidents with hostages** | **2.18** | **1.76** | 1.26 | 0.21 |
| Domestic violence | **2.18** | **1.80** | 1.04 | 0.30 |
| **Suicide victims** | **2.06** | **1.66** | 1.28 | 0.21 |
| Traffic deaths | 1.59 | 1.49 | 0.45 | 0.65 |
| Homicide victims | 1.82 | 1.60 | 0.82 | 0.42 |
| Paperwork | 1.82 | 1.34 | 1.70 | 0.09 |
| **Other Administrative tasks** | **2.06** | **1.27** | 2.70 | **0.01** |

Similarly, officers felt that there are gender differences in coping with stress related to handling violent suspects and in critical incidents. Table 7.6 shows the results of officers' perceptions of the *coping skills* of male and female officers with respect to stress engendered by various tasks. The male officers clearly felt that there are significant differences between how female and male officers cope with stress, whereas the female officers did not concur with this perception. The only exception to this was in the ability to cope with violent suspects, where both male and female officers felt that there are gender differences in coping with violent suspects. Further research is necessary to determine whether the male officers' perception that female officers cope differently is correct, and also to elucidate whether they feel that women are *more* or *less* able to cope with stress. Chapter 2 also has a discussion of previous literature with respect to gender differences in stress and stress management in law enforcement personnel.

Table 7.6
PERCEPTION OF GENDER DIFFERENCES BY OFFICERS

| Ability to Cope with the Stress of | Males Mean Rank | Females Mean Rank | t-value | p |
|---|---|---|---|---|
| Violent suspects | 2.75 | 2.36 | 0.97 | 0.33 |
| Traffic violators | 1.75 | 1.44 | 1.06 | 0.29 |
| Critical incidents with hostages | 2.63 | 1.71 | 2.86 | 0.01 |
| Domestic violence | 2.25 | 1.56 | 2.19 | 0.03 |
| Suicide victims | 2.56 | 1.51 | 3.55 | 0.00 |
| Traffic deaths | 2.25 | 1.52 | 2.68 | 0.01 |
| Homicide victims | 2.31 | 1.49 | 2.94 | 0.00 |
| Paperwork | 1.75 | 1.27 | 1.88 | 0.06 |
| Other Administrative tasks | 2.25 | 1.18 | 3.80 | 0.00 |

**Deputy Chief Wilson:** The differences in handling violent or critical incidents help and have evolved improvements in handling suspects by police with respect to both gender and ethnicity, as well as acceptance of differences. Male versus female strategies are different. It's been beneficial to have women in the force because it has changed the role of police from using violence to subdue suspects to using more cognitive strategies.

**Chief Kirkpatrick:** A male officer might use force whereas the female might say, "if you don't cooperate, I'll have backup and you'll be subdued anyway." The suspect knows this is true and may then cooperate with no force at all. On the other hand, it is particularly helpful for female police officers to know defensive tactics well and be able to utilize those skills if this approach fails.

**(Ret.) Chief Brooks:** One particular instance that I experienced was when I responded to a disturbance in a bar early in my career. I was the first officer on the scene and went into the bar to sort things out. I was able to speak with the person causing the problems and had convinced him to leave the establishment with no problems. When we got to the door, one of my male counterparts was there. The person causing the problem (who was a male) immediately got his dander up and wanted to engage in a physical confrontation with my counterpart. I was able to convince my counterpart to move out of the sight line of this person but still keep me in his sight line for officer safety. Once the male officer was no longer in the line of sight of the person, the person calmed down and continued on his way out of the bar with no further problems.

### 7.7 Why the Differences in Handling Violence?

Multiple explanations may be advanced for these perceived gender differences. It is clear that with rare exceptions, female officers are smaller, lighter weight, and physically weaker than their male counterparts. However, some female officers may possess martial arts skills which make them as skillful or more skillful at "taking down" violent suspects as their male counterparts without such training. Additionally, use of the Taser and firearms further levels the playing field as the use of these weapons is independent of size. Indeed, when one diminutive female officer was asked how she handled large, violent suspects, she stated that she quietly advises them that (a) she has larger, stronger backup officers en route to the site; (b) that she has firearms and will use lethal force if necessary; and (c) that compliance is inevitable.

Another dynamic relates to the medieval notion of chivalry in which males defer to females out of courtesy and gallantry. Another ancient dynamic from earlier civilizations which may still operate at times is the phenomenon of protection of females by males. This dynamic was cited as a major reason for excluding women from fighting positions in the military by opponents of such changes. One argument was that men would not jeopardize missions because of trying to protect a female colleague. However, it may also work to female police officers' benefit as suspects may be less likely to harm a female officer. This protective dynamic is clearly not applicable in cases of certain rape or homicide suspects with sadistic tendencies towards women. In cases of accosting sexual predators or serial murderers of women, a female officer might be in more jeopardy.

Other possible explanations for gender differences in the handling of violent incidents include psychodynamic differences between male and female authority figures in the U.S. There are several TV commercials that portray large male sports players who bow respectfully to commands from their tiny mothers. In contrast, media often portrays the successful physical rebellion of sons against their fathers in which the sparring of son versus father eventually results in the male child becoming stronger than the father. These portrayals of physical matches in which the child bests dad contrast to the portrayals of adult males deferring to mom's commands even when he dwarfs her.

While it would be completely inappropriate for a female officer to flirt with a male suspect, there is no question that most males modify their behavior in presence of an attractive female. Males may also be embarrassed demonstrating certain behaviors in front of females, such as being arrested while they are sleeping naked or in the bathroom. Police often utilize these psychological dynamics to their advantage in interview situations as well as during arrests.

### 7.8 Ethnic Differences in Use of Force

There have also been concerns that the use of physical force is disparate between different ethnic groups (Schuck, 2004). In a study of this issue in Phoenix, Arizona, it was found that disparity in police use of physical force was found only for male citizens not in custody when analyzed by race and ethnic group between white, black, and Hispanic citizens. The findings suggest that assessments of racial and ethnic disparity do not necessarily support the public's fears that use of force is disparate in different ethnic groups. Further research in a variety of American cities and rural areas is necessary to compare the vastly different subcultures and environments across the U.S.

In a fascinating study on Navaho police officers, investigators assessed the spiritual beliefs of Navaho police officers (Gould, 2002). They compared the use of force that Navaho officers with traditional Navaho spiritual beliefs (which eschew violence) versus those Navaho officers with more "European" beliefs. They found that the officers' feeling of spiritual connectedness to their culture was inversely related to the strictness of the enforcement of European-based laws. The more spiritual the officer, the less likely the officer is to rely solely on European-based laws, including force, and the greater the reliance on *other* methods of problems solving. This suggests that it is not simply a question of *racism* that determines use of force, but rather a mind-set to choose violence or peaceful means of solving problems.

## 7.9 Gender Differences in Washington State Fitness for Duty Evaluations

A retrospective review of 58 police officers and corrections officers who were sequentially referred for a FFD evaluation (to the author, KD) from 1999-2004 was conducted. (Other results of this study were described in detail in Chapter 3.) Demographic variables were similar between male and female officers referred for fitness for duty evaluations. There was no significant difference between the mean age, which was 35 for females and 40 for males. The majority of officers were Caucasian for both genders. However, 92 percent of the male officers were Caucasian and only 77 percent of the female officers were Caucasian. There was one African-American female, one Hispanic female, and one African-American male, but because there were more male officers, the percentage was lower. The composition with respect to rank was significantly different: 38 percent of the female officers were corrections officers and 60 percent of the male officers were corrections officers. There was also a significant difference between the marital status of the officers by gender. Fifty percent of the male officers were in their first marriage versus only 7 percent (1) for female officers. Sixty-one percent of female officers were divorced and 15 percent were single, never married.

There was a gender difference between the psychiatric diagnosis of female officers and male officers referred for fitness for duty evaluations in this study. Statistically, significantly more females than males were diagnosed with bipolar disorder and more males were diagnosed with a probable Axis II personality disorder as the primary cause of being "unfit." There was also a difference between the fractions of officers with substance abuse as a primary or secondary diagnosis leading to "unfit" status. Thirty percent of the "unfit" female officers had a secondary diagnosis of substance use disorder, whereas only 12.5 percent males had a secondary diagnosis of substance use disorder. Of these, two females had a primary diagnosis of major depression and one had a primary diagnosis of bipolar disorder.

These gender differences must be interpreted with caution. The number of unfit female officers was smaller than that of the males, and the overall sample size is large enough to permit statistical analysis, but it would be preferable to see if these differences occur in a larger series of cases. Possible explanations for the discrepancies that were considered include examiner bias, referral bias, nonrandom referral pattern, regional or geographic variability, and differential hiring patterns between gender.

Table 7.7
PRIMARY PSYCHIATRIC DIAGNOSES IN "UNFIT" OFFICERS

| Axis I Diagnosis | Total Number Unfit | Total Unfit Percent | Unfit Female Officers Percent | Unfit Male Officers Percent |
|---|---|---|---|---|
| No Axis I Diagnosis[1] | 3 | 10.0 | 0 | 12.5 |
| Major Depression | 13 | 68.0 | 44 | 37.5 |
| Bipolar Disorder | 8 | 23.0 | 44 | 17.0 |
| Anxiety Disorder | 2 | 6.0 | | 8.3 |
| Posttraumatic Stress Disorder | 1 | 3.0 | 11 | |
| Psychosis | 2 | 6.0 | | 8.3 |
| Substance Use Disorder | 1 | 3.0 | | 4.2 |
| Attention Deficit Disorder | 2 | 6.0 | | 8.3 |
| Axis II Diagnosis as Unfit | 3 | 10.0 | | |

[1]Those officers were deemed "unfit" because of an Axis II Personality Disorder.

The issue of examiner bias towards a specific diagnosis was not felt to account for the diagnosis of Bipolar Disorder, as the officers diagnosed with this disorder (both male and female) had been evaluated and treated at emergency psychiatric facilities and the diagnosis was based on severely disturbed behavior such as mania and/or suicide attempts. Similarly, the issue of substance use disorder was not felt to be due to examiner bias as in the majority of cases, blood alcohol levels and/or DUI's were obtained prior to the fitness for duty evaluation, making diagnosis clear.

It is quite possible that some police departments felt more comfortable sending a problematic female officer to a female so that more disturbed females were referred to the evaluator (KD). Thus, there might have been a referral bias on the part of the referring agency. It is also probable that officers of BOTH genders referred were referred to the author because they had more severe problems or were being prescribed psychotropic medications. The author is a psychiatrist and therefore better qualified to comment on medical and psychiatric conditions requiring medications than would be a psychologist evaluator.

However, it is likely that there were still significant differences in the psychological makeup of female officers referred for evaluation. An examination of the family history of the female officers revealed a much higher incidence of positive family history for substance use disorders as well as general psychiatric disorders, as shown in Table 7.8 below. A striking 67 percent of female officers described both general psychiatric and substance use disorders in first-degree family members. More of the male officers had no known family history (25% for males versus 5% for females), as well as a higher proportion of unknown family history (primarily due to adoption issues). However, male officers had a higher incidence of substance use disorders than did female officers. It could be that the female officers were either more aware of psychiatric problems in their families, so a further analysis of the data will be undertaken to address this issue.

Table 7.8
FAMILY HISTORY OF MENTAL HEALTH DISORDERS

| Family History | Female Officers Percent | Male Officers Percent |
| --- | --- | --- |
| Negative History of EITHER Psychiatric or Substance Use Disorders | 0.0 | 25.0 |
| Positive History of Psychiatric Disorders | 17.6 | 12.5 |
| Positive History of Substance Use Disorders | 11.8 | 25.0 |
| Positive History of BOTH Psychiatric and Substance Use Disorders | 64.7 | 22.5 |
| Unknown History | 5.9 | 15.0 |

## 7.10 Ethnic Differences in Fitness for Duty Evaluations

The author (KD) has encountered significant ethnic differences in the acceptance and compliance of medication treatment, which is well documented in the literature as well. Some of these differences are discussed in Chapter 5. Specifically, certain Hispanic individuals in the current study referred for evaluation resisted or declined to take medications for depression because it creates the impression of disability or being "loco" within their extended family. However, the number of cases of non-Caucasian officers was too low in the current data presented from Washington State to draw any statistical conclusions.

It is very difficult to examine nationwide trends with respect to minority or gender issues in the police force, as each region has different constraints, subcultures, and composition. However, one agency that is similar to a national police force is the Drug Enforcement Agency. This agency has officers throughout the country, but has more uniform regulations with respect to conduct than do individual local police departments. The DEA conducts periodic external reviews regarding the disciplinary activity of its agents. In a recent discussion of the findings of external reviews (DEA OPR, 2004) conducted over more than a decade, no disparity by race, ethnicity, or gender was found. The review examined disciplinary action taken by position and grade level for all DEA employees.

First, an early study in 1987 by an external contractor examined disparity related to race, gender, DEA office size, and geographic region (Korotkin, 1987). A more recent study in 2001 on the DEA focused on the issue of disparity in the discipline administered to Caucasian versus African-American special agents (Jacobs, 2001). The study analyzed disciplinary actions imposed from 1994 to 2000. The results presented in this study concluded there were no differences between Caucasian and African-American special agents in terms of the severity of the punishment issued.

The most recent study of the DEA was conducted by the General Accounting Office (GAO) in 2003. It included a review of racial, ethnic, and gender differences in the disciplinary process of special agents by the DEA (GAO, 2003). The study found that the proportion of African-American, Hispanic, and female special agents disciplined for misconduct was substantially higher than their representation in the DEA special agent workforce. The study was unable to completely explain this finding.

Although the review of the data for the DEA found some statistical differences in certain categories, the study concluded that the DEA's disciplinary system was fair and that the expected disciplinary proposals and decisions were the same for all races that were charged with similar offenses or offenses of the same level of severity (DEA, 2004).

## 7.11 Conclusions

There are differences between male and female police officers in terms of hiring, perception, and management of stress. Female officers are still underrepresented in the highest ranks of law enforcement.

Relatively simple interventions such as web-based efforts have been shown to result in dramatic improvements in recruitment. Gender differences are widely recognized in that the fashion in which male and female officers handle violent suspects is different-not necessarily better or worse, but necessarily different due to size and strength issues. However, both genders ranked the usefulness of interventions after a critical incident similarly.

Literature reviewed in this chapter suggests that although many of the stressors that affect male and female officers are perceived to be equally stressful to both genders, certain differences exist. For example, female officers tend to experience the impact of exposure to negative work environment, with respect to the need for camaraderie, and to exhibit different positive coping mechanisms. In some studies, female officers were also more "torn" between work and family roles. Data from the Washington State study presented in this chapter indicated few gender differences. Further surveys in the Washington State cohort need to focus on different questions to replicate the findings of role conflict or modify them, as roles continue to change.

Primary data from FFD evaluations on Washington State police and corrections officers revealed a higher percentage of female officers with bipolar disorder, and a higher percentage of males with attention deficit disorder. Because of the small sample size, the significance of this finding at a national level is questionable. Larger sample sizes and samples from different geographic regions are necessary to determine whether these trends are of broader significance. One trend that was striking in this study population was the much higher proportion of female officers with psychiatric and/or substance use disorders in their family history (65% vs. 23%). It is unclear whether this represents a difference in reporting bias (i.e., female officers are more aware of family problems) or accuracy of reporting (i.e., female officers are more truthful) or an actual difference in the incidence of disorders (i.e., more females are accepted that have a family history of psychiatric/substance use problems).

The Washington State sample was relative homogeneous: 92 percent of male officers referred for FFD evaluations were Caucasian and 77 percent of females referred for FFD evaluation were Caucasian. Therefore, the size of the sample did not permit any conclusions regarding differences between ethnic groups. Data was reviewed from the DEA's review of its disciplinary findings, and no consistent differences were reported. Further exploration of potential ethnic differences will require far larger sample sizes and/or comparisons between a number of geographic regions.

# REFERENCES

Acosta, F. X., & Sheehan, J. G. (1976). Preferences toward Mexican American and Anglo-American psychotherapists. *J Counsel Clin Psychol 44*(2):272-279.

Allen, R. Y. W. (2003). Examining the implementation of affirmative action in law enforcement. *Public Personnel Management, 32*(3):411-418 Fall.

Berg, A.M., Hem, E., Lau, B., Haseth, K. & Ekeberg, O. (2005). Stress in the Norwegian Police Service. *Occupat Med-Oxford, 55*(2):113-120 Mar.

Brandl, S. G., Stroshine, M. S., & Frank, J. (2001). Who are the complaint-prone officers? An examination of the relationship between police officers' attributes, arrest activity, assignment, and citizens' complaints about excessive force. *J of Crim Justice, 29*(6):521-529 Nov-Dec.

Drug Enforcement Agency.(2002). *Office of Professional Responsibility Report on Misconduct.*

Drug Enforcement Agency. (2004). *Review of the Drug Enforcement Administration's Disciplinary System.* Report Number I-2004-002, Jan.

General Accounting Office. *Equal employment opportunity: Hiring, promotion, and discipline processes at DEA.* GAO-03-413.

Gould, L. A. (2002). Indigenous people policing indigenous people: the potential psychological and cultural costs. *Soc Science J, 39*(2):171-188.

He, N., Zhao, J. H., & Archbold, C. A. (2002). Gender and police stress–The convergent and divergent impact of work environment, work-family conflict, and stress coping mechanisms of female and male police officers. *Policing–An International Journal of Police Strategies & Management, 25*(4):687-708.

Jacobs, L. (2001). *Drug Enforcement Administration Discipline System Study.* SHL: Litigation Support Group.

Korotkin, A.L. Schemmer, F. M., & Bruff, C. D. (1987). *A study of the Drug Enforcement Administration's current conduct and discipline system.* Advanced Research Resources Organization.

Milgram, D. (2002). Recruiting women to policing: Practical strategies that work. *Police Chief,* April.

Morton, T., (2004). Job-related stressors on African-American police officers. Dissertation Abstracts International Section A: Humanities & Social Sciences. Vol. 64(7-A): 2563. U.S.: Univ Microfilms International.

McElvain, J. P., & Kposowa, A. J. (2004). Police officer characteristics and internal affairs investigations for use of force allegations. *J of Crim Justice 32*(3):265-279, May-Jun.

Pogrebin, M., Dodge, M., & Chatman, H. (2000). Reflections of African-American women on their careers in urban policing. Their experiences of racial and sexual discrimination. *Int J of Sociol Law, 28*:311-326.

Pole, N., Best, S. R., Weiss, D. S., Metzler, T., Liberman, A. M., Fagan, J., & Marmar, C. R. (2001). Effects of gender and ethnicity on duty-related posttraumatic stress symptoms among urban police officers. *J Nerv Ment Dis,* Jul;189(7):442-448.

Pole, N., Best, S.R., Metzler, T., Marmar, & C.R. (2005). Why are Hispanics at greater risk for PTSD? *Cultural Diversity and Ethnic Minority Psychology, 11*(2):144-161.

Raganella, A. J., & White, M.D. (2004). Race, gender and motivation for becoming a police officer: Implications for building a representative police department. *J Crim Justice, 32*:501-513.

Rodichok, G. J. (1995). A quantitative and qualitative survey of job stress among African-American police officers. Dissertation Abstracts International: Section B: The Sciences & Engineering. Vol. 56(6-B), Dec: 3491. U.S.: Univ Microfilms International.

Schuck, A. M. (2004). The masking of racial and ethnic disparity in police use of physical force: The effects of gender and custody status. *J of Crim Justice, 32*(6): 557-564 Nov-Dec.

Stokes, L. D., & Scott, J. F. (1996). Affirmative action and selected minority groups in law enforcement. *J of Crim Justice, 24*(1):29-38.

Szalacha, L. A. et al. (2003). Discrimination and Puerto Rican children's and adolescents' mental health. *Cultural Diversity & Ethnic Minority Psychology, 9,* May (2): 141-155.

Worden, A. P. (1993). The attitudes of women and men in policing–Testing conventional and contemporary wisdom. *Criminology, 31*(2):203-241, May.

# Chapter 8

# DUTY DEATH: A MAJOR STRESSOR

Anne E. Kirkpatrick, Brian J. Wilson, and Kathleen P. Decker

In this chapter, the issue of how duty death affects law enforcement personnel and how their departments can help them cope with the stress are explored several ways. First, relevant literature will be discussed. Second, primary data was obtained by conducting a survey of 75 randomly selected law enforcement personnel of varying rank. They answered questions related to their views on duty death and interventions designed to lessen the stress of duty death. Both quantitative measures of their responses as well as their comments on the subject will be presented. The final component of this chapter is based on an interview Dr. Decker conducted of Chief Kirkpatrick and Deputy Chief Wilson. Their police department (Federal Way Police Department, Washington State) lost an officer in a fatal shooting by a domestic violence suspect while on duty. These command staff comment on these issues from the perspective of command staff who have managed the fallout of this event in the recent past (2003). This chapter will include a brief review of the literature in this area. The reader is referred to an excellent book which reviews police stress exhaustively (Violanti, 1999).

## 8.1 Recovery from Duty Death

An understanding of the similarities and differences in law enforcement personnel's response to a duty death compared to civilians is important in designing strategies to reduce the stress associated with this type of event. It is important for mental health professionals working with law enforcement professionals that coping mechanisms in law enforcement professionals are somewhat different from many other clients (Neylan, 2002, Neely, 1997). One way in which this is elegantly demonstrated is in the following chapter which deals with the response of police officers to death of another officer on duty. Most police officers tend to emotionally recover from the duty death of another officer much sooner than one might expect–50 percent of officers stated it took less than a year to recover and 17 percent endorsed that it only took a few weeks.

As one might expect, there was a wide range of responses regarding the amount of time it takes to recover from a duty death. There was no geographic variation in officers' responses in this study. However, somewhat surprisingly, female officers who responded to this survey stated that it took less time to recover from a duty death. Figure 8.1 show that almost half the male officers (47%) stated that it took less than a year to recover. In contrast, 60 percent of the female officers stated it took less than a year to recover from duty of a fellow officer.

Figure 8.1
Recovery Time from duty death by gender

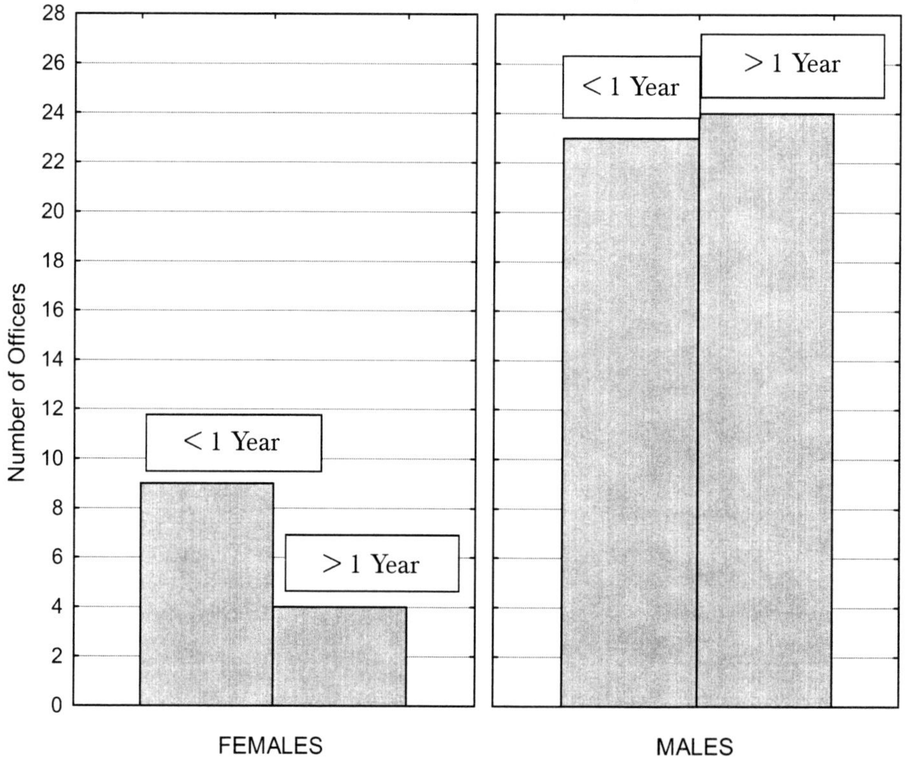

One hypothesis for this finding is that male officers bond differently with their partners and in certain cases, the loss of a partner may be more profoundly disruptive. This suggests topics for further research. Another hypothesis is that female officers may seek more external support for dealing with duty death and therefore recover earlier. A third hypothesis is that the women who currently comprise female officers are even more concerned with appearing tough than their male counterparts. A survey of psychological test results in successful pre-employment hires would help answer this question. A possible validation of the bonding explanation was offered by both the Chief and Deputy Chief:

**Deputy Chief Brian Wilson:** "Men attach more tightly to their (police) partner so they are harder hit."

This "gut feeling" on the part of the Chief and Deputy Chief is indeed supported by research indicating that male candidates for law enforcement show a greater tendency to choose this career in part based on a drive for comradeship in their work environment (Raganella, 2004). Thus, loss a of a comrade is a more threatening experience than for their female counterparts who are more likely to view their family as a primary support system, not their colleagues.

### 8.2 Relationship to the Victim

The most common factor that police officers identified as contributing to emotional difficulty with duty death was the nature of their relationship to the victim. The loss of a comrade is one of the major factors in stress related to duty death. Pre-employment testing shows that most law enforcement professionals are more group-oriented than self-oriented (Fabricatore, 1978). In fact, they are specifically chosen as individuals who will be most comfortable in a group setting. Therefore, loss of a comrade is a major blow to group unity and a threat to the group as a whole. This sentiment was frequently expressed by police officers as in the following statements made by police officers in survey responses:

*This is dependent upon the relationship between the victim employee and the co-worker. I believe the length of relationship and how close that relationship was will determine partially the length of recovery, i.e., working on the same squad with the fallen officer vs. never meeting the officer.*

*Only (hard) if you were personally involved with the individual, i.e., relationship out-*
*side of work, friendship.*
*Variables to consider are how close you worked with the officer, e.g., on the same squad,*
*specialty team etc.*
*It depends on the individual and their relationship (to him).*

## 8.3 Participation in the Critical Incident

Some officers stated that their feelings about duty death of a colleague were influenced by their participation in the critical incident.
These comments illustrate the point:

*It depends on the relationship the officer has to the incident.*
*It depends entirely on the circumstances regarding the death and one's involvement in the*
*incident.*

For example, officers attempting to respond to the call and arriving
late might feel more survivor guilt after the incident. Officers present
at the time of death might feel more loss of control if they perceived
themselves as "helpless" to assist or resuscitate their colleague. This
may lead to increased survivor guilt as described in the following statement by a police officer:

*I think that the trauma fades with time, but the loss and feelings of possible guilt last*
*forever based on the dynamics surrounding a death, e.g., survivor guilt, unable to get*
*to the officer, etc.*

## 8.4 Factors Influencing the Grief Process

Many officers acknowledged *differential* responses based on circumstances of the officer's death or the age of the officer.

*There are a vast number of reasons that could change this time, such as how close you*
*were to the person, were you there when the death occurred, and so on. Plus, each per-*
*son processes traumatic events in their own way and time frame.*
*I have lost a number of fellow officers. Some you can "get over" fairly soon, others you*
*may never get over.*
*It's based on age of the surviving officer and years on the job. It takes more time to get*
*over the death of a young officer.*
*I think it's an ongoing process of healing when an officer experiences that type of trau-*
*ma.*
*I don't know if the officer is ever totally "over" the death of a fellow officer. Follow-up*
*is very important.*

## 8.5 *Vulnerability: A Police Officer's Nightmare*

Duty death awakens safety concerns and "second-guessing" critical incident procedures in surviving officers. The greatest stress in duty death is the awareness of mortality and vulnerability. Most law enforcement professionals are proud of their strength and although they are invested in being helpful to people they perceive as weak or vulnerable, they resist identifying with traits associated with weakness. Therefore, duty death is very stressful as it forces survivors to contemplate the limits of life and the reality that we are all vulnerable. The consequence of this awareness of vulnerability is to worry that that the critical incident which resulted in the duty death was mishandled in some way.

It is natural for all concerned to review all possible factors involved in a critical incident to avoid another such incident. However, examining the incident may awaken concerns in surviving officers that other officers may not respond quickly enough to provide adequate backup; that superiors may not dispatch enough units or personnel to handle critical incidents; that equipment may be faulty, antiquated, or inadequate to protect officers.

Commanding officers should carefully evaluate these concerns and reassure surviving officers that these issues have been addressed. In the rare cases in which these concerns are justified, rapid response to address deficiencies is necessary to avoid long-term morale problems. These concerns were reflected in the following comments from officers completing the survey:

> *Trying to understand why it occurred.*
> *Officers reflect upon you or refer to the incident to remind themselves of what went wrong for future events to ensure that they'd not do the same thing to place themselves in jeopardy.*

Dynamically, these officers are attempting to establish what THEY can do to avoid the same fate and why THEY should not be worried about being vulnerable. Other common responses include officers seeking out heavier-duty vests or higher-caliber weapons after a duty death. In Federal Way, the response was to obtain different holsters. Literature review supports the contention that most police officers are uncomfortable with perceiving themselves as vulnerable and strive to avoid or reduce such vulnerability (Sawyer, 1988). Similarly, officers may attempt to avoid contact with surviving family members after a duty death to avoid reminders of vulnerability.

## 8.6 Sources of Support

What are useful sources of support in surviving police officers? In the survey results presented below, officers were asked to rate a number of different sources of support to deal with duty death. A total of 75 officers from a 14 different police agencies responded. The survey population was composed of 18 officers from urban police departments (Seattle and Tacoma), 28 officers from suburbs of those cities. Finally 19 of the officers were from rural areas of central Washington and northern Oregon within a 250 mile radius of Seattle and Portland.

The most important finding was that there was no consensus on one specific strategy or source of support. However, the major surprising finding was that immediate debriefing by the supervisor was rated as the most useful strategy. The second most frequent response was discussion with peers (unsupervised). There was no significant difference between different geographic populations (urban vs. rural officers). There was a statistically significant gender difference in that female officers who rated support from their spouse more important than did the male officers and female officers ranked immediate debriefing even more highly useful than did their male counterparts. All officers felt some type of intervention was useful.

Table 8.1
RATING OF INTERVENTIONS TO REDUCE STRESS
AFTER CRITICAL INCIDENTS

| Intervention | Number | Mean Rating | Standard Deviation |
|---|---|---|---|
| Immediate debriefing by supervisor | 56 | 3.0 | 3.2 |
| Peer discussion: no supervisor present | 56 | 3.7 | 2.0 |
| Discussion with spouse | 57 | 4.1 | 2.6 |
| Immediate debriefing by psychiatrist | 58 | 4.6 | 3.2 |
| Delayed debriefing by psychiatrist | 56 | 5.0 | 2.9 |
| Delayed debriefing by supervisor | 54 | 5.2 | 3.0 |
| Discussion with other family members | 55 | 6.4 | 2.6 |
| Informal discussion | 56 | 6.4 | 3.0 |
| Discussion with non-law enforcement friends | 56 | 6.7 | 2.4 |
| Discussion with religious figure | 56 | 6.8 | 3.0 |
| None | 54 | 10.7 | 0.9 |

**a. Peer Support:** Law enforcement colleagues are most likely to understand the response of the surviving officers. They understand the attraction of working in law enforcement in spite of the risk of harm or death and are matter of fact about continuing to do one's job in spite of risk. They also understand and have accepted the difficult choice of utilizing lethal force to defend one's own life or protect innocent bystanders. Thus, the support offered by colleagues may be quite useful in overcoming stress due to duty death.

Humor is an important method of defusing tension. Peers may reduce stress by joking or teasing each other regarding a fatal outcome. Such humor may be misunderstood by outsiders as callousness or insensitivity, but actually, multiple studies show that the use of humor as a coping mechanism lowers blood pressure and improves stress tolerance. It is well known that in law enforcement, as in many professions, there is a specific brand of humor that may be shared by other law enforcement professionals which may be somewhat incomprehensible or even distasteful to outsiders.

However, peer discussions may also result in increased stress at such times if the other officer(s) are critical of the actions involved in a duty death event. For example, some of the surviving officers may perceive (correctly or not) that the department or the individuals involved in the critical incident resulting in duty death were responsible for the event due to lax safety procedures, failure of backup, etc. They may then increase the concern of surviving officers that conditions are unsafe.

**b. Response from Superior Officers:** In some respects, the response of superior officers is similar to that of peers. The common acceptance of risk and the understanding that duty death is an infrequent but ultimate risk of working in law enforcement are shared perceptions with the surviving officer. This is reassuring. However, superior officers may have a broader understanding of the necessity of the outcome of a critical incident.

The superior officer may also have recourse to broader information on which to have based the decision to send an officer into danger. For example, in one critical incident, the officer accosting a suspect heard a radio transmission from a bank teller that the suspect "might have had a gun." However, a different officer listening to a description of the suspect at the same moment might radio headquarters that she/he had seen a suspect matching the same description the day before, who was carrying a gun. The knowledge that a suspect is armed and dangerous modifies an officer's behavior substantially, so that reaching into a pocket may elicit different behavior. The officer who was aware of only *possible* weapons will question the use of force to a much greater degree than one who is aware of documented danger.

On the other hand, this broader awareness of events may also be a burden for superior officers. If they are aware of mistakes made by the participants in a critical incident, if safety protocols were not followed correctly, this may result in great stress for the superior officer. Additionally, this knowledge is not something that they may share with the participants in the initial phase of the postcritical incident investigation. At certain times, it may never be appropriate to share all the details of how a critical incident occurred with their subordinate officers. Internal doubt in superior officers about the outcome of a critical incident may also limit the degree to which they reassure the subordinate officers.

### 8.7 Command Staff Perspective

The author interviewed command staff of a police department regarding departmental support and structure following a duty death in 2003. In the following exchange, Deputy Chief Wilson and Chief Kirkpatrick comment on the role of leadership and directions to officers in the immediate phase of a duty death.

**Deputy Chief Wilson:** Even the content of debriefing sessions is really important. I think the one thing that the Chief (AK) did that was just right on was at the first debriefing, it was very simple, but she said, "I have two missions. One is the family. Two is you." So everything just took off at that point. That was the clear direction of focus, was really important. Too, the first briefing was here's what's happened today. Here's what's going to happen tomorrow. That's all that was needed. Okay, what's going to happen to the rest of the day and what's going to happen tomorrow? And then here's when we're going to meet again.

| | |
|---|---|
| **Dr. Decker:** | So those debriefings were concrete, not emotional? |
| **Chief Kirkpatrick:** | No, there were also a lot of tears, a lot of hugs. I think at a time like that the normal, natural thing is for people to be emotional. |
| **Deputy Chief Wilson:** | But they are looking for that leadership, direction. They are looking for where we are going. |
| **Dr. Decker:** | So they want a plan. |
| **Chief Kirkpatrick:** | They need a plan. Because if there's no clear plan, one leaves them hanging and that is anxiety-provoking. They *need to know*. They need to know 'what I'm going to do tomorrow.' |
| **Deputy Chief Wilson:** | If there is a perception that there isn't a plan or that the staff doesn't know what the chief or the deputy chief doesn't know what they are doing, watch out! |
| **Chief Kirkpatrick:** | It's crucial; an agency can crumble if incidents like this are not handled correctly! |
| **Dr. Decker:** | What sort of elements of the plan do they want to know about? |
| **Chief Kirkpatrick:** | The debriefing says you are going to have a meeting with a psychiatrist. Then they know it and they have no choice. You get specific. 'You are going to meet with a psychiatrist at 4:00 tomorrow. And then another squad is going to meet with a psychiatrist on another day.' You remove the options and you are very direct about the mental health aspects and what they are going to undergo for debriefing. It's not a harsh message, it's just a clear delivery. This is THE plan. |
| **Deputy Chief Wilson:** | Seeing to the needs of the people, especially those who were directly involved in the incident. The issue of how the assessment is going to take place, the conveyance of concern for those affected. It has to be genuine. Even for us it's not something where you |

don't speak to a particular person for two years and then you have something like this. You have to draw on a prior relationship.

## *8.9 Limitation of Family Support*

Although family support is helpful to police officers, family members of law enforcement professionals are less likely to work through stress in the same way as police officers do, unless they are also in law enforcement. In part, this may be due to the fact that a law enforcement professional may have chosen a spouse with a lower risk tolerance than he or she does. If so, the spouse may not understand or accept the fact that the officer "shrugs off" a duty death in a colleague and "gets on" with the job. Often, spouses are severely shaken by the death of another officer as it reminds them that their spouse is doing risky work. Death in another reminds us all of mortality. This reminder may unmask the uneasiness that lies beneath the superficial acceptance that their spouse may not return from work one day. Thus, many law enforcement professionals feel that they tread a fine line between "protecting" their spouse from the stress that their job is dangerous and seeking support from them after critical incidents such as duty death. Deputy Chief Wilson illustrates this in his comments:

**Deputy Chief Wilson:** After another critical incident, the stress debriefing groups focused on families to be able to provide context and what to expect and what officers' role could be. There was a time in C . . . where we had like five or six fairly new officers in the two to five year range. Each was married with three kids. There were like seven of them. A variety of things were going on, but it almost a gigantic proportion (of officers involved in critical incidents). It came to the point where we wondered if we were missing something. People had thoughts of "we are not doing something that we should be doing to deal with this" because we had a couple of shoot-

|                          |                                                                                                                                                                                                                                                                                                                                                                                          |
|--------------------------|------------------------------------------------------------------------------------------------------------------------------------------------------------------------------------------------------------------------------------------------------------------------------------------------------------------------------------------------------------------------------------------|
|                          | ings and a couple officers were assaulted. These things contribute to an environment where people become concerned about their safety and they talk at home. With the death of an officer, the impact on the rest of the group includes questioning. We've looked at our entire agency and how many conversations took place, whether it's family members or significant others. |
| **Dr. Decker:**          | What sorts of issues do the family members have after a duty death?                                                                                                                                                                                                                                                                                                                       |
| **Deputy Chief Wilson:** | Questioning officers' jobs, like "Why are you doing this? You need to get out of here."                                                                                                                                                                                                                                                                                                   |
| **Chief Kirkpatrick:**   | I agree. Family members sometimes say "Why are you doing *this* job?"                                                                                                                                                                                                                                                                                                                     |
| **Deputy Chief Wilson:** | Or they may say, "This is a basically a, dangerous place. I need to be safe. I want you to be *safe*."                                                                                                                                                                                                                                                                                     |

## *8.9 Risk Tolerance*

Police officers are chosen to have specific personality traits that are necessary to their job. They are chosen to be psychologically "tough-minded." Police officers carry out a hazardous, physical, and unpredictable job in environment with violent and adversarial people. They must also be sensitive to victims and polite to citizens unless and until they are met with physical hostility. Then they are allowed to respond with judiciously graduated force, including lethal force. The selection of personnel who possess certain qualities of "tough-mindedness" reflects the demands of this unique job. Indeed, some psychiatrists and psychologists who screen officers for employment specifically look for this trait of "tough-mindedness." The 16PF is one psychological instrument which specifically attempts to measure this trait. This trait has been correlated with success in law enforcement personnel (see Chapter 4 for more detailed discussion of this trait).

Therefore, as expected, after duty death, most officers may prefer to focus on "getting on with the job." Indeed it would be a mistake for consulting psychiatrists or psychologists to focus attention for too long on the vulnerability and grief that officers feel after death of a colleague. This approach would foster regression and result in *more* trauma than in supporting the underlying personality style of most law enforcement personnel which is action-oriented. It is important that mental health consultants recognize the "special" personality makeup of law enforcement personnel and shore up their natural defenses, which may be different than those of other individuals (Hodgins, 1989, Patterson, 2000, 2002 and Robinson, 1997).

Another method of coping that is important in law enforcement personnel is exercise. Most law enforcement personnel endorse heavy physical exercise as a preferred coping mechanism for both anger and stress and state this is a preferred method of dealing with stress, ranking it above "talking out" stress (Decker, unpublished observation). It is likely that based on pre-employment attitudes and habits of law enforcement applicants, this is a very useful coping mechanism as well, and possibly one which is more important in police officers than in the general public. This coping strategy was not examined in the questionnaire utilized by this study. Indeed, few of the published articles on coping mechanisms to reduce stress in law enforcement personnel include examination of this factor. Subsequent studies should include examination of the role that physical exercise plays in stress reduction in police officers. The following comment summarizes the responses from a police officer that parallels the literature: "I have experienced several deaths of close friends–the other a mentor. Needed grief time but also knew work was important."

### 8.10 Mental Health Professionals' Roles

How can mental health professionals assist officers and police department to deal with duty death? The following interview of Chief Anne Kirkpatrick and Deputy Chief Brian Wilson illustrates thinking of police command staff have about the role that psychiatrists and psychologists may play in assisting police to work through issues surrounding duty death.

**Dr. Decker:**                    If a psychiatrist or psychologist is familiar with the department, are the officers going to feel that that person is adequately impartial? For civilians, patients prefer to go to a stran-

|  |  |
|---|---|
|  | ger for mental health treatment. It's comforting to go to a stranger because they have confidentiality. |
| **Chief Kirkpatrick:** | I think we (police) do prefer someone we *know* to deliver care. |
| **Dr. Decker:** | You phrased an interesting question. It starts with the subject of duty death, but it's actually a broader question. Would you say that most of the time law enforcement professionals prefer to be *ordered* to get mental health help, or do you think that's highly individual? |
| **Deputy Chief Wilson:** | Mandatory, absolutely. |
| **Chief Kirkpatrick:** | It's even in our policy. |
| **Deputy Chief Wilson:** | It's got to be mandatory. |
| **Dr. Decker:** | So you're saying you think the system would completely fail, for example, if you had a critical incident and you made any of the debriefing elective. |
| **Chief Kirkpatrick:** | It would fail. |
| **Deputy Chief Wilson:** | It would fail. |
| **Chief Kirkpatrick:** | And with it being mandatory, there is an acceptance with it. It's an interesting thing. |
| **Dr. Decker:** | Right, "because they made me do it kind of thing." |
| **Chief Kirkpatrick:** | They made me do it so there is no stigma. There's no feeling that "You are the one who's not handling it." The last thing a cop wants to be viewed as is you are not strong enough to handle it. They are saying to themselves, "I don't want anyone think I'm not strong enough. I don't want *me* thinking I'm not strong enough." That will be the number one obstacle to contact with mental health professionals. Any time you go see the MHP, that's the number one mark you're going to get a black mark. It says, "you're not handling it." |
| **Dr. Decker:** | So if everybody is told to handle it by going, then does it take away the whole issue of weakness? |

**Chief Kirkpatrick:**            Yes. Then everybody benefits too when they
                                  all go to the debriefing. They can say, "Gee,
                                  I'm really glad I spoke to Dr. Decker." In the
                                  end, they like it and they want it and they
                                  know they need it.

The above interview demonstrates that police officers look to and
appreciate support from the police department after a duty death.
Command staff must move swiftly to reduce anxiety and restore order
to the police structure following a duty death. The literature supports
the comments made above. A great deal of work was done by Violanti
and colleagues in the mid-1990s on the impact of certain interventions
by police departments. It supports the above statements that cohesive
and supportive environments improve coping in survivors of police
death. For example, Violanti found that increased quality of interactions with police groups lowered psychological distress scores following duty death (Violanti, 1996). Some studies found that concrete steps
were useful at ameliorating stress such as assistance with funeral
arrangements, transporting children to school, guarding the surviving
spouse's house, and so forth (Cook, 1990). A group called COPS,
Concerns of Police Survivors, is specifically oriented towards reducing
the long-term stress and helping with postduty death adjustment of
surviving family members. This group offers both moral support,
counseling, and specific assistance with basic needs.

### *8.11 Conclusions*

In conclusion, there are multiple approaches that law enforcement
agencies can utilize to reduce the negative impact of duty death on
their officers. First, research presented at the beginning of this chapter
shows that debriefing helps officers begin to put duty death in perspective. Debriefing by superiors is intended to gather information to
analyze the incident and to ascertain the factors leading to duty death,
but it has a positive effect on officers' morale. As Chief Kirkpatrick
and Deputy Chief Wilson stated above, the direction of superior officers to surviving officers regarding specific steps following duty death
is a valuable method of reassurance. Emphasis on an orderly process
to analyze and deal with the department's loss allows officers to con-

tinue work while processing the event. Literature review supports the contention that departmental structure and support is key to reducing police officers' stress after duty death.

It is crucial for departments to recognize that successful stress reduction mechanisms after a duty death are *different* for different surviving officers. As the data from the survey of police officers presented above show, *no single* method of reducing this stress is likely to produce optimal results in all officers. Therefore, it is overly simplistic for departments to settle on a rigid protocol of utilizing either chaplains, mental health professionals, or any other single method to help their officers cope. Rather, it is reassuring to officers to state that the department has a RANGE of options to help its officers manage the stress and return to duty with a minimum of disruption. This may include Employee Assistance Programs, training sessions regarding critical incident procedures, and new safety protocols.

Immediate, rapid debriefing of surviving officers involved in the duty death critical incident is a key element. An emphasis on shifting the energy of surviving officers to new assignments may be helpful as well. Reminding the officers that they need to "get on with the job and that there are other lives to save supports the internal coping style of most law enforcement professionals. Mental health professionals working with law enforcement personnel need to recognize key differences in the psychological makeup of this population and support must be tailored to their style of coping.

## REFERENCES

Carlier, I. V., Lamberts, R. D., & Gersons, B. P. (2000). The dimensionality of trauma: A multidimensional scaling comparison of police officers with and without posttraumatic stress disorder. *Psychiatry Res*, Dec 4:97(1):29-39.

Carlier, I. V., Voerman, A. E, & Gersons, B. P. (2000). The influence of occupational debriefing on posttraumatic stress symptomatology in traumatized police officers. *Br J Med Psychol*, Mar; 73( Pt 1):87-98.

Cook, J. D., & Bickman, L. Social support and psychological symptomatology following a natural disaster. *J Traumatic Stress,* 3:541-556.

Fabricatore, J. et al. (1978). Predicting performance of police officers using the sixteen personality factor questionnaire. *American Journal of Community Psychology*, 6(1) Feb, 63-70.

Hodgins, G. A., Creamer, M., & Bell, R. (1989). Risk factors for post-trauma reactions in police officers: A longitudinal study. *J Nerv Ment Dis*, Aug:(8):541-7, 1989.

Neely, K. W., & Spitzer, W. J. (1997). A model for a statewide critical incident stress (CIS) debriefing program for emergency services personnel. *Prehospital Disaster Med,* Apr-Jun:12(2):114-119.

Neylan, T. C., et al. (2002). Critical incident exposure and sleep quality in police officers. *Psychosom Med,* Mar-Apr;*64*(2):345-352.

Patterson, G. T. (2002). Demographic factors as predictors of coping strategies among police officers. *Psychol Rep,* Aug;*87*(1):275-283.

Patterson, G. T. (2002). Development of a law enforcement stress and coping questionnaire. *Psychol Rep,* June, 90(3 Pt 1):789-799.

Raganella, A. J., & White, M.D. (2004). Race, gender and motivation for becoming a police officer: Implications for building a representative police department. *J Crim Justice, 32*:501-513.

Robinson, H. M., Sigman, M. R., & Wilson, J. P. (1997). Duty-related stressors and PTSD symptoms in suburban police officers. *Psychol Rep,* Dec;81(3 Pt 1):835-845.

Sawyer, S. Support Services to Surviving Families of Line-of-Duty Death. Maryland: Concerns of Police Survivors, Inc.

Violanti, J. M., & Paton, D. (1999). *Police trauma: Aftermath of civilian combat.* Springfield, IL: Charles C Thomas.

# Chapter 9

# POLICE SUICIDE AND FITNESS FOR DUTY

KATHLEEN P. DECKER

### 9.1 Suicide Risk: High or Low?

Many studies have demonstrated that police officers have a higher risk of suicide than civilians. Many of the earliest studies found that police officers were almost twice as likely to commit suicide as the general population (Guralnick, 1963; Nelson, 1970; Labovitz, 1971; Richard, 1976). One early study examined mortality causes of municipal workers that utilized accumulated data from 1950 to 1979 in Buffalo, New York (Vena, 1986). The mortality rate for police officers was almost three-fold over that seen in all other categories of municipal employees. They found that the suicide rate of officers was similar to that of the general U.S. population, but when compared to other working professionals, the rate was higher. This is because working professionals have a lower rate (with the exception of dentists and physicians) than does the general population. In a related study on firefighters, the cohort of firefighters had a lower suicide rate than other municipal workers (Vena, 1987). Therefore, when they removed firefighters from the municipal cohort, there was a 2.4-fold higher rate of suicide in police officers.

In a later study, Violanti examined trends in police suicide over five-year intervals from 1950-1990 (Violanti, 1995). He found that police suicide rates in Buffalo, New York, have not fluctuated much over the 40 years. There were certain periods with higher average suicide rates than others, but more importantly, the suicide rate was shown increased over the decades of the eighties and nineties.

179

Other studies have failed to demonstrate higher suicide rates among police officers (Hem, 2001). In a recent meta-analysis of data from a number of different countries, Loo (1986) found that there were higher rates of suicide in the Americas and Europe were than in the Caribbean and Asian regions. There were differences in rates between federal, regional, and municipal police forces. Finally, he found that suicide rates based on short timeframe studies were significantly higher than for longer timeframe studies. This demonstrates that it is not possible to make sweeping generalizations about the risk of suicide in law enforcement personnel, either across cultures or across agencies as supported by other studies (Weissman, 1999).

### 9.2 Misreporting May Contribute to Underestimates of Suicide

Violanti made the point even in early studies that investigators of potential police suicides are investigating colleagues or friends. Thus, they may tend to minimize or conceal evidence of suicide to protect the surviving family. In addition, police officers are trained to recognize clues that differentiate suicide from accidental death or homicide. Therefore, those officers who successfully complete suicide may have an edge over civilians in terms of protecting his/her family by masking suicide as an accident or homicide.

To examine the issue of misreporting, Violanti et al. performed a study on 138 cases (Violanti, 1996). These investigators compiled a panel of auditors that included medical examiners to review a variety of data, including death certificates, medical examiner reports, autopsies, and police investigation data. They then undertook a review to ascertain whether cases were correctly classified based on detailed scrutiny of the more exhaustive data used by the panel. The results of this study indicated that police officers had a higher number of total suicides than other municipal workers. They also found that police officers had a higher suicide rate than other municipal workers for all types of external causes of deaths.

### 9.3 Geographical Variations in Social Violence

A second factor that may result in underestimates of police suicide includes the fact that different localities and countries have very different levels of violence and stress, which may lead to significant variability in suicide risk. One extreme is represented by the Norwegian police force, in which social violence is lower than in the U.S. In fact, duty death is so scarce, it was eliminated as a stressor from their studies on police officers (Berg, 2005). These investigators then assessed suicidal ideation in over 3,000 Norwegian police officers (Berg, 2003) by asking respondents to answer questions on an anonymous questionnaire. The questionnaire included both questions on passive suicidal ideation and suicide attempts. They found a very low percentage admitted to having made suicide attempts (0.7%) while 24 percent endorsed having felt life was not worth living on occasion and 6.4 percent had seriously considered suicide.

The opposite extreme of the social violence spectrum is arguably represented by South Africa. The incidence of PTSD is far higher in the South African police force (49%) than in most other police forces (Kopel, 1997), in large part due to the high level of violence due and civil unrest (Emsley, 2003). They found that frequent and prolonged exposure to trauma contributed to PTSD–80 percent of officers who had PTSD related it to multiple experiences, although only 13 percent of officers attributed it to a single event. A high percentage (18%) of officers had delayed PTSD.

Although there no specific study linking PTSD to suicide in South African police was found, there are reports linking chronic PTSD with suicide in U.S. veterans (Drescher, 2003). They found that behavioral causes accounted for 62.4 percent of deaths among 110 deceased male veterans out of 1,866 treated for posttraumatic stress disorder (PTSD). The breakdown was: accidents, 29.4 percent; chronic substance abuse, 14.7 percent; and intentional death by suicide, homicide, or suicide by police accounted for 13.8 percent of deaths. In a recent study on risk factors for suicide in U.S. police officers, the combined impact of PTSD and increased alcohol use was associated with a tenfold increase risk for suicide ideation (Violanti, 2004a).

The effect of the surrounding culture on violence and violent behavior in police officers was also highlighted by a study on Navaho police in which Navaho police officers who affiliated more with "European" versions of law enforcement were more likely to use force to resolve problems (Gould, 2002). It remains to be seen if this cultural dynamic applies to suicide as well, but it certainly suggests further studies regarding cultural and subcultural values and suicide. It also suggests that police officers can be educated to seek other solutions than violence.

## *9.4 Police Subculture Values Affect Attitudes to Suicide*

Certain values of police subculture may also account for increased risk of suicide (Hackett, 2003). There are a number of factors that contribute to this problem. First, police officers are hired with the assertion that they have "passed" the psychological evaluation. From day one, they see themselves as "fit" and mentally healthier than the general population. To some extent, this is true; police officers are chosen because of superior stress tolerance and ability to handle critical incidents (see Chapter 4). In fact, some investigators have written about the "police personality," which is said to embody values such as an action-oriented approach. One article distilled the police working personality to three primary traits: danger, authority, and efficiency (Skolnick, 2000). A recent review of the literature on this topic concluded that police officers do have some particular personality characteristics but that experience on the job is what truly forms the psyche of the officer (Twersky-Glasner, 2005).

However, as discussed in Chapter 3, many psychiatric conditions may develop later in life such that older officers who had no prior psychiatric history develop psychiatric conditions. Besides, long exposure to trauma also increases the risk of PTSD as described above. Then, officers experiencing psychiatric symptoms for the first time may see themselves as "unfit." They are liable to perceive themselves as "unfit' rather than as suffering from a temporary, correctible condition because law enforcement personnel value strength and decline to see themselves as weak or vulnerable. Removing their weapon (which is advisable during a FFD evaluation) and putting them on administrative leave leads officers to perceive themselves as idle. This may reinforce their perception that they are nonfunctional, rather than *temporarily* pursuing deserved rest and/or treatment to restore them to fitness.

Also, as discussed in Chapter 6, most law enforcement professionals are reluctant to seek psychiatric help as their experience with mental health professionals is limited to either pre-employment evaluations, FFD evaluations, or occurs in the context of mentally disturbed persons. Therefore, they often carry negative expectations of mental health professionals.

Finally, law enforcement personnel are chosen to be active and extraverted, rather than introverted and reflective. These qualities are appropriate for police work, but these same qualities may make it difficult for such officers to understand their emotions when they *do* experience psychological problems. Another consequence of being a very active as opposed to a reflective individual is that one may be more impulsive and therefore more prone to *acting* on negative emotions, rather than to explore emotions in therapy.

Agencies use a number of different Employee Assistance Program (EAP) models designed to address and alleviate stress in law enforcement professionals. The advantage of such programs is that if a mental health professional is specifically recruited and trained to work with law enforcement professionals, she/he may be able to better relate to them than therapists chosen randomly in the community. Unfortunately, law enforcement personnel frequently mistrust EAP counselors because of confidentiality concerns. There is an excellent review of the use of various EAP models in suicide prevention (Pinals, 2004).

### 9.5 Factors that Increase Risk of Suicide: Sex!

Certain risk factors increase the risk of suicide in police officers. Major contributors include marital difficulties and alcohol and substance use, according to many studies (Janik, 1994). An early study reviewed records of police officers referred for FFD evaluations during the five-year period 1985-1990 in an outpatient Public Safety Program at a large midwestern U.S. medical center. They found that of the 2 percent of active duty personnel referred each year for FFD evaluations, 55 percent admitted to previous suicide attempts. Psychosocial factors such as marital discord may contribute to increased risk of suicide. Results indicated that officers who reported marital problems were 4.8 times more likely to have attempted suicide, and that suspension was associated with an even higher risk at 6.7 times the baseline risk. They did not find that age, race, gender, or substance use accounted for the variance in suicide attempts.

Another recent, large study of suicidal ideation found that marital separation or divorce, general medical issues, job dissatisfaction, and older age were associated with higher risk of suicidal ideation (Berg, 2003). They collected questionnaires filled out by over 3,000 Norwegian police officers. However, as they pointed out, the accuracy of this study depended on whether officers were forthright in completing the questionnaire. Certainly it may be expected to be a more honest response than in a FFD evaluation in which the officer believes his/her career hinges on the outcome. On the other hand, officers who are referred for a FFD evaluation have already been "caught" with suicidal ideation and thus might be more likely to be forthright than those who are still on active duty and have the ability to conceal it.

### 9.6 Factors that Increase Risk of Suicide: Alcohol!

Alcohol use has been associated with a higher risk of suicide in a wide variety of studies. Many studies have examined the association of alcohol and suicide in civilians. Authors of a study on individuals diagnosed with major depression found that current (6-month prevalence) alcohol or drug substance use disorder increased the risk of suicide (Dumais, 2005). In another study on civilians, postmortem examination was conducted on a large series of individuals (1,018) who had been treated in Helsinki University Central Hospital emergency room for overdoses over a 14-year period. The investigators found that 222 (22.7%) died by the end of the follow-up period. A large proportion of the deceased suicidal individuals (38.5%) showed clear postmortem evidence of long-term alcohol misuse (Suokas, 2005).

There is evidence that military personnel, as well as civilians, have higher risk of suicide when alcohol is involved. A recent study of former peace-keeping soldiers in Norway found that individuals who died from alcohol-related fatal accidents had common risk factors with those who died by suicide. They had a higher incidence of depression, alcohol and substance abuse, and various social problems compared to individuals who died of nonalcohol-related accidents (Thoreson, 2003).

In a study of police officers, the rate of cirrhosis of the liver was significantly higher for 55-to-69-year-old officers between 1970 and 1990 (Violanti, 1998). An examination of the liver post-mortem of police officers that have committed suicide has not been conducted (to the author's knowledge). However, this study confirms the contention that many on-duty older police officers suffer from alcoholism undetected and whether some fatal accidents and suicides are alcohol-related.

## Case Scenario 1

A 32-year-old female officer had several documented episodes of inebriation on the job. Her overall job performance had deteriorated over a three-year period and she had been using excess sick leave. She had two citizen complaints regarding unprofessional conduct and other members of her squad indicated that they felt she was "not safe" on the job. She admitted she had been diagnosed with alcohol dependence but assured her primary provider (a nonpsychiatric nurse practitioner) that she would abstain from alcohol and take Disulfiram (Antabuse) to quit drinking. However, she was found to have alcohol on her breath on two subsequent occasions and observed to be drinking alcohol in a bar while off duty by another officer.

In the course of the FFD evaluation, the officer disclosed that she had been to three different alcohol treatment programs over the last five years at her own expense, without departmental knowledge. She had been admitted overnight for emergency psychiatric treatment on one occasion because of suicidal ideation. Her blood alcohol level was 2.0 at the time of admission. When she became sober, she denied any suicidal ideation and did not have vegetative (physical) symptoms of depression. She had been released with no psychiatric treatment except for the recommendation to pursue more aggressive alcohol treatment. The evaluator discussed the officer's treatment to date with her primary provider, a nurse practitioner who said "the officer was trying" to remain sober as an outpatient. She stated the officer had relapsed so many times that the Antabuse was a last resort.

### Possible Outcome 1

The evaluator communicated her findings to the referring institution. She indicated that given the relapse history to date that the potential of the officer relapsing on the job was a great forensic liability risk to the department. The evaluator recommended a course of inpatient substance use treatment but the evaluee declined stating she "had already been through programs and they don't work." She demanded to "do it herself." The employer then chose a medical separation.

### Possible Outcome 2

The evaluator communicated her findings to the referring institution. She indicated that given the relapse history to date that the potential of the officer relapsing on the job was a great forensic liability risk to the department. The evaluator recommended a course of inpatient substance use treatment. The evaluee reluctantly agreed and was placed on medical leave. She completed a 30-day inpatient program and returned to work thereafter. The employer then chose to provisionally return her to duty with random urinalysis monitoring for a one-year period, proof of AA attendance once a week, and periodic letters from treatment professionals that she was complying with psychiatric (including substance use) treatment.

### Comments:

The two different outcomes above illustrate several points. First, the officer might not be regarded as disabled from many civilian occupations with this history of alcoholism. However, even such industries as construction or those that involve machinery operation might also view intoxication on the job as an unacceptable risk. Indeed, many corporations have a "zero-tolerance" for substance use in their employees. Intoxication in an on-duty officer is clearly unacceptable, but even off-duty intoxication is relevant to the employer as it may result in impaired judgment, memory, and emotional lability.

There are major differences between isolated episodes of alcohol abuse and chronic relapses. As described above, the incidence of alcohol abuse in law enforcement personnel is higher than in the general population and it is a high-stress profession. Individuals also have a higher risk of suicidal thinking and behavior when inebriated. Therefore, chronic alcohol abuse or dependence, resistance to treatment, or repeated treatment failures are all serious problems which must be addressed by the employee and the employer both in terms of FFD issues and to minimize the risk of suicide in the officer. Finally, the two different outcomes above highlight that the treatment of alcohol or substance use is highly dependent on the individual's motivation to recover. The employer must take steps to ensure officer and public safety above all.

## 9.7 Factors that Increase Risk of Suicide: Guns!

Law enforcement personnel are trained to use firearms and are encouraged to practice shooting regularly. They usually maintain a duty weapon while off duty and often store it at home. Thus, they have instant access to firearms daily. This ready access and omnipresence of a lethal means of suicide may increase the risk of suicide by firearms. One study found that police officers were 6.4 times more likely to use a firearm when committing suicide than people in other professions (Violanti, 1996). Another early study on police officers in Chicago found that 95 percent of officers who committed suicide over a ten-year period used a firearm (Cronin, 1982).

Ready access to firearms is associated with untoward events in those diagnosed with PTSD. In a study on U.S. veterans, individuals with PTSD were four times more likely to possess firearms than other veterans being treated for other psychiatric problems such as substance use disorders or schizophrenia (Freeman, 2003). They assessed psychopathology and found that high levels of aggression, impulsive and dangerous weapon use, and ready weapon availability were all significant factors in gun-related violence in the PTSD patient population.

An association between PTSD and elevated risk for suicide was also found in a recent national study on Canadian civilians (Sareen, 2005). They surveyed a nationally representative sample 5,877 civilians aged 15–54 and examined the relationship between anxiety disorders and suicidal ideation or suicide attempts. They found that PTSD was significantly associated with suicidal ideation (odds ratio = 2.79; $p < 0.01$) and suicide attempts (odds ratio = 2.67; $p < 0.01$). None of the other anxiety disorders were significantly associated with suicidal ideation or attempts.

Thus, as both law enforcement professionals and civilians have been shown to have a higher risk of suicide when affected by PTSD, it seems likely that law enforcement personnel with PTSD and a firearm may have a higher risk of suicide as well. However, most studies on police officers have not examined this subtopic, so further conclusions must await specific research.

Ready access to firearms facilitates impulsive suicide attempts. Studies have shown that between 66–95 percent of police officers commit suicide using their guns (Violanti, 1995, Aussant 1984). This is higher than the rate for other firearms owners, who commit suicide with firearms in 58 percent of cases (Kellerman 1992, 1993). In the Canadian study by Aussant, 50 percent of officers who committed suicide with a firearm had a history of psychiatric problems and many of them had alcohol dependence.

It has been shown that individuals often change their mind in the course even when they utilize a high lethality means of suicide such as jumping off a bridge (2003). A study conducted by the FBI reviewed data obtained from its database on hostage/barricade incidents. They found that 50 percent of individuals who survived after jumping off a bridge changed their mind on the way down. In addition, when crisis negotiation teams were able to engage subjects who were poised to jump, 80 percent were willing to talk to negotiators, and 17 percent were successfully negotiated off the bridges. The other 79 percent completed the jumps and 4 percent were subject to physical intervention to get them off the bridge.

They also examined the substance use of would-be and completed jumpers. They found that 34 percent of all individuals involved in jumper incidents had used some form of drugs, medication, or alcohol but that 75 percent of the completed jumpers had used alcohol, methamphetamine, or antidepressants. Unfortunately, the FBI database in 2003 did not include the blood level of antidepressant. It would be a fascinating complement to this study to determine whether the blood level of antidepressant was suboptimal, therapeutic, or toxic in these individuals.

The above study suggests an important follow-up study—namely, a similar analysis with HOBAS data on suicide or suicide by cop with firearms. The number of instances of suicide in police officers or stand-offs is rare enough that there might not be adequate data to analyze such cases involving police officers. But even a review of civilian patterns during such incidents might assist with developing further strategies to reduce fatalities, as the above study does. The hypothesis generated by the data in both civilians and veterans suggests that ready availability of firearms and constant exposure to violence may predispose police officers to utilize firearms as a means of suicide. Since there is essentially no ability to change one's mind when a gun is fired, suicidal individuals may complete suicide at higher rates than if they had chosen a different means such as overdose or even jumping, as above.

## Case Scenario 2

Officer Wonderlic was hospitalized after an emergency evaluation. The evaluation was precipitated by a remark he made to another officer on duty that "I'd like to taste (gun) oil right about now." During the course of the evaluation, he revealed that he was recently separated and had lost custody of his three children. His wife, a school teacher, had moved to another state and he had not been able to prevail to stop the move. His finances were in disarray as he had to pay child support and they had sold their house in the course of the divorce. His wife had cited his preoccupation with chronic low back pain and knee pain as factors in the divorce.

In addition to the stress of the divorce, he revealed he was stressed because he had been transferred a year earlier out of the motorcycle division. In an on-duty accident while chasing a suspect, he was injured and left with residual chronic pain in his back and leg although he was still able to carry out patrol work. Upon questioning, he felt that his life was no longer worth living. "I can't do what I want to do, I'm almost a cripple, and I can't see my kids. There just isn't much left to live for–I can't provide, I don't like patrol, it's like they demoted me. Motorcycle cops are different; we're the cowboys. Anybody can do patrol work." The officer had had low-grade symptoms of depression throughout the year prior to the evaluation but had performed satisfactorily on the job. The additional stress of the divorce "put him over the edge" and he had developed vegetative symptoms of depression such as weight loss and insomnia a month prior to the evaluation.

### *Possible Outcome 1*

The evaluator recommended that the officer commence medication treatment for depression, as well as short-term psychotherapy related to the issues of divorce and partial disability. The officer complied with medication treatment for a month, then discontinued seeing the psychiatrist, stating, "I can handle my problems now; I don't need to see a shrink." He initially appeared to be functioning well and boasted he'd "got on with life." However, six months later, his ex-wife increased her demands for child support. Two days later, he was found dead in his car of a gunshot wound with a suicide note that referred to his "failures as a cop and as a man."

## Possible Outcome 2

The evaluator recommended psychiatric treatment, including medication for depression and psychotherapy for divorce and partial disability. The officer reluctantly agreed to a course of medicine and psychotherapy. His depression improved rapidly and the medication prescribed also resulted in some reduction of his chronic pain. He also underwent a course of physical therapy that increased his mobility although not to an extent to allow resumption of motorcycle duty. Although he discontinued sessions with the therapist after six weeks, he stated that "talking about the divorce made me realize it's just something that happens, that I can build another life. It wasn't my fault; maybe I need someone who understands cops' lifestyles better. An' there are a bunch of different things to do in law enforcement that are cool." He returned to duty without further incident, requested a transfer to an undercover position and remarried two years later to another police officer.

## Comments

It is frequent that law enforcement personnel view both medications and psychotherapy or counseling as signs of weakness. Most law enforcement personnel are initially screened to value "mental toughness" and therefore they are less likely than other individuals to accept the need for psychiatric treatment. However, when the resistance is overcome, they often demonstrate the resilience for which they were selected. Even relatively brief treatment may result in rapid stabilization if their ego is restored and they are made to feel productive and strong. Hence, therapy should be aimed at shoring up defenses and emphasizing alternate ways to contribute to law enforcement.

## 9.8 Primary Data: Washington State FFD Study

Data was collected sequentially from 58 police and corrections officers who underwent a FFD evaluation over a five-year period by the author. The demographics of the study population are described in detail in Appendix II. Thirty-one percent of evaluees admitted recent suicidal ideation and a high percentage (11%) of the FFD evaluees had made a suicide attempt immediately prior to evaluation. This is not surprising, as they were referred for behavioral problems and serious psychiatric symptoms. A large percentage (20%) also admitted to having suicidal ideation in the remote past, although only 5 percent admitted to having attempted suicide in the remote past. (Normally, the selection criteria for pre-employment include "weeding out" officers who have attempted suicide in the majority of agencies, although clearly, this is not a universal practice.)

Some officers had been *interrupted* while planning or attempting suicide by other police officers or supervisors, which precipitated the FFD evaluation. Table 9.1 shows the means of suicide planned or utilized by these officers–the most frequent method was overdose, followed by passive suicidal ideation, then by firearms. Only two officers planned or attempted suicide using multiple means simultaneously (overdose and firearms). The relatively low proportion of firearms-related attempts compared to the literature cited above is probably because these were suicide *attempts*, not *completed* suicide, as opposed to the studies reviewed in Section 9.7.

Table 9.1
METHOD OF PLANNED SUICIDE ATTEMPT

|  | *Count* | *Percent* |
| --- | --- | --- |
| **None** | 40 | 70.1 |
| **Firearms** | 4 | 7.0 |
| **Overdose** | 6 | 10.5 |
| **Passive** | 5 | 8.8 |
| **Multiple** | 2 | 3.5 |

The gender distribution of officers who planned suicide was similar to those who did not plan: 33 percent of planners were female and 29 percent of nonplanners were female. More of the suicide planners came from rural areas: 83 percent vs. 43 percent, but the number of subjects in this study was too small to draw statistically significant conclusions. Interestingly, as discussed in Chapter 3, psychiatric care was less available in rural areas and primary care providers provided psychiatric medications in those areas. Of those who did not attempt suicide, 22 percent were taking medications prescribed by a psychiatrist, while *none* of those who made a suicide attempt were receiving medications prescribed by a psychiatrist. This may support the contention that inability to access psychiatrists for psychiatric treatment is associated with poorer outcomes.

Table 9.2 shows that half the officers who attempted suicide were either single or divorced, and the other half were married. This was not very different from the proportion of those who did not make a suicide attempt, 41 percent of whom were married. However, more of those who did not attempt suicide were in their *first* marriage. Although the sample is too small to be compared statistically, it suggests that the details of marital status warrant exploration in future studies.

Table 9.2
MARITAL STATUS OF SUICIDE ATTEMPTERS AND NON-ATTEMPTERS

| Marital Status | Suicide Count | Non-Attempters Percent | Suicide Count | Attempters Percent |
|---|---|---|---|---|
| Single | 5 | 9.8 | 2 | 33.3 |
| 1st Marriage | 18 | 35.3 | 1 | 16.7 |
| Remarried | 5 | 9.8 | 2 | 33.3 |
| Divorced | 16 | 31.4 | 1 | 16.7 |
| Multiple Divorces | 6 | 11.8 | 0 | 0 |

None of the suicide attempters in this study had received previous treatment for substance use, while 33 percent of the nonattempters had had prior substance treatment. Of those receiving treatment for substance use, outpatient substance treatment was the modality in all but one case. However, more of the attempters were *diagnosed* with substance use disorders (either definitive or probable) during the course of the FFD evaluation: 25 percent of attempters had substance use disorders vs. only 8 percent of nonplanners. **Thus, the data here suggest a higher risk of suicide attempts in impaired officers who are undiagnosed and have untreated substance use disorders prior to the FFD evaluation.**

Table 9.3 shows the means of suicide utilized by those who attempted suicide immediately prior to the FFD evaluation. If "firearms" and "multiple means" are combined, half the officers chose relatively lethal means and half chose a relatively less lethal method, overdose.

Table 9.3
METHOD OF SUICIDE ATTEMPT

|  | *Count* | *Percent* |
|---|---|---|
| Firearms | 1 | 16.7 |
| Overdose | 3 | 50.0 |
| Multiple Means | 2 | 33.3 |

Table 9.4 shows the breakdown of **planned means of suicide** in all officers referred for FFD evaluation with current suicidal ideation whether they made an attempt immediately prior to the evaluation or not. Thirty percent of officers had planned suicide and of those, the distribution between planned means of suicide was fairly even.

Table 9.4
PLANNED MEANS OF SUICIDE: ALL FFD EVALUEES

|  | *Count* | *Percent* |
|---|---|---|
| None | 40 | 70.2 |
| Firearms | 4 | 7.0 |
| Overdose | 6 | 10.5 |
| Passive | 5 | 8.8 |
| Multiple means | 2 | 3.5 |

Table 9.5 shows that twenty-five percent of officers diagnosed with a substance disorder planned suicide versus only 8 percent of officers who had no substance use diagnosis. Unfortunately, no statistical significance can be assigned because the sample size was too small. Also, 12.5 percent of those with a diagnosis of substance use disorder had past suicide attempts versus only 4 percent without this diagnosis. Again the sample is too small to draw statistical conclusions. Certainly it suggests further directions for research, and additional subjects will be added to this series. One interesting difference is that those officers diagnosed with substance use disorder planned on using firearms or multiple means at a higher frequency than those without a substance use disorder.

Table 9.5
PLANNED MEANS OF SUICIDE BY SUBSTANCE USE DIAGNOSIS

| | Officers without Substance Use diagnosis | | Officers with Substance Use diagnosis | |
|---|---|---|---|---|
| | Count | Percent | Count | Percent |
| None | 37 | 75.5 | 3 | 37.5 |
| Firearms | 3 | 6.1 | 1 | 12.5 |
| Overdose | 6 | 12.2 | 0 | 0 |
| Passive | 3 | 6.1 | 2 | 25.0 |
| Multiple means | 0 | 0.0 | 2 | 25.0 |

By definition, the Washington State study does not address completed suicide with respect to FFD issues, but it does represent a unique window into the mindset of officers referred for FFD that were on the brink of suicide or who attempted it.

### 9.9 Family History of Suicide

A very high percentage (16%) of FFD evaluees in this study had a positive history of suicide or suicide attempts in their first-degree relatives. A subsequent paper will explore details of family suicide history and its potential role in shaping police officers' attitudes toward suicide (Decker, 2006). The finding of frequent suicide history in first-degree relatives is surprising in that the pre-employment evaluators would be expected to explore psychiatric problems in the evaluee as well as in first-degree family members, as many psychiatric conditions have a strong genetic component.

One would expect, if anything, a *lower* percentage of family suicide history than in the general population if applicants were being screened carefully. This may again highlight that the sample of officers referred for FFD evaluations represents a very different subpopulation than law enforcement personnel in general. It also suggests that evaluators may need to focus more carefully on family history during pre-employment—perhaps many evaluators are not focusing on these issues due to ADA issues or confidentiality concerns of applicants. Finally, it may be that this question should be asked on pre-employment polygraph examinations since it is much easier to deny a family history of psychiatric problems or suicide to an evaluator than it is to dissemble on polygraph. The polygraph might provide a useful cross-check for suicide history as it does for other important questions such as those regarding prior antisocial behaviors and criminal associations. (This is not to say that applicants should be rejected because of positive family history of psychiatric problems or suicide, but it would be helpful to improve accuracy of historical information.)

### 9.10 Conclusions

Law enforcement professionals' suicide has a profound impact on their families, friends, other officers, and agencies. While there may be variations in the risk of suicide in different regions or departments, implementing procedures to diminish suicide risk is always helpful. Departments may wish to consider procedures that ensure that officers can seek help at an early stage, particularly for marital issues, general stress management, and substance use disorders.

Also, although it is difficult to explore experimentally, higher suicide rates may accompany the higher level of violence in certain countries or regions in which violence is more prevalent. The author feels great caution must be exercised when attempting to draw conclusions about suicide in police at a global level. **Suicide may be one topic where it is more helpful to determine the magnitude of the problem on a local or agency level. Then, targeted solutions can be developed that apply to the specific agency or local problems in order to prevent suicide.**

## REFERENCES

Aussant, G. (1984). Police suicide. *RCMP Gazette, 46*:14-21.

Berg, A. M. et al. Suicidal ideation and attempts in Norwegian police. *Suicide and Life-Threatening Behavior, 33*(3):302-312.

Berg, A. M. et al. (2005). Stress in the Norwegian police service. *55*(2):113-120.

Cronin, T. J. (1982). *Police suicides: A comprehensive study of the Chicago police department,* 1970-1979. Master's Thesis. Romeoville, IL.

Decker, K. P. (2006). Suicidal ideation and attempts in law enforcement professionals referred for fitness for duty evaluations. *Am J Psychiatry,* submitted.

Drescher, K. D., Rosen, C. S., Burling, T. A., & Foy, D. W. (2003). Causes of death among male veterans who received residential treatment for PTSD. *J Trauma Stress, 16*(6):535-543.

Dumais, A. et al. (2005). Risk factors for suicide completion in major depression: A case-control study of impulsive and aggressive behaviors in men. *Am J Psychiatry, 162*(11):2116-2124.

FBI (2003). Jumpers: An ongoing HOBAS study. FBI Academy. Presented at American Academy of Psychiatry and Law, October.

Freeman, T.W., Roca, V., & Kimbrell, T. (2003). A survey of gun collection and use among three groups of veteran patients admitted to Veterans Affairs Hospital treatment programs. *South Med J, 96*(3):240-243.

Gould, L. A. (2002). Indigenous people policing indigenous people: The potential psychological and cultural costs. *Soc Science J, 39*(2):171-188.

Guralnick, L. H. (1963). Mortality by occupation and cause of death among men 20-64 years of age: 1950. *Vital Statistics Special Reports, 53.* Bethesda, MD: U.S. HEW.

Hem, E. Berg, A. M., & Ekeborg, O. (2001). Suicide in police—A critical review. *Suicide Life Threat Behav, 31*:224-233.

Hackett, D. P., & Violanti, J. M. (2003). *Police suicide: Tactics for prevention.* Springfield, IL: C C Thomas.

Janik, J., & Kravitz, H. M. (1994). Linking work and domestic problems with police suicide. *Suicide & Life-Threatening Behavior, 24*( 3):267.

Kopel, H., & Friedman, M. (1997). Post-traumatic symptoms in South African police exposed to trauma. *J Trauma Stress, 10*:307-317.

Labovitz, S., & Hagehorn, R. (1971). An analysis of suicide rates among occupational categories. *Soc Inquiry, 41*:67-72.

Langston, E. (1995). Police suicide. Presentation at American Criminal Justice Society Annual Conference. Boston, MA.

Loo, R. (1986). Suicide among police in a federal police force. *Suicide and Life-Threat Behav, 16*:379-388.

Loo, R. (2003). A Meta-analysis of police suicide rates: Findings and issues. *Suicide Life-Threat Behav, 33*(3):313-25.

Marzuk, P. M. et al. (2002). Suicide among New York City police officers. *Am J Psychiatry, 159*:2069-2071.

Nelson, Z. & Smith, W. E. (1970). The law enforcement profession: An incidence of high suicide. *Omega, 1*:293-299.

Pinals, D.A., & Price, M. (2004). Forensic psychiatry and law enforcement. R.J. Simon & L.Z. Gold (Eds.), In *Forensic psychiatry for the clinician.* Washington, DC: American Psychiatric Publishing, pp. 393-423.

Richard, W. C., & Fell, R. D. (1976). Health factors in police job stress. In W. Kroes & J. J. Hurrelll (Eds.): *Job stress and the police officer.* Washington, DC: USGPO, DHEW Publ. 76-187. NIOSH, pp. 73-84.

Roth, S. D. (2004). Suicide among police officers (letter). *Am J Psychiatry 161*(4):766.

Sareen, J. et al. (2005) Anxiety disorders associated with suicidal ideation and suicide attempts in the National Comorbidity Survey. *J Nerv Ment Dis, 193*(7):450-454.

Skolnick, J. (2000). Code blue. *The American Prospect, 11*(10).

Suokas, J., Suominen, K., & Lonnqvist, J. (2005). Chronic alcohol problems among suicide attempters-post-mortem findings of a 14-year follow-up. *Nord J Psychiatry 59*(1):45-50.

Thoresen, S., & Mehlum L. (2004). Risk factors for fatal accidents and suicides in peacekeepers: Is there an overlap? *Mil Med, 169*(12):988-993.

Twersky-Glasner, A. Police personality: What is it and why are they like that? *J Police and Crim Psychology, 20*(1):56-67.

Vena, J. E. et al. (1986). Mortality of a municipal worker cohort: III: Police officers. *American Journal of Industrial Medicine, 10*:383-397.

Vena, J. E., & Fiedler, R. C. (1987). Mortality of a municipal-worker cohort: IV: Fire fighters. *Am J of Indust Med 11* (6):671-684.

Violanti, J. M. (1995). Trends in police suicide. *Psychol Rep, 77*:688-690.

Violanti, J. M., Vena, J. E., & Petralia, S. (1998). Mortality of a police cohort: 1950-1990. *Am J Indust Med, 33*:366-373.

Violanti, J. M., & Hackett, D. P. (2003). Suicide and the police subculture. In D. P. Hackett & J. M. Violanti (Eds.), *Police suicide: Tactics for prevention.* Springfield, IL: Charles C Thomas.

Violanti, J. M. (2004). Suicide among police officers (letter). *Am J Psychiatry,161*(4):766.

Violanti, J. M. (2004a). Predictors of police suicide ideation. *Suicide Life Threat Behav, 34*(3):277-283.

Violanti, J. M., Vena, J. E., & Marshall, J. R. (1996). Suicides, homicides and accidental deaths: A comparative risk assessment of police officers and municipal workers. *Am J Indust Med, 30*:99-104.

Weissman, M. M. et al. (1999). Prevalence of suicide ideation and suicide attempts in nine countries. *Pscyhol Med, 29*:9-17.

# Chapter 10

# THE MANAGEMENT OF MISFIT OFFICERS

KATHLEEN P. DECKER

## 10.1 Unfit vs. Misfit Officers

Certain officers may be unfit for their previous position but fit for another position within the department, or law enforcement. The preceding chapters have focused on the multitude of problems precipitating FFD Evaluations. Attention has also been paid to the question of how the agency may proceed to deal with unfit officers. In this chapter, we will take a more positive stance and explore through case scenarios how agencies may use creative thinking and diplomacy to "retool" an officer's career path. In other words, some officers are not totally unfit for duty; they may just be or have become a poor match for their current assigned duties. In these cases, careful attention to their skills and strengths may allow retention of the officer in a different capacity. The focus on the system dynamics of individual performance and placement within the system is a feature of good organizations. The ability to place individuals in a job where they may contribute to the overall organization and feel successful also furthers the cause of smooth functioning of the organization.

Why retain officers if their behavior has been unsatisfactory enough to necessitate a FFD evaluation? There are several reasons. The first is that departments spend significant care, money, and time training officers. Especially in the case of veteran officers, it is not cost-effective to terminate individuals for inadequate performance. Second, if the behavior is the result of a remediable psychiatric illness, terminating officers for a single episode of psychiatric problems is akin to firing them for contracting pneumonia.

The statistics are especially compelling for depression. It is the most common psychiatric problem in any population. One in five people experience clinically significant depression during their lifetime and it is treatable. One in three of those individuals will never have another episode of depression. This means that one in 15 people will have a single, circumscribed episode of reduced functioning. Finally, police work is highly stressful and performance of job duties itself may be part of the precipitant for the depressive episode. Agencies owe their officers some understanding when the job itself exposes the officers to high levels of stress, as they do for physical risk.

Issues like "burnout" may be equally destructive to both the individual police officer and the agency for which they work. Even though it may not be a specific psychiatric syndrome, burnout is a major problem for veteran law enforcement personnel, as in Chapter 2. Strategies to deal with the individual's burnout and the agency's need to assert proper procedure and discipline can be challenging. These factors are explored in the case examples below.

### 10.2 Suitability

An officer may not be "mentally ill" but may be experiencing difficulty due to personality traits, which are undesirable in law enforcement personnel. The issue of suitability for law enforcement positions occurs in the course of FFD evaluations and is similar to that when selecting candidates during pre-employment evaluations. When considering applicants for law enforcement positions, psychiatrists, psychologists, police chiefs, and sheriffs recognize that an individual may be mentally healthy but "wrong" for the position. One of the primary factors sought in law enforcement personnel is "mental toughness." This characteristic is measured on certain personality tests such as the 16-PF as (discussed in Chapter 4) and verified during the clinical interview. There are many occupations such as psychotherapy, teaching, or nursing in which mental toughness is not only not required, but could be counterproductive. Mental toughness can be experienced as lack of empathy or patience in others. However, due to the grinding nature of dealing with violence, death, and corruption on a daily basis, mental toughness is regarded as an essential characteristic. It is possible that through burnout, major depression, or PTSD, law enforcement personnel may lose some of this trait.

Similarly, the quality of introversion is a normal component of many people with normal personality profiles in terms of interpersonal or overall psychological functioning, but it is not particularly useful in police officers. Officers may change over time and become less extroverted as officers age. As an extreme example, it would be problematic for an officer to stop and speculate on the past history and psychodynamics of a bank robber with a hold-up in progress.

Obsessive-compulsive traits are often seen in law enforcement personnel, as they are focused on the rule of law and tend to value order. It is clear that the major psychiatric syndrome of obsessive-compulsive disorder is problematic in law enforcement personnel, as an officer would not accomplish tasks if she/he were constantly preoccupied with internal thoughts or had to complete rituals. However, most people become more "set in their ways" as we age, and so the threshold of compulsive thinking that is acceptable in a young officer may rise as she/he ages, to the point where it becomes a problem.

Another trait that is crucial to routine performance of law enforcement duties is the ability to convey an authoritative presence without being threatening towards civilians. Individuals who develop bipolar disorder may manifest traits of grandiosity, irritability, and impatience alternating with traits of poor self-esteem, inability to assert themselves and fearfulness. It is clear that neither of these attitudes is desirable in law enforcement personnel. The job requires calm, unflappable individuals who can quietly but firmly assert their authority over a wide range of subjects and suspects. Similarly, individuals who "freeze up" because of anxiety or PTSD symptoms will not be able to carry out this function adequately.

The above factors represent just a few ways in which an evaluee may no longer be "suitable" for law enforcement but may not be disabled for other jobs in the community.

## 10.3 Role Availability

There are several factors that determine the ability of an agency to respond with the kind of flexibility described above. The first is size. It is obvious that a large agency with many officers has a larger number of positions, often with a greater variety of job tasks than does a small one. However, small agencies often have an advantage of a closer rapport between chief or sheriff and officer, which may facilitate sensitive discussions of reassignment. In certain case scenarios described in previous chapters, the outcome of a FFD evaluation was different based on the availability of light-duty options. The availability of administrative, clerical, or training slots will determine whether an agency can afford to reassign a patrol officer to another capacity.

## Case Scenario 1

Officer Jones was a 35-year-old, six-year veteran of a suburban police department comprised of five officers. He was referred for a FFD Evaluation because of excess traffic accidents, which clearly showed poor judgment. The evaluator was asked to determine if there was a psychiatric condition causing the poor judgment. Otherwise, he had already been subject to progressive discipline and was likely to be terminated. However, he had been an extraordinary inspiration to children while teaching a DARE (Drug Addiction Resistance Education) program at the local school and had prepared a host of informative teaching materials for the program. The officer was found to have no psychiatric illness, which explained the traffic accidents; he simply was a poor driver. He had successfully completed vehicle training as a police officer but continued to make mistakes when driving, possibly because of difficulty multitasking. The evaluator pointed out the officer's strengths to the agency during the evaluation process. However, the response was that the agency was too small to have a full-time dedicated training position in the schools and he was let go. He subsequently went back to college, obtained a teaching certificate, and obtained a job teaching high school.

### 10.4 Financial Issues Limiting Roles

In some agencies, there is a financial disincentive for officers to change their status. In general, clerical positions and/or purely administrative positions entail acceptance of lower pay. However, it may be a choice of reassignment or termination, in which case many officers may find such terms acceptable.

## Case Scenario 2

Officer Smith was a 56-year-old, 19-year veteran of a rural sheriff's office. She had had a solid career, although she had always been aggressive about firearms display. She had been a SWAT team member at one point in her career and was happiest at that time. She was referred for a FFD evaluation after she brandished her weapon in her personal vehicle off-duty in an incident where she felt threatened. She also had a history of having used unnecessary force on two occasions in the year prior to evaluation, including having tased a teen suspect. The evaluator conducted exhaustive tests, but the officer steadfastly denied symptoms of depression, anxiety, or other psychiatric conditions. However, collateral interviews with her supervisors as well as several peer officers revealed that all felt she had become "trigger-happy" and was becoming a liability to the agency. Her peers stated that she had a way of escalating situations and they no longer felt comfortable responding to calls where she was involved. She was interviewed on two different occasions, but neither interview nor psychological testing revealed a major psychiatric syndrome. The only explanation that emerged was that the officer felt she was more vulnerable as she was aging and she felt she needed to control suspects more quickly to reduce the risk of injury to herself.

The evaluator discussed the case at length with the referring department. The department decided the officer was a forensic liability and that that the department would have an indefensible position if the officer shot or injured another civilian. The evaluator suggested that as the sheriff's office also had positions in local corrections facilities, perhaps the officer could be provisionally reassigned to a corrections position. There she would not be armed (inmate transport jobs were separate and the only armed position) and she could finish her career in a more strictly controlled environment. The officer was unhappy about her perceived lower status of shifting to corrections work and stated it was a financial hardship as well. The agency found a supplemental source of funding for her so that her income dropped significantly but to a level upon which they were able to agree. She then transferred to corrections where she worked satisfactorily until retirement.

## 10.5 Litigiousness

Sometimes, preoccupation with legal issues creates barriers to evaluation and disposition that may harm the officer's case. In the course of some FFD evaluations, officers may have sought legal counsel prior to the evaluation. In some evaluations, the Policeman's Guild may attempt to influence the conduct or outcome of the evaluation. If an officer is contentious or litigious, the agency may not be willing to enter into a second set of negotiations regarding the disposition of such an officer. The author has performed a number of FFD evaluations during which the Guild or the officer was initially quite hostile to the process. However, when the officer decided that the evaluator was attempting to remain impartial and to find a workable solution for both agency and officer, the officer realized it was in the best interest of both to cooperate. As discussed in Chapter 3, there are many misconceptions police officers maintain regarding the FFD evaluation and mental health professionals in general. Often, a frank discussion of these stereotypes and concerns regarding impartiality may defuse litigious behavior from the outset and facilitate acceptance of alternative solutions like reassignment.

## Case Scenario 3

Officer Blank was a 28-year-old, 2-year veteran of a suburban police force. He was referred for evaluation because of excessive use of sick leave, negative attitude and two citizen complaints for rudeness. His evaluation was preceded by three phone calls from the Police Guild president and two emails from the Police Guild's attorney. The Police Guild president stated that the agency had "no grounds" to refer the officer for evaluation ("he missed work, he's not a psycho") and the Guild attorney threatened to sue the evaluator on behalf of the officers if she proceeded with the evaluation. The Police Chief went through a hearing before a judge regarding the legality of the evaluation. She made the case that the officer was being offered a chance to determine whether he had any underlying psychiatric reasons for his behavior prior to termination. The judge agreed that the officer would be better served by having such an evaluation than merely being subject to discipline.

When the officer presented for his evaluation, he was initially quite apprehensive and hostile to the evaluator. He repeated a concern that the evaluator "would railroad" him and declare he had major psychiatric problems "so the chief could terminate him." After discussion of the FFD process and reassurance that the evaluator had no vested interest in whether he had a psychiatric diagnosis or not, he agreed to cooperate with the interview. The interview and psychological testing both revealed that the officer was suffering from clinically significant depression and mild chronic pain from a previous duty-related injury. He had refused to reveal his symptoms to both  the chief and Guild representative out of pride—he did not want to be identified as weak. The evaluator outlined the process of treatment for depression and reported back to the department. The officer sought treatment for depression once he was reassured that merely seeing a psychiatrist and getting physical therapy would not result in termination. The chief granted him a one-month leave to commence treatment and followed with a three-week period of light duty and then she reinstated him to full duty. His behavior on the job improved markedly as his chronic pain and depression remitted.

### 10.6 "Attitude" Problems

What do people mean when they say an officer "has an attitude?" Most people understand immediately that the person in question is either rude, negative, critical, or argumentative.  None of these traits are *necessarily* markers of mental illness. Individuals can exhibit these traits for a wide variety of reasons. Simple examples include sleep deprivation, fatigue, and preoccupation with family problems. On the other hand, deeper reasons for "attitude" problems include psychiatric illnesses such as depression, which is associated with negative thinking and sometimes with irritability and thus rudeness. Individuals who are manic (as in bipolar disorder) may be euphoric and grandiose, which may be viewed as imperious and demanding. They may also be irritable and angry, which will also seem like an "attitude" problem. And finally, there may be other social reasons why officers may begin to exhibit "attitude problems." The following scenario illustrates one such explanation.

## Case Scenario 4

Officer Zebra was referred for a FFD Evaluation because of rudeness and poor communication skills with coworkers and superior officers. She had been an adequate employee of an urban police department for 15 years. However, her performance had gradually deteriorated in the year prior to the evaluation and she had been subject to disciplinary actions several times. The police chief referred her for evaluation to see if the officer had developed a psychiatric disorder that was causing interpersonal problems.

She presented for the evaluation but while she was filling out psychological tests, she sought out the evaluator and declined to continue the evaluation. The evaluator asked why and she said, "it's none of the department's d--- business what my sex life is like!" A 20-minute conversation ensued in which she explained she was afraid of the evaluation process. The limits of confidentiality and reporting techniques utilized by the evaluator were discussed in great detail. Once she realized that the frequency of her sexual activity would not automatically be disclosed to the agency, she continued the psychological tests and completed the evaluation process.

However, her attitude during the evaluation process was reflected in her psychological test scores. Her personality profile did not reveal a personality disorder, but 16-PF and other structured testing were consistent with the interview, which revealed her to be an intensely private person who was a "loner." Her hobbies were all solitary activities and she avoided contact with fellow officers off duty. As the years had gone by, she had become more isolated and was having interpersonal difficulty working in the primarily group setting of an urban police department. She stated that she was "tired of crime and criminals" but "wanted to retire when I have full benefits, and no sooner." Her symptoms did not meet the criteria for major depression or any other major psychiatric disorder.

The police department was informed that although the officer was found "Fit for Duty," further difficulties would be expected based on the evaluation as above. The psychiatrist recommended that assignment to police activities requiring less interpersonal contact would improve the chances that the officer could complete her service record. The evaluator also recommended brief psychotherapy focused on the issues of retirement and proper support systems. The police chief reviewed the recommendations and transferred the officer to the records department. As it was a large metropolitan department, the agency was able to maintain the officer in a position that reduced the officer's interpersonal contact. Officer Zebra attended only three of the five counseling sessions but did join a social club with nonlaw enforcement personnel on the recommendation of the counselor. Follow-up a year later showed she was performing adequately on the job with no further incidents. She reported an improved attitude and a determination to "make it through" her career.

The reader is referred to Chapter 2 for a discussion of the reduced coping skills often seen in older law enforcement personnel. Older law enforcement personnel often have fewer coping skills than younger officers and have many years of prolonged stress on the job. Both individual and group efforts aimed at stress reduction are necessary for police forces to retain valued veterans.

### 10.7 Personal Growth Affecting Suitability

As with "attitude" problems that may begin long after hiring, the suitability of an individual for law enforcement may change over time. We recognize that law enforcement is a profession which requires not only mentally healthy individuals, but those with a very particular mind set. Internal psychological change may be a positive event for the individual, but if an officer does not recognize the change as growth or ignores the call to a different lifestyle, the consequences can be negative. The following case illustrates this dilemma.

### Case Scenario 5

A 38-year-old African-American male officer, Officer Powers was referred for a FFD evaluation after serving five years as a police officer. He was referred when he demonstrated abuse of his sick leave over a one-year period. When confronted about this issue by his superior officer, he began sobbing and stated he was "afraid of being hurt on the job." The command staff were concerned he might be suffering from a major depression. Officer Powers completed a clinical interview and psychological testing without incident. He was polite and cooperative with the interview. However, he began to cry when asked about his statement that he was afraid of being hurt.

Officer Powers stated that he had grown up in a somewhat violent neighborhood and witnessed many incidents of domestic abuse, two stabbings, and many fights. He had not been abused as a child and he had a good home life. He had entered law enforcement thinking he would be fulfilled "getting the bad guys" and "putting them away." However, he had found that the long days of "waiting for stuff to happen" while he cited motorists for minor violations were very boring. When violent incidents did happen, he found himself taken off-guard and anxious. After each incident, whether it involved a physical scuffle to subdue a suspect or a domestic violence call, he would spend days replaying his response to the incident, wishing he'd done something differently and worrying about both the victim and the fate of the offender.

The officer did not meet criteria for any psychiatric disorder. He did not have flashbacks, nor posttraumatic stress disorder symptoms, but rather an increasing conviction that he did not want to be around violent people. The crying instances were explained by his fierce desire to appear "manly." He was ashamed that violent critical incidents turned out to be intensely disturbing to him. In turn, he had begun to fantasize about other careers. He had taken a night course in business, and found he had a flair for finance. His abuse of sick leave turned out to be due to fatigue after attending night classes. He admitted to the evaluator that "I want to make a change, but I don't know how."

The evaluator submitted a report to the agency and explained the problem. She also recommended that he engage in counseling to help him reconcile his view of "manhood" with his personality. The department requested that the evaluator schedule a follow-up session with the officer to discuss his options. The Chief did not want to fire the officer, and felt it was important that the officer understand the results of the evaluation. The Chief felt that in retrospect, he could see the officer was "not a typical cop anymore."

During the follow-up interview, she explored the concept of "suitability" to the officer. In lay terms, she discussed the concept of tough-mindedness versus empathy. Police officers tend to score high on tough-mindedness. It is typical that they are grounded, and pursue a solution, rather than introspective. Indeed, the officer had scored very low on tough-mindedness and although his score fell short of a disorder, he had significant obsessive-compulsive tendencies. In this case, his pre-employment test data were available and his psychological profile showed an increase in empathy (or decrease in tough-mindedness) and a slight increase in obsessive traits. The evaluator indicated that although Officer Powers still wanted to work with people, the evaluation results suggested he was evolving into a person who preferred a different kind of interpersonal interaction.

The officer was relieved to finally engage in open discussions about his career dilemma. He attended three sessions with an EAP counselor and explored career counseling through a local college. He resigned from the force, took out educations loans and obtained a partial scholarship to attend business school. A year later, he called the evaluator and informed her he had obtained a position in a stock brokerage. He expressed his gratitude that he had "not been spinning his wheels anymore" and stated he was very happy in his new endeavor.

### 10.8 Conclusions

These vignettes are used to illustrate some of the complex issues that distinguish a forensic FFD evaluation from a routine psychiatric evaluation. Each case should be judged on its own merits with careful attention to the department's particular needs, the compliance of the officer with treatment, and the specific prognosis. The cases below illustrate individuals who might well productively return to employment in other sectors of society, but continue to represent liability risks (both legal and physical) in a law enforcement setting. These examples are *not* meant to be absolute, but to illustrate *possible* difficulties. Each case should be dealt with individually and its resolution can be quite complex.

# Chapter 11

# LEGAL CONSIDERATIONS: DISCIPLINE VERSUS ILLNESS

ANNE E. KIRKPATRICK AND KATHLEEN P. DECKER

## I. GENERAL PRINCIPLES

This chapter focuses on the process of differentiating "simple misconduct" from psychiatric illness that is associated with misconduct. First, the types of conduct that are considered misconduct from the law enforcement perspective will be presented. Then examples of cases will be presented which demonstrate that episodes of misconduct may be a symptom of psychiatric problem during the course of a FFD evaluation. As discussed in Chapter 3, FFD evaluators should make no comment on proper police disciplinary procedures; that is the purview of the employer. The job of the FFD evaluator is to diagnose possible underlying conditions that may be *associated* with misconduct and to make recommendations regarding the medical or psychological conditions. However, a brief overview of the disciplinary process is provided in this chapter so evaluators can gain an understanding of employers' and employees' rights and limitations. This chapter also explores conflicts between the employee's right to privacy and due process versus the employer's legitimate right to obtain information pertaining to the employee's fitness to perform her/his job. There is an excellent comprehensive review of this subject (Aitchison, 2004).

## 11.1 Negligence in Hiring

The issues in this area may be summarized humorously as Gordy Graham's[1] Mantra:

"If it's predictable it's preventable!" Employers have a duty to utilize caution in hiring and maintaining workers. Negligent hiring refers to the situations in which the employer is held responsible for "bad acts" committed by an employee because of lack of diligence on the part of the employer to adequately screen or supervise the employee's behavior. This is also referred to as the "Theory of Respondeat Superior." An employer is liable for the harmful acts committed by an employee where the employee was *"acting within the scope of his/her employment."* One example is when a police car crashes during pursuits. Another example might be if a police officer commits domestic violence and the employer knew of her/his propensity for such behavior and did not proceed to thoroughly evaluate and/or discipline the officer.

## 11.2 Duty in Hiring

The duty of the employer to adequately screen and maintain employees leads to the conclusion that employers should screen prospective employees and should use methods such as psychological testing and background checks including domestic violence inquiries as well as general ethical inquiries. Indeed, failure to utilize careful screening methods prior to employment may leave the employer liable for negligence. However, primary data from psychological testing or similar methods need not be released to the agency directly, only the conclusions as discussed below.

In one example of a negligent hiring case (*J.H. v. West Valley City*), a police department was sued by a juvenile who was molested by a city police officer. The officer was in charge of the Explorer Scout Program. However, the molestation occurred while taking the boy home. The court ruled in favor of the city because the background check performed on the officer prior to his employment as a police officer was sufficient and did not indicate he was a pedophile.

---

[1]Gordy Graham, J.D. is a Captain of the California State Highway Patrol who teaches extensively at the FBI Academy on Risk Management for Law Enforcement Professionals.

## II. DISCIPLINE INVOLVING CONDUCT

### *12.3 Conduct Unbecoming an Officer*

The largest numbers of disciplinary cases arise under the category of conduct unbecoming. The general public, law enforcement agencies, and officers themselves have a vested interest in aggressively rooting out police misconduct and/or corruption. Research by the IACP indicates that most officers recognize the need for guidelines that specify organizational expectations (IACP, 1977). Most officers also endorsed appreciation of the contribution that such guidelines can make in maintaining high standards of conduct.

One of the major difficulties with the issue of misconduct is that it does not fall squarely within a specific rule. In order to be punished for the violation, the agency must have a rule in place that specifically prohibits "conduct unbecoming an officer." This concept has often been challenged for vagueness. Some examples of Conduct Unbecoming include criminal conduct even where the officer has not been convicted of the crime (an officer who slapped the informant); driving crimes while committed off-duty (an officer who crashed his DARE car while passing on a curve–late for a PTA meeting); sexual misconduct, particularly on duty (officer looking at pornography on his mobile data computer (MDC) while manning a busy intersection at the fair). Other types of conduct unbecoming an officer include substance abuse, including abuse of alcohol and drugs, e.g., while off-duty which draws police attention; mishandling of property; and verbal tantrums.

There is a branch of the federal government, that is responsible for the enforcement of civil law regarding police conduct. They have formulated a specific "Police Misconduct Provision." This law makes it unlawful for State or local law enforcement officers to engage in a pattern or practice of conduct that deprives persons of rights protected by the Constitution or laws of the United States (42 U.S.C. § 14141). The types of conduct covered by this law can include, among other things, excessive force; discriminatory harassment; false arrests; coercive sexual conduct; and unlawful stops, searches, or arrests. In order to be covered by this law, the misconduct must constitute a "pattern or practice"–it may not simply be an isolated incident. The DOJ must be able to show in court that the agency has an unlawful policy or that the incidents constituted a pattern of unlawful conduct. However, unlike the other civil laws discussed below, DOJ does not have to show that discrimination has occurred in order to prove a pattern or practice of misconduct.

### *11.4 National Statistics*

Although the subject of this book is primarily oriented towards an understanding of FFD issues in local law enforcement agencies, the United States represents a vast territory with high degrees of local autonomy. This makes it more difficult to evaluate national trends in police stress, misconduct, and fitness for duty than in small countries, such as Norway, which have a national police force which is monitored in a uniform manner, as discussed in Chapter 2. Therefore, it has been very difficult to develop and standardize regulations regarding misconduct as well as to analyze data about types of misconduct on a national scale in the U.S. However, it is possible to examine statistics from national law enforcement organizations in the U.S. regarding misconduct and discipline to assist with an understanding of the magnitude of national trends in the U.S. The Drug Enforcement Agency (DEA) was selected for illustration in this chapter because many, although not all, of its activities resemble local law enforcement duties such as arrest powers, search and seizure, and so forth. The reader is reminded that local law enforcement spends a far smaller part of its operations undercover and therefore police officers are subject to different pressures than DEA officers. Accordingly, they may have different patterns of misconduct.

The top five offense codes charged against DEA agents by the Office of Professional Review are presented in Table 11.1. "Poor judgment" and "conduct unbecoming an officer" together *only* accounted for 16 percent of charges against officers. This highlights the fact that although it is critical to understand issues such as misconduct and perform FFD evaluations, the vast majority of disciplinary actions result from much smaller issues. Thus, although the issues precipitating FFD evaluations and misconduct charges potentially represent the most problematic behaviors, they are *infrequent* behaviors.

Table 11.1
TOP FIVE OFFENSE CODES CHARGED AGAINST DEA OFFICERS (2001-2002)

| Offense | Number of Offenses | Percent of Total Offenses |
|---|---|---|
| Poor Judgment | 143 | 10 |
| Failure to Follow Written Instructions | 120 | 9 |
| Conduct Unbecoming an Agent | 77 | 6 |
| Failure to Report OPR Matters | 64 | 5 |
| Loss or Theft of a Defendant's Property or Funds | 58 | 4 |
| All other charges | 930 | 67 |
| Total | 1,392 | 100 |

## 11.5 Examples of Misconduct

The off-duty conduct of an officer can be regulated only to the extent that there is a direct relationship between the off-duty conduct and a provable impact on the job performance and effective functioning of the agency. Misconduct cases may be separated into several conceptual categories that include misuse of police powers, corruption, violence, and misbehavior demonstrating poor judgment.

A. MISUSE OF POLICE POWERS. Misuse of police authority is certainly an important area in which to govern misconduct. We (society) grant the use of lethal force and allow officers to carry a variety of lethal weapons on and off duty. We expect them to use these weapons judiciously, not maliciously. In one related case of misuse of police powers [*City of Meriden*, 1993 WL 800920 (Stewart, 1993)], an officer was fired after getting extremely drunk; he got into a fight, he escaped from two officers who were taking him home, and then he commandeered a tractor-trailer, telling the truck driver he had a pistol. Another case which was less dangerous but equally inappropriate involved an officer who was terminated for drinking while working an off-duty party and wearing a uniform [*Shields v. City of Shreveport*, 565 So.2d 473 (La.App. 1990)].

B. VIOLENCE. Similarly, law enforcement personnel are trained and retrained to administer deadly force and/or use nonlethal force to subdue suspects, if necessary. This use of force can and must be regulated to include its use only when appropriate for police emergencies. At times, when physical force is misused, the consequences are more severe for law enforcement personnel than for civilians. For example, in *Murray v. U.S. Dept. of Justice*, 821 F. Supp. 94 E.D.N.Y. 1993, an FBI Agent was fired for smashing in the windows of a car improperly parked in his space. This might seem harsh, but his misuse of violence might have indicated a hair-trigger temper that is inappropriate in law enforcement personnel.

On the other hand, occasionally courts have attempted to put "temper loss" into the context of the overall performance of the officer. In *City of Dayton v. Fraternal Order of Police*, 2000 WL 706829 (Ohio App. 2000), an officer was fired after he got involved in a dispute over change with a fast food cashier. The dispute culminated in the officer pepper spraying the clerk. The arbitrator overturned the termination and ordered a suspension because of the officer's good work record and this was a "single act of misconduct."

C. MISBEHAVIOR. Behavior which would not be considered newsworthy in civilians may at times be trumpeted by the media as typifying police behavior. Two examples of this include the following cases in which police officers certainly used poor judgment but may not have actually had serious psychological issues. For example, in the *City of Claremore*, 1992 WL 717429 (Shearer, 1992), an off-duty officer was involved in the illegal taking of two deer. Seventeen newspapers and CNN covered the story. The other case involved an officer who was terminated for selling t-shirts that read: "smoke 'em, don't choke 'em" after the chief banned the use of the carotid hold *City of Portland*, (Hanlon, 1985).

## 11.6 Misconduct Remedies

The remedies available under the misconduct law do not provide for individual monetary relief for the victims of the misconduct. Rather, they provide for injunctive relief, such as orders to end the misconduct and changes in the agency's policies and procedures that resulted in or allowed the misconduct. There is no private right of action under this law; only DOJ may file suit for violations of the Police Misconduct Provision. Individuals also have a private right of action under Title VI and under the OJP Program Statute; they may file a civil lawsuit under these laws as well as the complaint. However, individuals must first exhaust their administrative remedies by filing a complaint with DOJ if they wish to file in Federal Court under the OJP Program Statute.

Evaluators need to understand that different systems of discipline may be used by different agencies, even in the same geographical region. The IACP has determined that, "written directives serve as the foundation of effective discipline." However, each agency or department may craft different policies regarding such consequences.

### 11.7 Misconduct vs. Illness

The Americans with Disabilities Act (ADA) defines a covered "disability" as a physical or mental impairment that substantially limits one or more of the major life activities of such individual; a record of such impairment; or being regarded as having such impairment [42 U.S.C. § 12102(2)]. The key concept is the notion of "substantially limits" major life activities. If an individual has a mental or physical impairment that does *not* substantially limit his/her major life activities such as a past history of a psychiatric condition, he/she may not be eligible for such consideration.

The (ADA) covers mentally as well as physically disabled individuals. An employee who becomes a plaintiff who establishes liability for disability discrimination under the ADA is entitled to recover damages for emotional injuries relating to such discrimination. The concept of reasonable accommodation was originally established for employees with physical conditions, not mental disabilities. It is clearly easier to establish "reasonable accommodations" for certain physical conditions such providing wheelchair-accessible work environments. Clearly the concept of reasonable accommodation is more complex with the relatively intangible and invisible impairments involved in psychiatric conditions. The concept of what is a reasonable accommodation in an occupation involving chronic high stress is also challenging to define.

The ADA's intent to require employers to make reasonable accommodations was also not meant to cover all psychological conditions. If an individual is impaired by a condition not covered by ADA, the employer may not be required to make accommodations for such a condition. The reader is referred to an excellent review of the ADA as it applies to employers and a recent update of this material (McDonald, 1995, McDonald, 2005).

## Case Scenario 1

Officer Dyna Mite was a petite officer who was known for her "hair-trigger temper." She was often regarded with amusement because of her intolerance of others' mistakes and her dogged dedication to "getting the bad guys." However, she was referred for a FFD evaluation after she punched a civilian while off duty in a department store. She gave no explanation for the incident. At first, her supervisor followed the disciplinary route alone and charged her with conduct unbecoming. She was disciplined according to her department's regulations. However, a week after the incident, she began berating a fellow officer verbally for "slacking off." She used a four-letter word to describe the officer. As the conversation occurred on police radio, she was again called in again to discuss her behavior. When questioned about her behavior for the second time, she broke down into tears and explained that her father had died several weeks prior to the first incident. She had concealed the death from fellow officers because she was "not close" to her father and didn't want to explain or deal with condolences. She had been "trying to deal with it" by exercising more and by talking to her pastor. However, she had been sleeping more than 10 hours a night, had gained 10 pounds in a month, and was "not sure she could go on." She had not wanted to take leave as she was saving it for a family vacation with her husband later that year.

Officer Mite received appropriate discipline for both incidents from her superiors. The FFD evaluator diagnosed major depression. Her symptoms were more severe than just a grief reaction. He did not find evidence of a personality disorder. Because of the sleep and appetite changes, the evaluator recommended antidepressant medication treatment. At first, Officer Mite was defiant, but she grudgingly agreed to try medications and "go in for a few sessions of counseling" regarding death. Two months later, she presented for re-evaluation. She was polite, energetic, and had lost five pounds of the excess weight. She stated she was sleeping seven to eight hours a night and had more energy. She had discontinued counseling after eight sessions but felt "much more at peace" with her father's death.

Her superiors remarked Officer Mite was "not just better" than she had been immediately prior to the FFD evaluation, but "calmer and happier all 'round." They said she was more tolerant of frustration on the job. She told the evaluator she felt more self-confident than she had in years and "didn't sweat the small stuff." Accordingly, she planned to continue the antidepressant for an indefinite time.

### 11.8 Truthfulness

Truthfulness is an important reasonable expectation for police officers. Many agencies refer to a "bright line" regarding standards of truthfulness. On May 7, 1999, former-Mayor Paul Schell appointed a panel of citizens to evaluate the issue of employee accountability and the process by which reports of police misconduct are investigated by the Seattle Police Department, in part due to an incident in which a police detective was accused of first degree theft. He was accused of stealing $10,000 from the home of a Seattle resident. The panel made a series of recommendations, which include sections on the importance of truthfulness. They stated:

> Taken together, there is no question that the Seattle Police Department has a policy that requires its employees to report misconduct, that obligates employees to tell the truth in their statements, and that mandates anyone in a supervisory capacity to report misconduct to the Internal Investigations Unit.

The panel also made specific recommendations regarding the implementation of truthfulness and misconduct standards as follows:

> To ensure consistency of discipline, the OPA shall develop a formal range of discipline for misconduct cases. The OPA is urged to take note of the panel's recommendations regarding a "Bright Line" policy in this effort. The Chief shall be responsible for making the final determination as to discipline and may, for good cause and in writing, modify the adjudicative findings of the Director.

The policies and procedures manual of another city in Washington State, Federal Way Police Department also specifically addresses truthfulness. Its manual states that "Members of the police department shall be forthright and truthful at all times which pertain to their duties, conduct, observations, or any other area pertaining to the official business of the Federal Way Police Department." This statement provides the structural support for reasonable discipline for infractions of this policy. However, it may be important to differentiate between forthright vs. truthful, which is based on deception. Therefore, more recent versions of the policy treat statements that are based on the concept of truthfulness separately from forthright statements. Truthfulness is particularly important because police officers sustained (found guilty) of lying must by law disclose a background of lying to defense attorneys, which may result in their impeachment as witnesses in any case in which they subsequently attempt to testify. These issues received increased attention following the *United States v. Gill*, 99 F.3d 484, 485 (1st Cir. 1996) in which an officer was found guilty of criminal contempt after he refused to testify.

In the following case involving dishonesty, an officer falsely claimed to have stopped an intoxicated individual when in fact, he was en route to his mother's house to take a bathroom break (*City of Hialeah*, LAIG 5316 (Lambert, 1997).) *In re Radlinger*, 782 N.E.2d 1215 (Ohio App. 2002) Officer failed to appear in court, later giving the excuse that he was investigating a homicide. In fact, the officer was taking his dad to the doctor. In the *City of Lawton Oklahoma*, 2001 (WL 574317), an officer responding to a suicide scene moved the victim's gun, unloaded it, and placed it on an egg carton on top of an automobile hood all before the crime scene personnel arrived. Then the officer made inaccurate report regarding the order of events. The arbitrator overturned the discipline on the grounds that the officer was not intentionally untruthful, although his account was "contradictory and confusing and did not provide a complete picture of the events that transpired."

### 11.9 Intimate Relationships

The clearest case of a nexus between an officer's sexual activities and on-the-job performance is when that activity is illegal. Less clear cases usually involve illicit but not illegal activities such as marital affairs. The courts are willing to allow agency regulation in such cases if the affair is so open and notorious that it can be truthfully said that the officer's image has been significantly tarnished. In a case entitled *City of Sherman v. Henry*, 11 IER Cases 1569 (Tex. S. Ct. 1996), a police officer had a sexual affair with the wife of a fellow police officer. The officer was denied a subsequent promotion based on the affair. The Texas Supreme Court upheld the denial finding there was is no privacy deprivation and no constitutionally protected right in having an affair.

In *Dawson v. State Law Enforcement Division*, 7IER Cases 629 (D.S.C., 1992), a police officer was fired after he and a coworker's husband were caught masturbating in a room together while off-duty. The officer claimed he had a constitutional right to engage in private homosexual conduct. The court disagreed, but with *Lawrence v. Texas*, this ruling would be overturned. In 1986, in the case of *Lawrence v. Texas* (539 U.S. 558, 123 S.Ct. 2472), the Supreme Court ruled that state laws can make homosexual sodomy a crime. Officers could be discharged simply for their homosexuality on the theory that the officer failed to comply with the law. A Federal Court of Appeals upheld the FBI's policy of not hiring homosexuals on the grounds that they must be able to comply with the law in every state.

In 2003, the United States Supreme Court ruled that the Dallas Police Department's refusal to hire homosexual applicants violated the Fifth Amendment right to privacy. Hence, the court ruled that the Fifth Amendment granted individuals the right to engage in private, consensual homosexual acts, and struck down a state statute criminalizing such conduct.

## Case Scenario 2

Officer Don Won was spotted having sex in his patrol car on duty, in a parking lot on his beat with another officer. Both officers were initially charged with misconduct, reprimanded, and suspended for two days. The female officer returned to duty and ceased sexual activity on duty.

However, Officer Won was referred to the evaluator after he repeated inappropriate sexual behavior on duty on three subsequent occasions within the same month with three different females. Officer Won presented for the evaluation, laughed loudly, and was jovial. He interrupted the evaluator constantly and made sexual innuendos. He explained his grandiose plan to become mayor of the town and "build skyscrapers that trump the tallest towers." He also revealed that he had been sleeping less than two hours a night for several weeks, and that he had lost 15 pounds "without trying–I don't need food anymore."

To the evaluator, the diagnosis was clear–Officer Won was suffering from a manic episode. Further history, testing and investigation was consistent with this diagnosis. He was removed from duty but hospitalization was narrowly averted by emergency psychiatric treatment.

In this case, the difference between the two officers' conduct is that the female officer was guilty of simple misconduct (and poor judgment). However, Officer Won had a psychiatric illness causing his behavior. This case underscores the need to follow both the disciplinary path *and* to consider FFD evaluation if officers' misconduct is repeated or bizarre. The chief could not have foretold after the first incident which officer was merely misbehaving and which had a psychiatric illness. Thus, discipline was warranted for both officers. But after *repeated* incidents, the index of suspicion rose that Officer Won had a psychiatric problem that might respond to treatment, rather than intentional misbehavior. It required a psychiatrist to evaluate the medical and psychiatric symptoms.

### *11.10 Insubordination*

There are six steps that are required to establish insubordination.

1. Officer is to be given a direct order to perform or not perform.
2. If a direct order was not given, were clear and specific rules distributed to the officer.
3. The officer was specifically advised that the failure to comply would subject the officer to the discipline imposed, including and up to termination.
4. The officer disobeyed.
5. The order does not require unlawful conduct or jeopardizing safety.
6. The employer did not provoke the insubordination.

One instance labeled insubordination occurred when an officer disobeyed an order to terminate a pursuit in the *City of Green Forest v. Morse*, 873 S.W.2d 155 (Ark. 1994). Another example termed insubordination occurred when an officer refused to transport a prisoner with AIDS. *City of Philadelphia*, LAIG 4254 (Ryan, 1989). Other examples include a School Resource Officer (SRO) who violated the chief's order to not meet privately with a 14 year old girl who was intimating her romantic intentions toward the SRO [*City of Piqua*, 107 LA 1158 (Heekin, 1997)]. Finally, an officer who refused to cut his hair after being ordered to comply with grooming code. was labeled insubordinate [*Hamilton County*, LAIG 4164 (1988)].

## III. THE DISCIPLINARY PROCESS

*The following sections are not meant to be an exhaustive review of discipline policies and procedures but are intended to give FFD evaluators a glimpse of the type of reasoning used by law enforcement professionals. There may be wide fluctuations in the approach to discipline taken by different agencies and departments, as with other material in this chapter.*

### 11.11 Progressive Discipline

Progressive Discipline is a useful concept and consists of stepwise increase in severity of disciplinary measures to enforce conforming behavior. The steps include:

**Step 1: Nonconsequential Discipline.**
This may consist of coaching counseling or training as well as a verbal reprimand to delineate nonconforming behavior.

**Step 2: Consequential Discipline.**
In step 2, behavior, which recurs after step 1, has already been implemented, may consist of a written reprimand which is usually not subject to appeal, suspension, and/or termination.

However, a department may circumvent the progression depending on the seriousness of an offense. It is important that a department utilize a consistent and predictable approach to progressive discipline. The discipline should fit the offense and be systematic so that it is not vulnerable to charges that a superior is arbitrarily subjecting an officer to discipline. For an excellent review of the potential advantages and disadvantages of specific penalty schedules, the reader is referred to a white paper by Maloney (Maloney, 1999).

### 11.12 Policies and Procedures

The foundation for discipline lies in having well-crafted policies. In the OPR's report on DEA discipline, referenced above in Section 12.4, documentation of discipline was lacking at times. The conclusions of the report included the statement that "it is important that the official personnel files contain the appropriate documentation to ensure that the imposed disciplinary actions were taken and to serve as permanent records of employees' disciplinary histories." In the author's experience, this is a common pitfall encountered by local law enforcement agencies as well. Many sheriffs or police chiefs believe that if an officer is suffering from a psychiatric problem that they should "go easy" on discipline. However, if the officer later turns out to have further disciplinary problems and no documentation of the earlier events has occurred, it circumvents the progressive discipline procedures. *It is important for police executives to view and administer discipline as a separate process than a FFD Evaluation, which concerns itself with an illness, not merely misconduct.*

Departments must use just cause for discipline. Just cause may be thought of as satisfying ten rules:

1. Did the employee violate a known reasonable rule or order?
2. Did the employee receive an adequate opportunity to correct his/her behavior through the use of progressive discipline?
3. Was the employee treated consistent with other similarly situated employees?
4. Was the employee at fault either in whole or in part?
5. Did the employer conduct a full and fair investigation?
6. Did the employee receive the benefit of all procedural protections?
7. Did the punishment fit the crime?
8. Were there any relevant mitigating circumstances?
9. Has the employer complied with all provisions of the agency's personnel rules and standard operating procedures?
10. What was the previous record of the employee?

## IV. LEGAL PROTECTIONS AND FFD EVALUATIONS

*The following sections include cases and legal decisions that ARE NOT relevant to all agencies or jurisdictions. For example, the Garrity rule, the Loudermill hearing, and the Weingarten decision apply only to agencies or departments that employ UNIONIZED officers. These decisions are therefore also inapplicable to federal officers. The reader is cautioned that case law changes quickly. Local, state, and even federal laws may change substantially with respect to legal protections of both employers and employees. The safest* *practice is for evaluators to discuss issues that arise during FFD cases with attorneys if there are legal aspects of which they are unsure. These topics are presented here as **examples** of how the employee's legal rights may at times conflict with the process of a FFD evaluation.*

### 11.13 The Garrity Rule

The handling of statements compelled by police departments of police officers was raised in *Garrity v. New Jersey*, 385 U.S. 493 (1967). In the 1967 landmark case, which arose out of a ticket fixing investigation whereby the suspected police officers were ordered to answer questions or lose their jobs. The court ruled that the compelled statements of police officers could not be used against them in a subsequent criminal proceeding. The rationale was that it violated a person's Fifth Amendment right against self-incrimination. There are three steps of the Garrity rule:

- *Order* the officer to answer the questions under threat of disciplinary action.
- Ask questions that are *specifically, directly, and narrowly* related to the officer's duties or the officer's fitness-for-duty.
- *Advise* the officer that the answers to the questions will not be used against the officer in criminal proceedings.

If the officer then refuses to answer appropriate questions, the officer can be terminated for insubordination. The scope of Garrity includes written or oral statements, although written statements are preferred. The officer has no right to have an attorney present before giving a statement but she/he does have union representation rights as established by the Weingarten case. The *National Labor Relations Board v. J. Weingarten*, 420 U.S. 251 (1975), was a landmark case in 1975 where an employee was denied his request to have union representation present during a disciplinary interview. The court ruled that the purpose for the National Labor Relations Act was to *equalize power*. Hence requiring a lone employee to face such an interview perpetuates inequality.

The scope of Weingarten applies to all members of a bargaining unit regardless of rank and confers the right for representation only where the supervisor is eliciting information from the officer (even if it is

elicited only in writing). However, the officer *must request the representation.* The officer's union, and not the employer, gets to select the
union representative. The union's representative may be the union
lawyer, but the officer has no right to have his/her private attorney.
Having a delay in the interview in order to secure representation cannot "unduly interfere with the agency's need to have an investigatory
process."

The Garrity rule automatically attaches whenever an officer is
required to answer a supervisor's questions as a condition of employment. When an order is absent, the employee has no obligation to
answer questions. An employer has no obligation to utilize the Garrity
rule if the agency does not want to give any protections. If the officer
volunteers to give a statement, there is no protection [*Bodette v. Cox
Com, Inc.,* (9th Circuit 2004) (366 F.3d 736)]. At present the law is
unsettled as to how the Garrity rule applies when an officer is merely
writing a required police report as opposed to answering questions.

### 11.14 The Officer's Representative

The role of the representative includes:

• The right to consult with the officer prior to the interview.
• The right to know the charges prior to the interview (charges can
  be amended later).
• The right to privately consult with the officer during the interview.
• The right to offer investigatory leads *at the conclusion of the interview.*
• The right to offer mitigating circumstances *at the conclusion of the
  interview.*
• The right to object to inappropriate questions *during an interview*
  (watch out for the Perry Mason's. Tape these interviews when pos-
  sible and *note* the objection, then move on).

### 11.15 The Officer's Defense

The officer has a right to defense in disciplinary actions.  In a case
between the *Cleveland Board of Education v. Loudermill,* 470 U.S. 532
(1985), the case required a hearing in order to allow the officer a reasonable opportunity to make a defense. This case noted, "the right to

be heard, to present one's side of the story, is a fundamental requirement of any fair procedural system."

The scope of Loudermill states that notice is required with a letter
of intent to suspend or terminate including the date, time, and location
of hearing. The hearing applies to both union employees and at-will
employees and is subject to constitutional protections.

Loudermill, Garrity, and Weingarten apply only to unionized
employees but not at-will employees. Finally, the employer must balance liberty and property interests for both union and nonunion
employees. It derives from the constitutional umbrella protecting citizens from unreasonable or unlawful treatment.

Conduct during the disciplinary process with respect to both the
Garrity rule and the Loudermill hearing is different than during a FFD
evaluation, which is *not* a disciplinary process. Occasionally, unin-
formed union guild representatives and/or law enforcement personnel
request or demand that a third party be present during an evaluation.
Challenges have been raised repeatedly, but the conduct of psychiatric or psychological evaluations may be impaired or invalidated by
the presence of third parties during the interview. This is partly
because of the nature of probing psychological questions and partly
because the individual may be divulging deviant or intensely personal values which he/she might not do in the presence of third parties.
However, interviews may be audio or videotaped as long as the
evaluee agrees and copies are available to both the evaluee and the
evaluating agency.

### 11.16 At Will Employees

Sworn officers may be subject to different disciplinary action than
certain other employees at an agency. At-will employees are subject to
termination for any reason, *even arbitrary ones*, but they still have constitutional protections and they may have protections as a result of
public policy. These may include constitutional issues such as race,
color, national origin, age, sex, religious creed, marital status, disability, or sexual orientation[2] [*Lawrence v. Texas* (2003)]. There are also Civil
Service rules to consider. If the department has a Policy and Procedure

---

[2]Employers have occasionally argued that employees can be fired for exercising their free speech
rights since they can be fired for any reason. A Supreme Court ruling in *Sperry v. Sinderman* said that
is not so.

Manual, these guidelines must be utilized, and finally, the past practice within the department must be considered.

### *11.17 Conclusions*

The foregoing chapter outlines disciplinary issues and methods for police departments to deal with such issues in a progressive, impartial, and fair manner. However, the FFD evaluation is *not* a disciplinary action. This has a number of ramifications that the evaluator must consider and may occasionally need to remind the employee, employer, or him or herself. First and above all, disciplinary issues are *not* the province of a FFD evaluation. The existence and handling by both employer and employee may contribute to understanding the nature of the employee's difficulties and resolving the issue of fitness. However, evaluators should decline comment on the appropriateness or means of discipline to both employee and employer. Psychiatrists and psychologists are unfamiliar with the specific policies and procedures for such discipline and in order to provide an unbiased expert opinion on fitness, they may comment only on the *cause* of untoward actions, not the employer's disciplinary solution to the problematic behavior.

Officers and/or union representatives may accidentally or purposely try to approach them as though they were disciplinary hearings, requesting friends, union representatives, or even attorneys or their representatives "sit in" on the evaluation. The presence of third parties during a psychological interview interferes with the conduct of the interview and may compromise the evaluation. Employees may either conceal socially undesirable information in the presence of a third party or make statements based on their perception of legal ramifications. However, one strategy that is useful to provide an accurate representation of the interview for the employee's later use is to audio or videotape the interview.

Additionally, discipline should be thought of as a separate, *parallel* track to the FFD evaluation. If an employee is found to have a psychiatric condition which precipitated the inappropriate behavior, that should be dealt with as a separate issue. Discipline can be administered concurrently, mitigated, or suspended until the employee returns to fitness, depending on the case.

# REFERENCES

Aitchison, W. (2004). *The rights of law enforcement officers* (5th ed.). Portland, OR.

Bodette v. Cox Com, Inc., (9th Circuit 2004) (366 F.3d 736)

City of Claremore, 1992 WL 717429 (Shearer, 1992).

City of Hialeah, LAIG 5316 (Lambert, 1997).

In re Radlinger, 782 N.E.2d 1215 (Ohio App. 2002).

Dawson v. State Law Enforcement Division, 7IER Cases 629 (D.S.C., 1992).

City of Green Forest v. Morse, 873 S.W.2d 155 (Ark. 1994).

City of Philadelphia, LAIG 4254 (Ryan, 1989).

City of Piqua, 107 LA 1158 (Heekin, 1997).

City of Lawton Oklahoma, 2001 WL 574317 (Prlogdky, 2001).

City of Sherman v. Henry, 11 IER Cases 1569 (Tex. S. Ct. 1996).

Cleveland Board of Education v. Loudermill, 470 U.S. 532 (1985).

E.D.Va.City of Portland, (Hanlon, 1985)

Federal Statute. The Health Insurance Privacy, Portability and Accountability Act (HIPPA), April, 2003.

Garrity v. New Jersey, 385 U.S. 493 (1967).

Hamilton County, LAIG 4164 (1988).

International Association of Chiefs of Police. (1977). *Managing for effective police discipline: A manual of rules, procedures, supportive law and effective management* (2nd rev. ed.).

J.H. West v. West Valley, 840 P.2d 115 (Utah 1992).

Lawrence v. Texas, cite as 539 U.S. 558, 123 S.Ct. 2472.

Philip, J., & Maloney, M. A. (1999). *The role of penalty schedules in managing police misconduct.* Memphis Shelby Crime Commission (1):4, September.

McDonald, J. J. Jr, Kulick, F. B., & Creighton, M. K. (1995). Mental disabilities under the ADA: A management rights approach. *Employee Relat. Law J., 20*(4):541-569.

McDonald, J. J. (2005). *Forensic practice in employment cases.* Workshop at the American Academy of Psychiatry and Law Conference.

Murray v. U.S. Dep't. of Justice, 821 F. Supp. 94 E.D.N.Y. 1993.

National Labor Relations Board v. J. Weingarten, 420 U.S. 251 (1975).

Shields v. City of Shreveport, 565 So.2d 473 (La.App. 1990).

# Chapter 12

# AFTERWORD

This book presents an overall perspective on the reasons for performing fitness for duty evaluations, the process of the evaluation, and details some of the problems encountered in officers referred for FFD evaluations. In Chapter 1, a detailed introduction to the evaluation process was presented. Chapter 2 focused on comparisons from the literature of prior decades on stressors and stress responses with data on perceived stress and interventions in current law enforcement personnel. One of the striking findings is that organizational stress remains highly stressful to officers. Rural officers experience more stress related to more restricted training opportunities. Duty death, although a relatively uncommon event, remains the most stressful event.

In Chapter 3, a systematic review of psychiatric conditions found in officers referred for FFD evaluations was presented for the first time in the literature. Major depression was the most common condition, and the most common secondary diagnosis was substance use disorders. Bipolar disorder and attention deficit disorder were other common diagnoses. PTSD was not a major reason for referral in this series. Certain officers who were evaluated for fitness were found to be fit in spite of having an Axis I condition such as major depression, as successful treatment of some conditions may allow officers to resume duty. It is likely that as officers age, no matter how strong their mental health was during pre-employment testing, they may develop certain psychiatric disorders as a result of stress, such as posttraumatic stress disorder or depression or because of later age of onset such as bipolar disorder. The psychiatric diagnosis of officers referred to psychologists for evaluation may be different than those referred to the author (a psychiatrist). One topic of future research will be to obtain a wider sample of officers referred for FFD evaluations.

The material in Chapter 4 comprises a review of psychological tests and their use to characterize the psychological mindset of law enforcement personnel. A number of standardized tests have been used in pre-employment evaluations to attempts to select individuals with specific qualities such as "tough-mindedness," high integrity, and a grounded approach to problem-solving. Suitability, not just mental health, is the key to choosing good law enforcement personnel. Careful attention to substance use issues is important as this is a frequent problem later. These tests may also be utilized in FFD evaluations, either to compare to the current level of psychological functioning or to assess whether the individuals has developed characteristics that make him/her unfit for duty. The most important concept presented in this chapter is that *no one psychological test* will provide an adequate means to assess fitness. A battery of test which assess different aspects of psychological functioning should be used. It is important for psychiatrists performing FFD evaluations to collaborate with psychologists to perform and interpret such tests, unless they undergo *thorough* training and education in the administration of such tests.

The vast majority of officers referred for FFD evaluations in the Washington State study were taking psychoactive medication prior to the evaluation (80% of metropolitan and 63% of rural officers). Chapter 5 explores the effects on officer performance of prescription medications and a few nonprescription medication. The wide use of medications to treat chronic pain and insomnia, many of which have deleterious effects on vigilance, judgment, and reaction time makes an understanding of these issues crucial. In addition, primary care providers prescribe a wide variety of psychiatric medications. Many of these primary care providers are not only untrained in psychiatry but are not aware of the special performance requirements and circumstances in law enforcement personnel. Thus, it is important to further education of primary care providers. Law enforcement personnel should be referred for psychiatric evaluation and treatment to ensure that officers are prescribed medication in a manner that will restore them to duty quickly and safely. Psychologists who perform FFD evaluations should collaborate with psychiatrists when medication issues are involved, as psychiatrists are qualified to diagnose and treat serious psychiatric disorders and to understand complex medication interaction issues which are crucial in law enforcement personnel.

What do law enforcement professionals think of mental health professionals? The answer to this question, presented in Chapter 6, is that a number of negative stereotypes and negative perceptions predominate. This is truly unfortunate, as the two disciplines have similar goals in terms of helping others and public safety, and must frequently collaborate in cases of mentally ill persons in the community. A number of strategies may be employed to improve mutual understanding. These include increased focus on mental health training for police officers, an awareness by psychologists and psychiatrists of the fear that most law enforcement professionals have of evacuator bias, and establishment of more formal relationships to improve contact between the two disciplines. Finally, more strategies need to be developed to ensure that mentally ill persons who first come to police attentions receive streamlined mental health treatment rather than becoming incarcerated in jail.

Although female and minority representation in police work has increased, these groups are still underrepresented in upper level police management. They also experience more stress associated with promotional activity than Caucasian males. These topics of gender and ethnic differences are explored in Chapter 7. Data from the literature was reviewed which suggests that women face more stress associated with "role ambiguity" than do men. Both women and minority members demonstrate primarily *similar* issues with respect to stress, but both experience promotional activities more stressful and in many studies, both of these subgroups experience stress associated with being "different" from the majority of Caucasian, male officers. Because the U.S. is so diverse, it is difficult to delineate national trends in FFD evaluations with respect to gender or ethnic differences. This suggests that a broader review of FFD cases from a number of different departments or agencies in different regions would be helpful to reveal national trends.

Duty death, although an uncommon event in police work, remains a critical stressor. Chapter 8 utilizes a multi-pronged approach to analyze this subject. Literature review supports the contentions that departmental structure and support is key to reducing police officers' stress after duty death. This was verified in interviews with command staff of a police department which suffered a recent duty death of an officer. Command staff endorsed the view that critical incident debriefing needs to be mandatory after such an event. The perceptions of officers surveyed, as well as literature, show that departmental interventions need to be tailored to specific needs of the individual. Female officers stated that they recovered emotionally from duty death more quickly than did males in the Washington State study. This finding needs to be replicated.

The issue of whether police officers commit suicide at a higher rate than do individuals in the general populations is controversial and is discussed in Chapter 9. However, there is no question that *when* law enforcement personnel make suicide attempts, they have lethal means at their disposal more readily than do civilians. They use firearms more frequently, which results in higher lethality of attempts. Factors associated with higher risk of suicide in police officers include: marital discord, alcohol abuse and certain police sub-cultural variables.

Chapter 10 utilizes a series of case scenarios to illustrate the point that although and officer may exemplify typical law enforcement attitudes when hired and be mentally suited to the job, individuals may change over time and become mismatched with their position in law inforcement. This may occur not just through illness, but because of personal growth or changes in their family structure or needs. When such mismatches are discovered, departments or agencies and the officer should work together to either find and alternate position or recognize that there are other careers available than police work. Greater emphasis needs to be placed on educating law enforcement professionals about career development and role shifts, so that changing needs are not viewed as strange or signs of weakness.

The vase field of legal issues encountered in FFD evaluations is touched upon in Chapter 11. Specific legal cases that illustrate misconduct and discipline are presented by Chief Anne Kirkpatrick to educated FFD evaluators about the approach that law enforcement agencies utilize. Some of the legal rights of the officer that may limit agencies' actions are also presented. The read is cautioned that because of variations in state and local laws, many of these practices vary widely by region. Also, discipline is administered in different fashion according to whether an agency is local, regionals (i.e., state police), or national and depends on whether officers are unionized.

The vast majority of the men and women who constitute our law enforcement community work extraordinarily hard, frequently under adverse circumstances including the possibility of fatal outcomes. This book is designed to assist the law enforcement community to hire and retain individuals suited for this unique profession. The author hopes that the book also provides a framework for potential evaluators to raise and maintain the highest ethical and practical standards of evaluation in cases where fitness is questioned.

# APPENDIX I

# SAMPLE NOTES AND REPORTS

*The following cases are presented to illustrate the stages of a FFD evaluation from case notes to report to follow-up. Clearly, each FFD case is unique and presents a different set of issues. However, the two scenarios below present some typical issues exemplifying the best and worst outcomes. The other point that is demonstrated is the comprehensive nature of the information gathered versus the brief communications in the Fitness for Duty report. The reports are designed to reduce exchange of nonessential confidential information to the essentials needed by support officers in order to return officers to duty.*

## Case Scenario 1

**A. Session Notes:**

**Identification:** Officer T. Roma is a 44-year-old African-American male who presents for a psychiatric evaluation.

**Relevant History:** The evaluee first noted symptoms of increasing anxiety since coming home from Vietnam. He was in combat and participated in two firefights. When he came home, he had several panic attacks but didn't get treatment for it. He felt they were because friends were so critical of "Nam."

For last year and a half, he has had many more panic attacks. He had a divorce and that wasn't too bad as his wife was primarily maternal, not romantic, and the divorce was mutual. He met another woman after that, and hew was "crazy about her." He left police work because "something wasn't right." He got a job in sales. He had a panic attack and his significant other was "*not* supportive." He came back to law enforcement one year later. His significant other was also in law enforcement. She has been drinking too much (not on duty) and refuses to get treatment. He had not pursued his hobbies for one and a half years, but is back to them since he began taking Nefazadone. He studies insects for fun.

He saw his family therapist and was on "same medication family in Valium" for less than 30 days. Had another severe panic attack a month later when his significant other left him. He has felt better since the breakup, although he was still having panic attacks at the time of the evaluation. Has not been violent but has been quite agitated when these happen, e.g., threw a glass by accident through a window. He

233

has been on Nefazadone since February, and has felt well until recently; then anxiety came back. He accidentally discharged his weapon, which triggered a panic attack. He handed off the weapon and discussed it with his commander who has been supportive. They talked and he got better, but felt he couldn't work. He stayed off work for two days and then went back to work. He had no weapons at home. He has annual requalification and did one a week after accidental discharge with no problems.

He had no symptoms of PTSD after Vietnam and has had no flashbacks.

His primary care doctor "said he could go back to work last week," and he has been doing much better since (but still not sleeping, is jittery). He feels lately that his memory had been poorer, and loses track of things. He suffers anxiety attacks once a day or once a week at this point.

**Vegetative symptoms: Wt:** stable **Sleep:** was decreased to a few hours per night with frequent awakening, had no nightmares

**Suicidal ideation:** never, "loves life" **Suicide attempts:** Number 0

**Medications:** Nefazadone 150 bid

**Past medical history:** Problems s/p MVA head-on collision 2 years ago, no LOC had seatbelt

**Medical hospitalizations:** none

**Allergies:** nka

**Past psychiatric history:**

**Outpatient treatment:** had counseling 1 1/2 yrs., with Counseling Ctr. for a few sessions

**Inpatient treatment:** none

**Substance use:**

| | Frequency *low=<1/wk.* *medium=<1/day* *high=daily* | Comments |
|---|---|---|
| **Caffeine** | high | 2 cups/day, get anxious with more |
| **Nicotine** | high | 1 pack/wk |
| **EtOH** | no more | quit when depressed, 3 beers in pas max |
| **Marijuana** | once in VietNam | got "paranoid and scared" |
| **Cocaine** | none | |
| **Heroin** | none | |
| **Amphet.** | none | |
| **LDD** | none | |

**Social history:** Has 6 grandchildren (by marriage), no kids. Married for 8 years, currently is divorced. He has 1 sister and 5 brothers; he was the middle child. Parents were divorced at age 10 and he went with his father. Father was in law enforcement. He suffered mild abuse by mother. On good terms with father.

**Family History: Father:** psychiatric: none known **Paternal relatives:** grandmother–EtoH **Mother:** psychiatric: EtOH, not known, but sexually abusive **Maternal relatives:** UNKNOWN **Siblings:** none known

**ASSESSMENT:** Officer Roma has a history most consistent with the diagnosis of major depression with panic attacks. Other diagnoses considered included: bipolar disorder, dysthymia, or adjustment disorder, or ADD.

**RECOMMENDATIONS:** (1) Medications: add Trazodone 50 mg at bedtime and increase to 100 mg if no improvement. Consider another antidepressant if symptoms are not better. Continue Serzone 150 mg twice a day.

(2) Medical Psychotherapy to focus on: relationship with significant other and her substance use in context of his life.

**DIAGNOSES:**

1. Major psychiatric syndromes: Major depression with panic attacks (primary)
2. Personality disorders: None
3. Major medical problems: None
4. Psychosocial stressors: Mild stressors
5. Impairment: Mild

**B. INITIAL CONCLUSIONS:**

Officer Roma has a strong history of good psychiatric functioning, even under stress. He apparently has a subclinical (mild) episodes of depression with panic attacks during periods of severe stress which went untreated. The current episode is associated with clear psychosocial stressors, and has been partially treated with Nefazadone and counseling. I recommend adding a sedating antidepressant (Trazadone) at night and continuing with Nefazadone and counseling.

Officer Roma has a good prognosis for returning to work in good condition, providing his sleep improves. Careful monitoring of his sleep and attention to psychosocial stressors are recommended for the next month. If he begins sleeping 7-9 hours a night in the next few days, he may return to work. If no, he may need further interventions.

**Sara Saddler, M.D.**
**Forensic Psychiatry**
**21 Blue Lane, Suite 245**
**San Diego, CA 93873**

## INITIAL FFD EVALUATION REPORT:
## CONFIDENTIAL

Name: Officer Tomas Roma          Position: Corrections Officer

Sheriff Smaling
New England Department of Corrections
275 State Street
Boston, MA 22222

Dear Sheriff Smaling:

This letter is in response to your request for evaluation of Officer T. Roma. He presented for a Fitness for Duty Evaluation on time and was polite and cooperative with the evaluation process. He was seen for a clinical interview for one and one half hours and completed psychological testing including the following tests: MMPI-2, MCMI-III, PAI, 16-PF and the SCL-90. In addition, the following materials were reviewed:

1. Letter of reprimand from 12/2/04
2. Commendation for heroism from 7/2/03
3. Sick leave usage records from 2003, 2004, and 2005
4. Memos and incident report from March, 2005 (accidental discharge)

In your referral letter, you posed the following questions:
**Questions #1:**
Is Officer Roma Fit for Duty at the current time?
**Answer #1**
Officer Roma is UNFIT for duty at the current time.

**Question #2**
If not, what is the nature of his problem–temporary or permanent?
**Answer #2**
The nature of his problem is: Axis I (Major Psychiatric Syndromes): Major Depression, in partial remission. Axis II (Personality Disorders): None. Officer Roma has a strong history of good psychiatric functioning, even under stress. He apparently has had subclinical (mild) episodes of depression with panic attacks during periods of severe stress before which went untreated. The current episode is associated with clear psychosocial stressors, and has been partially treated with and antidepressant, Nefazadone and counseling.

**Question #3**

If the officer is fit for some limited duty in their current state, what are the limitations? Are there reasonable accommodations the department can make?

**Answer #3**

Officer Roma should not be returned to full duty or armed until his sleep had normalized and he is not longer having panic attacks. He may assume light duty for the next two weeks but should be reassessed after successful completion of light duty for potential return to full duty.

**Question #4**

What is the prognosis for Officer Roma to return to full duty?

**Answer #4**

Officer Roma has a good prognosis for returning to work, providing his sleep improves and the panic attacks subside. Careful monitoring of his sleep and attention to psychosocial stressors are recommended for the next month. If he resumes normal patterns of 7-9 hours of sleep per night in the next two weeks and the panic attacks cease, he may return to light duty at the end of that time. If not, he may need further interventions to stabilize his condition. It is recommended he returned for re-evaluation at the end of his light duty to ensure his symptoms are well-controlled and that he is fit for full active duty.

**Question #5**

Are there any specific treatment recommendations to assist with restoring Officer Roma to fitness?

**Answer #5:**

1. Addition of sedating antidepressant (Trazadone 50-100 mg) at bedtime to ensure proper sleep without the risk of addiction or side effects.

2. Continuation of counseling once a week or twice a week to focus on his relationship with his significant other AND her alcohol use.

## C. INITIAL FOLLOW-UP: (THREE WEEKS):

**Subjective/Objective:** Officer Roma is feeling "ok." He was anxious on the first day—there were a lot of rumors. But he handled it. He has been working too much overtime—performed three overtime shifts in one week because he had "mandatory overtime and didn't want to say no." Supervisor Smith sent a memo stating he had been completing his detail with "a good attitude and more confidence" than previously.

He had one panic attack where he started sweating at work. He had "pulled a double" the night before and was in "intensive (inmate) management." He feels he has been doing better. His former significant other started several rumors at work, so he decided to stop seeing her. In the past, he would have gone into panic—now he is relieved he doesn't have to deal with her alcohol abuse anymore. They mutually decided to stop seeing one another a week ago. The evacuator discussed issues to follow up on in his counseling. His father has been asking him to move closer to him. Has had one armed detail and did fine. He feels "much more positive" about the job and his ability to handle it. He had been taking 50 mg of Trazadone and occasionally 100 mg at bedtime.

**Mental Status Exam:**
**Affect:** more confident, direct **Mood:** consistent with affect
**Thought content:** see above
**Sleep:** 8, no awakening Appetite: good; he has gained 5 lbs.
**Assessment/Plan:** Continue tx. with PCP and PCP MD.
1. Advised to stay on meds for life to prevent future episodes–discussed early warning signs of depression.
2. Advised to go to the (target) range every month for several months to enhance confidence with weapons.
3. He was strongly advised not to pull "mandatory doubles."
4. Will contact chief to discuss the "mandatory double" issue.
5. Recommended he see psychiatrist rather than just his primary care doctor.
6. Called the department and discussed findings. He was approved for unrestricted duty but no mandatory doubles.

### D. EXTENDED FOLLOW-UP (SIX MONTHS):

Officer Roma went back to work for another 6 months. At the end of that time, Dr. Saddler called the agency and they stated he had been performing satisfactorily. The Officer called a few weeks later and verified he "felt better than he had in years, more confident, happier and calmer." He announced his intention to continue medication treatment indefinitely.

## CASE SCENARIO 2

### A. SESSION NOTES:

**Identification:** Officer Bill Cose is a 29-year-old male who presented for a psychiatric evaluation for fitness for duty referred by Chief Donegal of Whitcomb Police Department. He refused to sign paperwork for release of information to his health care providers. He says it "is none of my business." He stated, "you don't need to talk to the providers, it's not relevant," The evacuator explained several times that it was necessary to sign release, and he refused. Dr. Zen agreed to conduct the interview, but informed him that he may well suffer adverse consequences from not cooperating. He was distressed to be referred for a FFD evaluation and was in tears for portions of it. Overall, he was mildly agitated but polite.

**Relevant History:** The evaluee first noted symptoms of anxiety last year. He says he "wasn't aware he had fit for duty problems." He has had "a rough few months where he was drinking too much."

He has been taking medication from his family doctor. He says that taking Paxil was "like being on speed." Then they tried Luvox and "it didn't work because I was drinking too much alcohol." He couldn't take meds out of the hospital. He took a month off because he had been drinking and he couldn't function. One day at work he came it and had shaking episode, which she tried to treat by taking several over-the-counter antihistamines. He felt he improved, but a supervisor sent him home. Then two weeks prior to the evaluation, he was sent to the chief's office. He thought that it was "confidential seeing the psychologist," but he was pulled from his job. He was then referred her to see Dr. Zen for a fitness for duty evaluation. He says he wasn't informed of today's appointment until 6:30 a.m. today. He "didn't know if he is on paid administrative leave."

He was on Trazodone from an MD after a motor vehicle accident. He stated it helped him a lot, but his current MD declined to prescribe it. He has been on Anatbuse, Risperidone, Atarax, and Trazodone previously. He has also had the following antidepressants previously: Sertraline, Paroxetine—but both "felt like speed."

Dr. Zen invited evaluee to volunteer additional info about his symptoms, and he said "things happen, you move on." He stated he was "furious that nobody cared about these issues" until he had an incident at work with shaking and anxiety. He says he has had no difficulty with his supervisor, who has "been good to him." The supervisor did tell him Officer Cose had taken a lot of leave in the last year and he admits he had been cautioned several months ago not to take excess leave.

**EDUCATION: Elementary school:** "typical" **High School:** honor student
**College:** B.A. in Criminal Justice
**Vegetative symptoms: Weight:** variable 10-15 lbs lost or gained several times in the last year **Sleep:** was decreased to hours/night
**Suicidal ideation:** "not my type of thing" **Suicide attempts:** Number 0
**Psychosis:** denies **Mania:** denies, but then endorses staying up for 5 days at a time frequently a couple years ago
**Medication:** none in the last 4 weeks
**Past medical history:** Problems: possible irritable bowel syndrome
**Medical hospitalizations:** none
**Allergies:** none know
**Past psychiatric history:**
**Outpatient treatment:** seeing PCP now; she refuses to Rx trazodone, won't prescribe psychotropics
**Inpatient treatment:** 1 inpatient dual diagnosis hospitalization

**Substance use:**

| | Frequency low=<1/wk. medium=<1/day high=daily | Quantity | Treatment | Comments |
|---|---|---|---|---|
| **Caffeine** | high | high | | 3-4 cups/day, gets "wired" with more |
| **Nicotine** | med | | | occasional cigarettes |
| **EtOh** | none now, high | | Impatient detoxification once | 17-18 high, and see above |
| **Marijuana** | used regularly at age 17-18 | | lots, none now | |
| **Cocaine** | tried 10 times | | | Denied euphoria |
| **Heroin** | denies | | | |

| | Frequency<br>low=<1/wk.<br>medium=<1/day<br>high=daily | Quantity | Treatment | Comments |
|---|---|---|---|---|
| Amphetamines | used regularly<br>age 17-18 | | | During withdrawal he<br>became<br>profoundly depressed |
| LSD | tried twice | | | |
| ecstacy | tried three times | | | |

**Social History:** Has 1 child aged 5. Divorced for 4 years, is now serious with another woman. Patients has been working as an officer at same department as his fiancée. He had 2 brothers. His parents were divorced at age 15. Father has been remarried at least 5 times. Mother remarried 3 times. He suffered a lot of abuse in childhood–"Dad was alcoholic and didn't attract healthy women." He suffered sexual abuse by his mother–primarily inappropriate fondling. On poor terms with family, has little contact with any of them.

**Family history: Father:** psychiatric: EtOH, was hospitalized in long-term psychiatric care **Paternal relatives:** EtOH in multiple members, PSA, 2 suicides by gunshot **Mother:** psychiatric: none known **Maternal relatives:** His grandmother became demented in her 50s–attacked and injured her horse. **Siblings:** none known **Social Contacts:** The officer has "few friends" other than his fiancée.

## B. DIAGNOSES:

1. Major psychiatric syndromes: probable bipolar disorder, type I (Primary), alcohol dependence, in remission
2. Personality disorder: defer
3. Major medical conditions: Irritable bowel syndrome
4. Psychosocial stressors: Moderate
5. Impairment: Moderate

## CONCLUSIONS:

Officer Cose continued to decline the sign release form, even when Dr. Zen informed him that it would be viewed as a lack of cooperation with the interview process. ("If they're going to fire me, let them do it!".) He was very concerned that he had no privacy left, and "did not want any more information circulating." The evacuator conducted the interview anyway at the request of the agency. Officer Cose presents with uncontrolled mood swings, with vegetative signs consistent with bipolar disorder. He also has had a traumatic childhood history, although he denies that accounts for his current symptoms.

**Bud Zen, M.D.**
**Forensic Psychiatry**
**46 Lake St., Suite 88**
**Billings, MT 99838**

**INITIAL FFD EVALUATION REPORT:**
**CONFIDENTIAL**

Name: Officer Bill Cose          Position: Police Officer

Chief B. Donegal
Whitcomb Police Department
555 Central Avenue
Billings, MT 99840

Dear Chief Donegal:

This letter is in response to your request for evaluation of Officer Bill Cose. He presented for a fitness for duty evaluation on time. He refused to sign paperwork for release of information to his health care providers. He says it "is none of your business." He stated "you don't need to talk to the providers; it's not relevant." The elevator explained several times that it was necessary to sign release, and Officer Cose refused. He stated he was distressed to be referred for an FFD evaluation and was in tears for portions of it. Overall, he was mildly agitated but polite. He was seen for one and one half hours in clinical interview and completed the following psychological tests: MMPI-2, MCMI-III, PAI, 16-PF and the SCL-90. In addition the following materials were reviewed:

1. Letter of reprimand
2. Citizen complaints from 3/2/04
3. Sick leave usage records from 2004-2005
4. Memos and incident report from

In your referral letter, you posed the following questions:
**Question #1:**
Is Officer Cose Fit for Duty at the current time?
**Answer #1:**
Officer Cose is UNFIT for duty at the current time.

**Question #2:**
If not, what is the nature of his problem—temporary or permanent?
**Answer #2:**
The nature of his problem is: Axis I (Major Psychiatric Syndromes): Bipolar Disorder, type I. Axis II (Personality Disorders)

## Question #3:

If the officer is fit for some limited duty in his current state, what are the limitations and are there reasonable accommodations the department can make?

## Answer #3:

Officer Cose should not be returned to full duty or armed. If he could be shifted to a "light duty" position within the department, e.g., primarily clerical work until his symptoms are stabilized, this would be a much more acceptable level of forensic risk.

## Question #4:

What is the prognosis for Officer Cose to return to full duty?

## Answer #4:

Officer Cose has a poor prognosis for returning to work as a patrol officer. The prognosis for return to work as an armed officer is poor for individuals with bipolar I disorder. This diagnosis represents a serious forensic risk in law enforcement positions. People with bipolar disorder may have long periods of high functioning, but they are also subject to intermittent, but potentially serious, lapses in judgement. When firearms are involved, this potential liability is usually unacceptable to most departments. Officer Cose show clear symptoms of bipolar disorder, and is *not being treated* for this condition. In fact, he has ceased taking all psychiatric medications.

## Question #5:

Are there any specific treatment recommendations to assist with restoring Officer Cose to fitness?

## Answer #5:

1. Officer Cose would benefit from treatment of bipolar disorder by a qualified psychiatrist. Officer Cose's current psychiatric care is being provided by a primary care provider. Since he declined to sign a release, Dr. Zen could not verify this information with his primary care provider, nor communicate these findings to him.

2. According to the evaluee, his primary care provider has not suggested mood stabilizers. If this is correct, he has not had a trial of the medications most likely to improve his condition. In addition, Officer Cose reports doing much better when on Trazodone, but he states primary care provider declines to prescribe it. The probable bipolar diagnosis is consistent with his response to Zoloft, Paxil, and amphetamines in childhood.

3. Officer Cose would also benefit significantly from further education and discussion of the importance of compliance with treatment for bipolar disorder.

## C. INITIAL FOLLOW-UP (FOUR WEEKS):

Officer Cose continued to decline to release information to both the evacuator and the department. Dr. Zen stated that he felt that there was enough information to make the diagnosis without that input. Chief Donegal and the city's attorney concluded that the town of Whitcomb did not have enough personnel to permit a permanent light duty assignment and that the city was not willing to run the forensic risk of retaining Officer Cose in an armed capacity. They therefore moved for separation of employment.

## D. EXTENDED FOLLOW-UP (ONE YEAR):

Dr. Zen was notified by the city that Officer Cose was terminated after exercising family medical leave (12 weeks). He did not pursue psychiatric treatment while employed as a police officer. However, he contacted Dr. Zen a year later to inform him that he had made a suicide attempt after being terminated, and then had a clearcut manic episode with a psychiatric hospitalization within two months of termination. At that point, he decided to begin treatment for bipolar disorder. He began mood stabilizers and had a good treatment response. He obtained a position selling real estate after beginning psychiatric treatment. He was stable, happy, and was designated number one sales for his region a year later.

# APPENDIX II

# DEMOGRAPHICS OF WASHINGTON STATE STUDIES

## WASHINGTON STATE STUDY I: POLICE OFFICERS' EXPECTATIONS OF MENTAL HEALTH PROFESSIONALS

A total of 250 questionnaires were distributed to 12 people departments with 75 responses. Of the 75 responses, 21 were from urban police departments (Seattle and Tacoma), 35 were from suburbs of those cities and the 19 were from rural areas of central Washington and northern Oregon within a 250 mile radius of those cities. The number of officers that identified themselves as female was 18, with 49 males, and eight individuals declined to identify their gender. Table A.1 shows the breakdown by rank of responding officers. The majority were patrol officers, but all ranks were represented.

Table A.1
FREQUENCY TABLE: RANK

|  | Count | Percent |
|---|---|---|
| Police Officer | 23 | 30.7 |
| Detective | 11 | 14.7 |
| Lieutenant | 11 | 14.7 |
| Sergeant | 5 | 6.7 |
| Commander | 6 | 8.0 |
| Deputy Chief | 7 | 9.3 |
| Deputy Sheriff | 2 | 2.7 |
| Police Chief | 2 | 2.7 |
| Sheriff | 2 | 2.7 |
| Support Staff | 4 | 5.3 |
| Missing | 2 | 2.7 |

## WASHINGTON STATE STUDY II:
## FITNESS FOR DUTY IN LAW ENFORCEMENT PERSONNEL

A retrospective review was conducted of police officers and corrections officers who were sequentially referred for a FFD evaluation (to the author) from 1999-2004. The results of this study were described in detail in Chapter 3. The FFD results of fifty-eight officers comprised of 36 police officers and 21 corrections officers were studied. Of these, 15 officers were from urban departments, 15 were from suburban departments, and 27 were from rural departments. There were 17 females and 40 males. The mean age was 39.7 and the breakdown by age range is shown in Table A.2. The majority of officers were Caucasian, as shown in Table A.3.

Table A.2
AGE RANGE OF FFD EVALUEES

| Age (Years) | Count | % |
|---|---|---|
| <30 | 5 | 8.8 |
| 31-40 | 28 | 49.1 |
| 41-50 | 15 | 26.3 |
| 51-61 | 9 | 15.8 |

Table A.3
ETHNICITY OF FFD EVALUEES

| | Count | % |
|---|---|---|
| Caucasian | 50 | 86.0 |
| African-American | 5 | 8.8 |
| Hispanic | 1 | 1.8 |
| Asian | 1 | 1.8 |

Most of the offices referred for FFD evaluation were married (45.6%). Table A.4 shows the breakdown in which those officers who were divorced and remarried were separated from those who were still in their first marriage. The rate of divorce was quite high: 41.7 percent of officers had been divorced at least once and 10.5 percent had been divorced multiple times.

Table A.4
MARITAL STATUS OF FFD EVALUEES

|  | *Count* | *%* |
|---|---|---|
| **Unmarried** | 7 | 12.3 |
| **Married, never divorced** | 19 | 33.3 |
| **Remarried** | 7 | 12.3 |
| **Divorced** | 17 | 29.8 |
| **Divorced multiple times** | 6 | 10.5 |

# AUTHOR INDEX

# SUBJECT INDEX

end dummies

*Note:* Mental Health Professional and Law Enforcement Professional occur too frequently to tabulate.